AF527978

Women in Contemporary Indian Society

Women in Contemporary Indian Society

Seema Pandey

RAWAT PUBLICATIONS
Jaipur • New Delhi • Bangalore • Guwahati • Kolkata

ISBN 978-81-316-0672-8

© Author, 2015

Reprinted, 2017

No part of this book may be reproduced or transmitted in any form or by any means, electronic or mechanical, including photocopying, recording or by any information storage and retrieval system, without permission in writing from the publishers.

Published by
Prem Rawat for **Rawat Publications**
Satyam Apts, Sector 3, Jawahar Nagar, Jaipur 302 004 (India)
Phone: 0141 265 1748 / 7006 Fax: 0141 265 1748
E-mail: info@rawatbooks.com
Website: www.rawatbooks.com

New Delhi Office
4858/24, Ansari Road, Daryaganj, New Delhi 110 002
Phone: 011 2326 3290

Also at *Bangalore, Guwahati* and *Kolkata*

Typeset by Rawat Computers, Jaipur
Printed at Nice Printing Press, New Delhi

Contents

List of Tables

Preface

'Empower women', 'down with gender inequality' – the impassioned words of feminists have rung out over and over again, but what is it that these activists want? What effect has this appeal had for society in general and individual mindsets in particular?

One positive aspect of this outcry has been that the status of women has become an important parameter to gauge the level of development and sensitivity in any society. The consciousness for empowering women has, over the decades, percolated from feminists and sociologists to the echelons of power at one end and to the dusty bylanes of our rural and tribal habitats on the other.

Although scores of data and secondary information are available to illustrate the status of women in specific segments of society, yet a holistic and comparative viewpoint of the women's status in tribal, rural and urban segments is not available. This study is a modest attempt to fill this gap and throw light on the status of women in the tribal, rural and urban society of Rajasthan.

While deciding the area for investigation, Jaipur seemed an obvious choice since it is the fastest growing urban conglomerate in the state, having all sorts of modernizing influences on its populace, particularly women. We made urban sample fraction as representative as possible by drawing in respondents from the household, informal and formal sectors.

For the rural segment, the focus of study was Dangarwara village (Jamua Ramgarh tehsil) of Jaipur district. This is an obscure, interior village having minimum urban influence and multi-caste inhabitants.

Tribal inhabitants in the vicinity of Jaipur have undergone major changes due to urban influences, hence we decided to move away and look for a tribe which has been relatively unexposed, and the Garasias, residing in Sirohi-Pali-Abu Road belt, fulfilled our criterion. We, therefore, selected Varli village (Pindwara tehsil) of Sirohi as a universe for tribal study.

While a questionnaire-cum-schedule was introduced for urban and rural respondents, we depended on intensive interviews with tribal respondents to probe deeper and gain an insight into their exact situation.

This research work has been organized into eight chapters. While Chapter I defines the concept of status of women and traces the historical perspective from the Vedic period to modern times, Chapter II provides an insight into the socio-cultural domain and explores in detail the patterns of marriage, rites and rituals, structure of family, socialization, issues of hierarchy and education in each section and sub-section of our study. In Chapter III, we uncover issues related to women's health, fertility and mortality and how they affect the status of women in general. Since empowerment of women cannot be achieved without their active involvement in the political process, we gauge the level of involvement of our women respondents in politics and its ramifications in Chapter IV of this study.

Economic value of women's unpaid labour in agricultural and family enterprises, particularly in the informal and household sub-sections of urban society, as well as tribal and rural set-ups, has been substantially undervalued and an attempt has been made to quantify their unrecognized contribution in Chapter V of this study. Modernization and exposure have made urban respondents bold enough to debate issues of female body and sexuality. The extent to which this awareness has filtered down to the rural and tribal women has been examined in Chapter VI.

The social structure and culture of a society have direct concomitance to the patterns of leisure, yet it apparently seems that leisure has remained a prerogative of males since it is they who have all the freedom to use leisure as they like. Women also have leisure but they face several restrictions and have to curtail their aspirations. Chapter VII of this study takes a roller-coaster ride into the wants, desires, ambitions and frustrations of our women respondents.

In Chapter VIII, we summarize the conclusions and draw comparisons between various segments and illustrate the major findings of this study.

It is hoped that this study would go a long way in presenting the true perspective regarding the status of women in various segments of Rajasthani society.

Acknowledgements

It gives me immense pleasure and satisfaction to acknowledge my heartfelt thanks and gratitude to all those who have provided me with guidance, encouragement and intellectual inputs to enrich this research work.

First of all, I remain indebted to my guide Dr Ishwar Modi, an eminent sociologist and formerly Associate Professor of Sociology in the University of Rajasthan, who very kindly allowed me to register under him for this research study. His guidance and constant encouragement, along with a liberal dose of intellectual analyses and stimulating inputs, have gone a long way in allowing me to complete this study.

Dr Anil Bharghava, Assistant Professor (Sociology), and Dr R.C. Swarnkar, Assistant Professor (Anthropology) in the University of Rajasthan, deserve special mention for their guidance and encouragement. I owe a lot to Dr Maya Unnithan Kumar and Dr B.L. Mehrada, whose academic inputs on the lifestyle of the Garasias have been liberally quoted in this research work. I am also grateful to the staff of MLV Tribal Research Institute, Udaipur, for extending help in consulting records, books, journals and other materials.

Thanks are also due to the Deputy Labour Commissioner, Pali, Shri P.C. Parmar and staff of Binani Cement Factory for facilitating my stay and movement during the close interaction with the Garasia community. Generous hospitality offered by Shri Babu Lal Garasia, Deputy Sarpanch, his wife Pavni and their children during my stay in Varli village overwhelmed me. I remain thankful to Shri Samera Ram, Sarpanch, Varli; Shri Moti Lal Garasia, ex-Sarpanch, his wife Gangabai and daughter Sita Kumari, who acted as the main interface with tribal respondents and provided a valuable insight into their life.

I profoundly thank Mrs Kamla, ANM, and Dr Sita Ram Chauhan, PHC, Pindwara, for providing first-hand information regarding health practices among tribal women. Likewise, I appreciate the willing cooperation of WCD worker Batto Devi and all inhabitants of Dangarwara village, especially Sarpanch Kamla Meena, for facilitating my study in various ways. Special mention may be made of Chanda Devi Sharma and her family for their generous hospitality.

Last but not the least, I express my gratitude to my father-in-law Shri R.P. Pandey, who left for his heavenly abode in 1996, my husband, Shri Punit Pandey, and my son Pulkit, who supported me in times of distress and despair and rejuvenated me with fresh zeal and enthusiasm. My younger sister Krishna Sharma was my constant companion and friend in this entire process.

I dedicate this research work to my parents, Shri Shyam Lal Sharma and Smt Vidhya Sharma, who nurtured, coaxed and fuelled my academic pursuits right from childhood.

Glossary

Adak	Clan
Ajwain	A kind of spice emitting a sharp smell and used for digestion
Anganwadi	Childcare centre
Angarkhi	Waist coat
Ardhangini	Wife
Asar	The fourth Hindu month occurring in June–July
Ata-Sata	Exchange
Bajra	Grain
Bania	A Hindu caste
Banna	Groom
Banni	Bride
Baosi	Term of respect for all deities and some men
Bhaboot	Ash with which a Hindu makes sectarian marks on the forehead or which mendicants rub over their bodies
Bhajan	Religious songs
Bhakar	Popular term for mountain terrain
Bhavli	Term sharing of water
Bhello	Benevolent
Bhoot	Ghost or evil spirit
Bhopa	Ritual mediator; Shaman
Chakki	A handmill
Channa	Gram
Chuda	Set of bangles worn all over the arm
Chudel	Witch, a female ghost or evil spirit
Churma	A preparation made from crushed bread, sugar, ghee
Dai	Local midwife
Dalia	Coarsely grounded grain

Dapa	Brideprice
Dava	Payment for wife-stealing
Devla	Grain deviner
Devra	Temple, sacred centres of village
Devrani	Husband's younger brother's wife
Dhamino	Fishing
Dhoti	Loin cloth
Diya	An earthen lamp
Dosh	Fault
Dussehera	A Hindu festival, victory of Rama over Ravana
Gaaba	Cloth, also symbol of menstruation
Gair	House
Gali	Street
Garam	Hot
Ghagar	Eczema
Ghagra	Women's thick-pleated long skirt
Ghatti	Also referred as Chakki – a handmill
Ghee	Clarified butter
Ghooghri	Boiled corn
Gobru	Malevolent
Gotraraj	Ancestor clan head
Haap	Snake
Haga	True
Hagai	Engagement
Hahu	Mother-in-law
Hahur	Father-in-law
Hakal	Long iron chain having 5 rings in the centre and 5 triangular rings at the end.
Hal	Plough
Helaru	Cooperative association of a large number of persons
Halmo	Friendship: To call
Hamara	Ours
Holi	Hindu festival celebrating spring
Hoo lagna	Heat stroke
Hoopra	A winnowing instrument used manually

Huavad	Special diet for newborn child's mother
Huhani	Also referred to as *dai* – local midwife
Huhara	In-laws' house
Huttak	Period of five to seven days of ritual impurity after childbirth
Jaapaa	Delivery of a child
Jachacha	Mother of newborn child
Jamai	Elder and younger daughter's husband
Jawar	Millet
Jeth	Husband's elder brother
Jhadphoonk	Method of treatment of local medicine men by using certain mantras
Jhulki	Woman's blouse
Kamzor	Weak
Kevka	Also referred to as *huavad* – special diet for newborn child's mother
Kharjavo	Treatment of wound
Khayo	Bit; to eat
Khichana	Marriage by capture
khichri	A kind of dish made of pulse and rice
Khoont	Ritual expert
Krishna paksha	Dark night
Kua poojan	Worshipping the well
Kuldevi	Clan mother
Kurta	Waist coat
Kutro	Dog
Laj kadhana	Veil
Lapsi	A kind of sweet dish prepared by fried wheat flour
Lota	Drinking pot
Maid	Honey
Maili veddya	Black magic
Makka	Corn, maize
Manauti	A vow or promise to worship a deity on the attainment of certain desired objective
Mantras	Sacred words of enchantment
Masa	Piles

Matar	Same as churma above, but salty rather than sweet
Moti	Big, large, higher
Mela	Fair
Morpankh	Feather of peacock
Mutho	Also referred to as *morpankh* – feather of peacock
Nach	Dance
Nadi	Pond
Nakor	Epistaxis
Namkaran	Naming ceremony of a child
Nanad	Husband's sister
Nanki	Small, young
Nichali	Lower, inferior
Niyat	Caste
Odhni	A big cloth worn by women with Kurti, Kanchli to cover head
Panch	A group of five or more arbitrators
Panchayat	A committee with selected persons to settle local dispute
Pani toda	Accidental termination of pregnancy
Pap	Sin
Patel	Person with primary legislative authority
Pavana	Guest
Peethi	The application of turmeric paste
Peravana	Clothing by mother's brother
Phalli	Spatial subsection of the village
Phera	Nuptial round
Pir	Muslim priest/saint
Piyar	Natal, parental house
Pooja	Worshipping
Poojapati	A brass plate in which articles of worship are kept
Potiyu	Turban
Rakshabandhan	A Hindu festival; festival of sisters seeking protection from their brothers
Rayda	Rape seed
Romkiya	Toys
Roti	Bread, chapati
Sanda	Wound

Sarpanch	The head of the jury or panchayat
Shadi	Ceremonial marriage
Shitla mata	Pox goddess
Shukla paksha	Bright night
Sookha Rog	Disease which reduces the body to mere sketelon. In medical terminology, known as Marasmus and Kwashiorkor
Taap	Fever
Tabar patakna	Abortion
Tabeej	Amulet
Tehsil	Smallest state administrative unit comprising a number of villages
Thanda	Cold
Ujli	Clean
Vadku	Metal dish of bride
Valro	Shifting cultivation
Vastuta	Placenta
Veer	Spirit
Vehu	Term of address for daughter-in-law
Visu	Scorpion

1 Conceptual and Theoretical Formulation

The Status of Women in Different Eras

India is one of the largest democracies but it is an undeniable fact that without equality and social justice, there can be no democracy. If the India of tomorrow is truly going to be more democratic, adequate emphasis has to be laid on the aspect of equality and social justice. Equality indicates a person-to-person relationship based on freedom and dignity. Equality is an inseparable corollary of liberty and the demand for equality grows in magnitude whenever there is a gap between theoretical equality and practical inequality. Equality of opportunity means that things without which life is meaningless must be accessible to all without distinction in degree or kind.

As far as women in emerging India are concerned, this factual inequality is expected to be taken care of by the paternalistic role which the state is expected to play. Legal paternalism is inherent in the directive principles of the Indian Constitution. The Preamble goes one step further and expresses the people's resolve to secure among other things, the dignity of the individual. Then, of course, the fundamental rights, clearly reflecting the egalitarian concept, proclaim manifestly the power of the state to take affirmative action for the benefit of women. So, at least, since Independence, it would seem that women in India are no more prisoners of tradition, culture and history, but their destination is governed by moral, natural and written laws, and also by the abiding creed built into our Constitution.[1]

The status of women in Independent India occupies an important place and all efforts are being made to establish the significant role a woman can play in the upliftment of her own self and the society at large. The Preamble to the Constitution of India resolved to secure to all its citizens 'justice, social, economic and political, liberty of thought, expression, belief, faith and worship, equality of status and of opportunities and to promote among them all fraternity assuring the dignity of the individual and the unity and integrity of the nation'. Indian women are entitled to these rights just as men are. Some of the specific Directive Principles are free and compulsory education for all children up to the age of 14, right to an adequate means of livelihood, equal pay for equal work, maternity relief, etc.[2]

With all this, women's development in emerging India poses special challenges and the existing structure, policies and programmes need to be reviewed and modified. Services to women cannot be provided without material resources being available in the first place. Even then, these services will be underutilized in the absence of adequate motivation to use them. India is an agrarian country and even emerging India needs a proper perception of development in the urban and rural sectors. In the rural sector, women have increasingly learnt to use the facilities of bank credit, income-generation schemes, health care programmes, and representation of women in village panchayats. But, these schemes should be enlarged in terms of dissemination of information to the landless and illiterates. Here, the role of mass media is imperative, and this should be matched by providing TV sets for community groups in the remote areas. The hopes and fears of women in emerging India are more based on non-social security and social insurance and these anxieties have extensive developmental consequences. Women anywhere can develop only when they are given special protection and treatment. Such measures as social benefits are justified and necessary for the women's total development.[3]

It is well known that women have been playing a vital role in the household. They have worked as one of the wheels of the family bullock cart and tried to put the household economy on a sound footing. Normally, they are engaged in a wide range of activities in addition to their routine domestic work. Various jobs done by women are not recognized as productive work and, therefore, they are engaged in a wide range of activities in addition to their routine domestic work. The status of women in a society is the true index of its cultural, social, religious and spiritual levels. It is one of the most important criteria for estimating with precision the degree of civilization attained by a particular society in various periods of its history.

History teaches us that the class or social group which plays the principal role in social production and performs the main functions in production must, in the course of time, inevitably take control of that production.[4] And these groups naturally emerge as victorious to play a vital role in the socio-economic and political development of a system. This is very true even in the case of women. Most of the primitive societies were generally considered to be matriarchal societies in which women played the principal role in production. Women performed both household and food production functions, while men roamed in the forest, in quest of games.[5] The release of new productive forces and desirability to increase production brought tremendous changes in the social relations and paved the way for the emergence of the concept of private property and new classes such as masters and slaves, exploiters and exploited emerged. The invention of fire, weaponry, cattle rearing, agriculture, domestic handicrafts, etc. gave further impetus to the release of new productive forces. Subsequently, the necessity for more labour went up to meet the requirements of increased productive forces.

The search for the new 'forces' began along with the urge and aggrandizement of private property. In the process, battles and wars erupted between groups of people and it provided the winners with prisoners, who were later converted into slaves. Women were also held as captives. Further, during the course of history, the idea of 'stable life' was developed to structuralize male-female relationships. The origin of family, men taking a major part by playing the role of 'savage warrior and hunter', relegated the women into a secondary position, confining her to domestic labour.[6] According to the division of labour within the family at that time, it was the man's part to obtain food and the instruments of labour necessary for the purpose. He, therefore, owned the instruments of the labour, and in the event of husband and wife separating, he took them with him, just as the wife retained her household goods.[7] The institution of marriage and specially 'pairing marriage' introduced a new element in social life, replacing the mother-right genes with a 'natural father' phenomenon. The division of labour within the family regulated the division of property between the men and the women. That division of labour remained the same, and yet it now turned the previous domestic relations upside down, simply because the division of labour outside the family had changed. The same cause which had ensured to the woman her previous supremacy in the house – that her activity was confined to domestic labour – now ensured the man's supremacy in the house. The domestic labour of the women no longer counted beside the acquisition of and the necessities of life by the man and the acquisition of latter was everything, the former an unimportant extra.[8] Thus, such a position of man rendered him more important both in the family and social life and he took undue advantage of this dominant position.

This system was fortified during the feudal age as the concentration of authority and economic power became the base for the prevalence of class structures in the social system. Exploitation became the prime concern of feudalism and women were the worst sufferers in all respects. The changes in the mode of production and emergence of a capitalist system although improved the status of 'dominant' class women to some extent, it further ruined the status of 'dependent' class women. Thus, women became secondary citizens in the family life cutting across the boundaries of class structure. And, the women of the 'exploited' class were relegated to a much lower position. Since the status of women was transformed along with the class relations in a society, the emancipation of women also depended on the emergence of a classless society. History teaches us the lesson of participation in a revolutionary struggle as the most potent liberator of women.[9]

The changes in the mode of production, and in the super-structural setting from time to time, introduced many variations in the status of women. Although the basic character of the system remained the same, yet a few noticeable variations could be observed in different countries. As a matter of fact, within the Indian sub-continent, there have been infinite variations on the status of women diverging according to cultural milieu, family structure, class, caste, property rights and morals.[10]

Historical evidence confirms that during the Vedic age, women enjoyed considerable freedom and equal opportunities with men.[11] They participated in every sphere of human life. Woman was man's friend, his co-worker and never his inferior. She had enjoyed the property rights and had access to the property of her father and husband. She struggled against the political as well as social problems freely with man. Women went to 'Gurukula' to receive education and married only after getting education. Thus, they occupied a high position in society. They were not kept in seclusion and could move about freely in society. *Purdah* was not prevalent. In social and religious functions, too, they occupied a prominent position. They had equal rights with men in the matter of selecting the life-partner. Marriage was well established and was considered a social and religious institution and a necessity which prevented sexual immorality to a great extent. It was made obligatory for all girls by about 300 B.C. because the society found that there are pitfalls in the path of an unmarried woman than those in the way of an unmarried man. From the religious point of view, a person who is unmarried is unholy and is not eligible to participate in sacraments.[12]

Educated girls had an effective voice in the choice of their husbands. Very often, there were love marriages which were subsequently blessed by the parents. Due to this, the marriage of the daughter was not a difficult problem for parents because she could select her own husband. A wife was her husband's equal partner, performed all religious ceremonies with her husband and was designated as *dampati*. Vedic literature mentions many a woman's names who attained eminence in the sphere of philosophy. The custom of *sati* was unknown in Vedic times. Widow remarriages were allowed by the society and were fairly common, if she liked. Women also had the privilege of adoption. Women in this period could be initiated in Vedic studies and were entitled to offer sacrifices to gods; the son was not absolutely necessary for the purpose. Even in the joint family, her authority was accepted and she had full liberty of action.[13] However, the position was subsequently altered. But, very little is known at present as to how and when the major change took place relegating the role of women into a secondary place during the course of Indian history.

Indications of a change in the status of women can be noticed in the early texts referring to the origin of the notion of the state.[14] Women along with the means of production lost this 'communal' identity and began to succumb to private ownership. It was from this point on that the status of women began to deteriorate as is evident from the narration in the texts of the Buddhist canon and the *Mahabharata*.[15] The texts of other Puranas and Dharma Shastras classified men and women as two distinct classes and equated women with Sudras.[16] Woman was considered as man's private property and was symbolized as the adjunct of low legal status and a ritual contempt. Though the deification of women was the creation of the early societies, it has continued as a compensatory gesture to suit to the changing conditions. It also reflects the dualistic character of Indian society. Thus, to quote Altekar, 'for nearly 2,000 years from 20 B.C. to 1,800 A.D. the position of women steadily deteriorated though she was saddled by the parents, loved by the husband and revered by her children. The revival of *sati*, the prohibition of remarriage, the spread of *purdah* and the greater prevalence of polygamy made her position very bad.' Thus, there was a vast gulf between the status of women in the early Vedic period and in the nineteenth century.[17]

Like various other sections of a society, women derive their ideological and moral basis for their status and institionalized roles from religion. Evidently, the various restrictions imposed on women and our notions about their proper roles in the domestic and social spheres have been greatly influenced by the religious conceptions with regard to their fundamental characteristics, their assumed virtues and vices, etc. which are substantiated by various legends and myths.[18] However, in the later stages, a few reform movements gave impetus to the elevation of the status of women to some extent. Buddhism and Jainism gave greater freedom to women, and due to the royal patronage the religion received, their teachings were promptly put into practice. The Bhakti movement and nationalist movement, process of modernization, impact of western culture, etc. have influenced to a great extent in bringing about changes in the social role of women. There are, however, sharp differences of opinion about the changes taking place over the years in the position of women in India. Some regard these changes as profound and pervasive. They point to the increasing participation of women in public life and to the changes introduced in their legal status.[19] Others maintain that the position of women has changed very little and that Indian society continues by and large to be a male-dominated society.

Women were usually uneducated, they were married at the age of 8 or 9 years. They were given training only in housekeeping to equip them for their married life. Society had a general prejudice against female education. During the Mughal period, the percentage of literacy among women went down rapidly and at the advent of the British era, female education had practically disappeared. Female education was confirmed only to the cultured and well-to-do families where the custom of child marriage did not take root. But, their number was generally very small.

The son is considered more important in the family compared to the daughter because religiously and economically, the former is more useful. Not only does a son perform the funeral rites necessary for salvation, but he is also a potential wage-earner and support for his parents in their old age. The *purdah* system was prevalent among royal and noble families in a restrictive form even before the Muslim conquest. After the Muslim conquest, the system of *purdah* became quite common among higher and richer classes in India to provide protection to beautiful women against kidnapping by Muslim rulers. Hindus adopted the *purdah* system as a protective measure to save the honour of their womenfolk.

There are various reports which throw light on the position of women's education during the last two centuries. Neera Desai has presented a very useful picture of this. The position of female education during the nineteenth century was very bad. 'It was an age when the mass of people were steeped in complete illiteracy. Education was restricted even among boys only to a small section. Education among girls was still more meagre.'[20]

Mahatma Gandhi, who championed the cause of women, made extensive and meaningful efforts to stress the need for women's education. 'Education not only develops and sharpens one's intellect, but also increases one's capacity of doing good.'[21]

Chandrakala has given a brief account of the progress of education among women during the last century. In the year 1882, the position of female education was really alarming. At the primary level, there were only 0.12 million girls under instruction, which increased to 3 million at the primary school stage by 1946–47. Nearly two decades later, that is, by 1965–66, the number increased to 18 million. The number of girls to every 100 boys had also risen from 36 to 55. But, this does not approach 100% even at the basic stage.[22] It is further stated that though proportionately more girls are taking advantage of this education, there is still a great lag between boys and girls.

Another significant event that had a far-reaching impact on the women's cause was the establishment of the Indian National Congress in 1885. It drew a certain number of women into the vortex of the country's political life. The Indian National Social Conference provided a forum for deliberations about the changed position of Indian womanhood. It was here that the urgent need for re-orienting the traditional institutions was felt on the political plane.

Gandhiji emerged on the Indian political scene in 1918. He appreciated the qualities of Indian women: 'To call woman the weaker sex is libel; it is man's injustice to woman. If by strength is meant moral power, then woman is immeasurably man's superior. Has she not greater intuition, is she not more self-sacrificing, has she not greater powers of endurance, has she not greater courage? Without her, man could not be. If non-violence is the law of our Being, the future is with women.'[23]

Having envisioned these qualities of women, Gandhiji thought women's entry into the fields of politics, education and economics will have a civilizing effect: 'Woman is the embodiment of sacrifice and suffering, and her advent to public life should, therefore, result in purifying it, in restraining unbridled ambition and accumulation of property.'[24] Thus, Gandhiji pleaded for equality and economic independence for women but advised them not to practise these rights, for, they were fitted to the 'brute nature' of man.

Though Gandhiji was able to mobilize a large number of women to participate in the national movement, it is evident that only women of the well-to-do classes, with good education, well-placed husbands and servants could satisfactorily perform the dual role, implied in the Sita model, that is, of service to the family and service to the nation. Most of the women leaders of this time came from feudal or bourgeois families, e.g. Sarojini Naidu, Durgabai Deshmukh, Kamla Devi Chattopadhyay, to mention a few. For all of them, service to the society was a voluntary activity, not an economic necessity. It did not come in the way of their family roles.

The nationalist movement brought women from their homes to face *'lathis'* and bullets and gave them not only a consciousness of their own strength, but also a new vision of their true place in society. This had several implications for women. First, in the wake of the nationalist movement, it became easier for women to leave their homes for the national cause as the movement was supported by their husbands and guardians. Secondly, women themselves became aware of their capacity for work, suffering and leadership and organized themselves to fight for their due place both in the home and in the society. Thirdly, the nationalist movement provided a suitable forum for women to assess their own work, which began in the earlier part of the century with the creation of several women's organizations.

The women's movement in India grew out of male reformist efforts in the late nineteenth and early twentieth centuries.[25] It was a bourgeoisie feminist movement involving middle-class women who campaigned for extension of educational opportunities and property rights. The reformists of the last century infused in their women relatives their favourite ideologies and encouraged them to participate in public life through forming associations and holding conferences. The idea was to project a progressive image to impress Britain in order to win more political power.[26]

Socially accepted rights and expected roles of women are closely affected by the stages and methods of development and the position held by the group in the social hierarchy. All this makes broad generalizations regarding women's status unrealistic. The status of women and their social relationship as necessitated by the new social, political and economic organizations in society (on the larger canvas) has come out only through the routine factors of process of social change, namely, education, urbanization, influence of modernism or modernization.[27]

In the pre-Independence period, the women's movement was very much a part of the nationalist movement. The liberal approach to women's issues and overall middle-class urban leadership emerged as significant features of the first phase of women's movement. With Independence, when the constitutional equality was guaranteed and the social welfare departments, both at the Central and state levels, evolved grant-in-aid programmes for women's organizations, a period of acquiescence began. Achievement of freedom not only generated optimism, but it was also felt that legal enactments against social evils and welfare-oriented programmes for women would ensure gender equality. Recognition of the vital reality that a struggle is necessary for implementing the principles of gender equality was yet to come. Stereotyped activity by women's organizations and apathy towards crucial issues concerning women marked the period of first two decades after Independence. During the 1960s, though specific women's issues did not surface prominently, women were mobilized in large numbers and they joined the general struggles of the rural poor, tribals, industrial working class and other mass movements. Participation of women in the Naxalbari movement, anti-price rise demonstrations, Navnirman youth movement in Gujarat and Bihar, rural revolt in Dhule district in Maharashtra and Chipko movement provided a backdrop for the ensuing struggles on women's issues. However, the fact that women participated in other larger struggles but had not evolved their own platform for focussing and pressing for their own issues till the mid-Seventies has been observed by various scholars.

The National Committee on Women in India considered a 'Draft on National Perspective Plan for Women, 1988 to 2000'. The subjects of the draft *inter alia* included education and employment of women, discrimination against women, social legislation affecting women and other social customs having a bearing on the status of women. The terms of reference included advice from time to time on specific policy, legislative and administrative measures necessary for removing economic and social inequality affecting women and to suggest ways and means to enable them to achieve their full potential and use their capacity to contribute to the development process, and also to review the progress regarding implementation of policy and programmes designed for development of Indian women.

The position of women in the Indian society is clearly evident in the process of transformation and will also have an important impact on future social development. Three major trends are discernible in the process of transformation. First, in the socio-economic sphere, the continuing absorption of women into the workforce is likely to continue. Further access to higher education is expanding the boundaries of women's social roles, which results in an increased sharing of responsibility within the family, more continuous employment in jobs, lower fertility patterns and greater participation in social and political activities. Secondly, science and technology in relation to birth control and reduction in their drudgery will minimize the present imbalance in the capacity for personal decision and action between the sexes. Thirdly, the present redefinition of the moral and psychological assumption that a single-parent family is the only legitimate form of sexual cohabitation is likely to continue. These three emerging trends in the Indian society are likely to generate specific and continuing courses of action, particularly on the part of organized women's groups, governments and large private corporate organizations. Social policy in both public and private sectors will increasingly respond to the demand that society should no longer exploit the dual role of women but acknowledge it as a chargeable contribution to socio-economic development. The extension of equal treatment and equal consideration to women would go a long way in ensuring equal social justice, the struggle for which has been a basic theme of political and social movements for the past several centuries. For a long time, this goal will best be achieved by organized women action.[28]

Appreciation of this complexity led the Committee on the Status of Women in India to admit that 'the status of women in the Indian context cannot be defined simply. General concepts like equality, role differentiation, legal, social and political rights, dependency or independence, are not applicable to all sections of our population'.[29]

Since a very large section of our society still continues to be under the influence of traditional standards, we had to juxtapose the role conceptions, norms and values in all their wide variety in traditional society, against the new dimensions in women's status and roles introduced by the Constitution and the processes of social change. Traditional India had seen women only as members of the family or a group as daughters, wives and mothers and not as an individual with an identity or rights of her own. The radicalism of the Constitution and its deliberate departure from the inherited social system lay in its implicit assumption that every adult woman, whatever her social position or accomplishments, will function as a citizen and as an individual partner in the task of nation-building.[30]

According to M.N. Srinivas, a noted sociologist, it is extremely difficult to make general statements about Indian women because of regional, caste, class and other differences. The upper castes have a bibliocentric view of Indian culture and society, including the place and role of women in it, and how that has acted as a barrier to the observation and interpretation of actual behaviour. This has been compounded by the heterogeneous character of scriptures, their differential authority and finally, inconsistencies which are to be found in the scriptures in the conceptualization of certain basic roles and relationships, particularly the conjugal one.[31]

In order to describe the position of women in India, Srinivas created a model of rural society and showed how the female role and behaviour varied at different levels of land and caste hierarchy and then viewed the model as a diachronic one in order to show how even traditionally, the caste system permitted a certain amount of mobility and how opportunities for mobility increased considerably during the British rule and afterwards. Since Independence, opportunities for mobility have greatly increased for the poor and low-status Indians, particularly the Scheduled Castes and Scheduled Tribes. In rural India, movement to the top layer of the rural hierarchy generally led to female 'immurement' among both Hindus and Muslims and possibly also among Christians. Another consequence of upward mobility among the Hindus was Sanskritization, which altered husband-wife relations. Whatever the legal and formal position of women in Hindu society, as a married couple gets older, and a wife becomes a mother-in-law and grandmother, she becomes a force to reckon with within familial matters. Conjugal relations became egalitarian and this was more or less effectively concealed under the well-developed symbols of wifely differences. Finally, migration to the urban areas, female political participation, education, the activities of social reformers, and the *inequalities* of dowry – all enabled women to make a relatively easy transition to new roles and responsibilities.[32]

The granting of equal status to women was followed by the need to provide education to them. It was widely accepted that for the progress of society, it was necessary to provide equal opportunities of education to women. The need for spread of education was also stressed. Education of women led to growth of confidence in them and also in developing in them an urge to play a more useful role in their families as well as in the society. They envisaged a new role beyond the confines of their household and began to take up employment for the betterment of their economic status. With the spread of education of women, more and more women began to take up non-traditional jobs and even progressed to higher posts involving decision-making. However, this change did not remove the patriarchal values and the traditional normative structure. It created many problems in the path of their smooth progress. Thus, in contemporary society, women have been relieved from many of the constraints of the previous times and significantly enough attained constitutional right of equality of status with men. Opening of educational opportunities has also helped them in breaking the barriers of confinement within the household as well as joining gainful employment for improvement of their economic progress. Yet, this state of improvement is mostly confined to the upper and middle classes of Indian society. Old bias against women is still present in the lower strata of the society, where ignorance and lack of education still persist in enormous proportions. However, the most gratifying feature lies in the fact that a beginning has been made in the direction of improving the status of women and redefining their role in society.

The available evidence, as pointed out earlier, suggests that women enjoyed a much better status in primitive society. During the feudal times, women were looked upon as chattel, the plaything of men, with childbearing and rearing as their main functions in family life. As capitalism was superimposed over the feudal and semi-feudal structures in India, particularly during the imperialist rule, new forms of exploitation and social oppression of women came into being. This was accentuated by the large-scale ruination of handlooms, handicrafts and other cottage industries and the increase in the landless agricultural population.

The present demand of the women for increasing opportunities outside home should, at best, be termed as a tertiary stage in the history of women's emancipation. There has been a switch-over from the traditional role of the women subservient to menfolk to the neo-traditional phase, in which the women have been up in revolt against all types of exploitation, reiterating their equality with men in all fields of rights and responsibilities ranging from education, employment, health, institutionalized welfare facilities coupled with the participation of women at different levels of social and national activity. Thus, there is bound to emerge a highly-developed society, based on harmonious relations, allowing no exploitation, economic, intellectual or otherwise, by eliminating all traditional taboos that had led to restricting the women's life to certain spheres only.[33] Patience and an endless wait for redressal of grievances has never been satisfying for women. A proactive approach through mass movements and collective opinion has been instrumental in changing of mindsets and forming organizations to take care of women's interests. Many feminists, therefore, are not only asking and fighting for the 'equality' of women, but for a just and equitable society for women and men.

Feminism

In addition to being action-oriented, feminism is also an ideology, a belief system. All actions are based on a set of beliefs. Feminism is a doctrine advocating social and political rights for women, equal to those of men. It is also the body of knowledge, thought and theory that feminist scholars/thinkers/writers have created to challenge patriarchal knowledge and ideology.

There are two definitions of feminism which were accepted by women from Bangladesh, India, Nepal, Pakistan and Sri Lanka in two South Asian Workshops. According to one, feminism is 'an awareness of women's oppression and exploitation in society, at the place of work and within the family and conscious action to change this situation'. The other definition is a little more explicit: '*Feminism is an awareness of* patriarchal control, exploitation and oppression at the material and ideological levels of women's labour, fertility and sexuality, in the family, at the place of work and in society in general, and conscious action by women and men to transform the present situation.'

According to this simple and rather broad definition, anyone (woman or man) who recognizes the existence of sexism (discrimination on the basis of gender), male domination and patriarchy and who takes some action against it, is a feminist. Feminists recognize that all over the world, simply because of their gender, women experience discrimination and unequal treatment in terms of basic food, nutrition and health care, education, employment and participation in decision-making in social, cultural, religious, political and economic arenas.

From the above, it is clear that a mere recognition of sexism is not enough; it has to be accompanied by action, by challenge to male domination.[34]

It would be in order to introduce at this stage the feminist ideology in detail. To be sure, there is not one unified feminism; rather, there are several. Some of the forms of feminism are presented in Chart 1.

Chart 1 *Varieties of Feminism*[35]

	Forms of Feminism	*Roots of Subordination of Women*
1.	Socialist Feminism	The system is the problem
2.	Marxist Feminism	Division of labour confines women
3.	Equal Rights Feminism	Prejudice and unequal opportunities for women
4.	Althusserian Feminism	Category of feminine is the reason for subordination
5.	Humanist Feminism	Alienation from traditional roles
6.	Unaligned Feminism	Feminine role expectations
7.	Feminism Seeking Wages for Housework	Exploitation, not oppression
8.	Radical Feminism	Men are the problem
9.	Revolutionary Feminism	Oppression and exploitation due to housework and childrearing
10.	Red Stocking Feminism	Male supremacist, capitalist, imperialist
11.	Cultural Feminism	Isolation of women as a source of their inferiority
12.	Feminism of Female Supremacist	Women are biologically and morally superior, men hold power by force

Most vocal and violent among various forms of feminism is radical feminism, for it assumes a radical posture on the sex role. The radical ideology believes in the absolute equality between the sexes. All forms of discrimination against women should be eliminated and the fight should continue till women and men are equally treated in terms of human rights and fundamental freedom in the political, economic, social, cultural, civil or any other field.

Feminism remains a controversial and misunderstood concept in the social sciences. It has been viewed both as an ideology of women's liberation and a women's movement aiming to create a world for women beyond simple equality. As a theory and an ideology, it remains inadequate in relating to life experiences of women cross-culturally. In this development, as a theory, its meaning has undergone tremendous change historically.[36] French in origin, the term 'feminism' referred to what was called 'women's movement' in the nineteenth century United States of America (USA), a movement which comprised a diverse collection of groups, aimed at advancing the position of women in society. In the early twentieth century, it was used to refer to a specific group of women's rights advocates, namely that which subscribed to the idea of uniqueness of women, the mystical experience of motherhood, and women's special purity.[37] Later, many groups and individuals engaged in raising women's issues came to the movement that has been seen as the major version of feminism in the contemporary western society.

Feminism and Feminist Theory

Feminism can be defined as the doctrine advancing the view that women are systematically disadvantaged and are advocating a collective or individual struggle for equality. Defined this way, feminism is a political position. Feminism and feminist are political labels, implying support for the objectives of the women's movement which emerged in 1960s and the feminist critique is a distinctive political discourse – a critical and theoretical exercise directed against patriarchy and sexism.[38] However, feminism can also be defined as a social movement to achieve certain specified aims. In other words, feminism is the review of past knowledge and also the font of new learning which offsets what was there earlier. But it is also a source of action based on knowledge, opposing all that which is not feminist, understanding male domination and demanding rectification. Feminist theory, similarly, is the critical analysis of the dynamics of gender and sexuality, a basic objective of which is to analyse gender relations – to see how gender relations are formed and experienced, how we think of them, or more importantly, how most of the time we do not think of them.[39] Feminism and feminist theory, in this sense, consist of a range of political opinions that seek to analyse and eliminate sexual oppression, in both theoretical and practical forms.

However, there is much evidence of an evolving Third World feminism, both linked to, and independent of the West. Kumari Jayawardana[40] provides the working definition adopted in her study. The word 'feminism' has now been expanded to mean an awareness of women's oppression and exploitation within the family, at work and in society, and conscious action by women and men to change this situation. The word 'feminism' is used in a larger sense, embracing the movement for equality within the current system and significant struggles that have attempted to change the system. Women all over the world, both in the past and the present, have been involved in what has been referred to as 'less conventional policies'. Their strategies include interpersonal networking, grassroots, economic development projects, protests of many kinds, use of traditional women's activities in the cause of national liberation and involvement in non-governmental and informal women's group and organizations. Schlesinger's[41] book was published in 1989, and as such is part of the rediscovery of science that occurred throughout the 1970s and 1980s, and issues connected with it by feminists. In one case, science and scientific community was a target for feminists, since in numerical terms it virtually excluded women. In fact, in some biographies, detailed descriptions were provided of the humiliation and marginalization endured by women in their professional life as scientists. These and other works attempted to underline the absence of women from science. Another tradition that developed was documenting not merely the liberal presence or absence of women, but the wider aspect of feminism and crucially and centrally, the relationship between the absence of women feminity and the findings and conclusions of science. Put most simply, what these and other women argued was that the questions that science identified were determined by the construction of the social world in which men occupied the public space and women the private space. The issues about child care, maternity leave, direct and explicit discrimination against women were central to feminist concerns, and more complex questions about the inherently gender-related form and content of knowledge were largely ignored or marginalized.

The issue around which much of the debate in the social sciences was organized was that of sexual division of labour. In fact, feminists began to ask questions about the assumed 'natural' responsibility of women to care for children, the aged and the infirm, and at the same time just as 'naturally' being excluded from anything corresponding to real social and political power. Thus, a new understanding and vocabulary was developed by feminist social scientists that identified women's work, the 'caring professions', the 'unpaid domestic labour', the 'double shift' and other manifestations of the apparently 'natural' social division of labour. In a way that was to have immensely radical and far-reaching implications outside the academy. Women collectively questioned their role as the providers of domestic care and emotional nurturance. Throughout the West, a generation of women identified with what they saw as unpaid labour in the home.[42]

Woman throughout the nineteenth century was Jane Eyre's cry from the battlements of 'Thornfield Hall'.[43] Women are supposed to be very calm generally but women feel just as men feel. In the opinion of some renowned sociologists, the idea of shared oppression that unites women in their struggle for liberation has been central to second-wave feminism. It is often seen as the emergence of women's liberation movement, while their subsequent fragmentation is linked to the recognition that sisterhood had differences and that women automatically shared neither interests nor identities. The uncomfortable acknowledgment of differences between women was precipitated by debates around sexuality and race and was associated with the emergence of identity politics and the fragmentation of the western women's liberation movement at the end of 1970s.[44]

In analysing the relationship between gender and politics, G. Waylen[45] says that politics does not have the same impact on women as it does on men. The political process often alters gender relations, and this needs to be explored. Also, women often participate in political activity in different ways to men, which raises questions about the distinctive nature of women's political activity.

According to Margaret Hall[46], feminism re-emerged in the US in 1970s. In the earlier periods, the emphasis was more on legislative reforms than on values and the everyday behaviour of an average woman. On the contrary, contemporary feminism in the US and other modern industrial societies influenced mainstream values related to equity. Feminists work towards personal and social empowerment, cooperation and community welfare. They promote alternatives to the patriarchal system of hierarchical differences, competition and coercion. Feminism is a value and belief system that can be adhered to women and men alike. When feminism can relate to the basic needs of all women in all times and in all places, it will become a more effective social movement and will make considerably more gains as well. Although there are still many gains to be made, some of the previous estrangements and perceived conflicts of interest among women have been reduced. Gains need to be made in the relationship between women's personal and public domains. They cannot participate comfortably as equals in public life for part of the day, and return home in domestic servitude each evening. This compartmentalization of roles and expectations persists in most women's lives, however, as they frequently assume full responsibilities both at the workplace and at home. Feminist gains need to be evaluated in the purview of accomplishing the goal of a cooperative society with equal opportunities.

Nisha Garg and Pradeep Kumar[47] are emphatic that in today's society there are women who may not have imbibed the essence of feminism, and whose enthusiasm may ironically prove counter-productive. It is important to see that the women's movement is not hijacked by such elements, either inadvertently or by jumping on to the popular bandwagon. It is, therefore, necessary to shift the real issues from the claptrap of all that goes with feminism today.

The women's liberation movement, as emphasized by Romila Thapar, does not have immediate relevance to the Indian social situation: 'It is the product of urbanized middle class with large number of women trained as professionals as a result of expanding education opportunities whose professional skills are wasted by limiting them to domestic work.'[48] Indian feminism, unlike in the West, did not take the form of a craving to acquire outlook, ambitions, freedom and power of men, as this transcends feminity and leads to a duplication of the virtues and the defeats of man and propagates a sexuality which is suicidal for the race.

Not only the concept of feminism but also its practice has changed over the last four decades. For instance, in the 1960s and 1970s, in the women's movement in the West, the term 'feminism' came to symbolize the efforts to forego a collective identity of women supposedly sharing similar experiences of oppression. Simultaneously, academicians were seen engaged in unearthing the causes of universal subordination of women.

By this time, political differences about conceptualization of the roots and agents of oppression became apparent and developed as liberal, socialist, Marxist and radical feminist theories. Nevertheless, the belief that women suffer injustice because of their gender remained the basic underlying assumption in all their interpretations. Linking to this notion, feminists offered different analyses of the causes or agents of female oppression, and worked at different strategies to counter them. These ideological positions inspired the women's struggles in other parts of the world.[49]

The main differences between earlier feminists and present-day ones is that earlier, the struggle was for the democratic rights of women. It included the right to education and employment, the right to own property, the right to vote, the right to enter parliament, the right to birth control, the right to divorce, etc. It is clear that earlier feminists fought for legal reforms, for a legally equal position in society; the struggles were essentially outside the home and the family. They were not looking at patriarchy as a system which perpetuates women's subordination. Today, feminists have gone beyond demanding mere legal reforms to end discrimination; they are working towards the emancipation of women. Feminism now includes the struggle against women's subordination to the male within the home, against their exploitation by the family, against their continuing low status at work, in society and in the culture and religion of the country, and against their double burden in production and reproduction.

In addition, feminism challenges the very notion of feminity and masculinity as mutually exclusive, biologically determined categories.[50]

Thus, feminists see that women have to not only fight against discrimination but also for emancipation and liberation from all forms of oppression by the state, society and men. Since women are victims of exploitation (e.g. unequal pay, low wages), subordination (e.g. under male domination), oppression (e.g. violence), they are in a position to understand the problems facing other women and know that they have to initiate the struggle to change their situation and society itself.[51]

Review of Literature

Sociologists have explored the status of Indian women right from the Vedic period to more recent times, and have created a part pool of secondary information which has divergent undertones given the richness and diversity of our country and its culture. To begin with, it would be pertinent to record viewpoints expressed by key sociologists in the above contexts.

D.D. Kosambi[52] has some very valid points to say in his article, 'Historical Perspective of Women', that appeared in the book *Status of Women in India* by H.C. Upadhyay: 'There was no caste or class differentiation within tribes. Agriculture was then the monopoly of women. Women were the first potters and weavers. Weaving was the speciality of the women, though male seers might weave a hymn as if it were patterned garment of the loom. Women were the rulers and the system of matriarchy prevailed before 400 B.C. in different parts of continent. During the early Vedic period, the women in India enjoyed almost an equal status with men in different spheres of life. Vedic studies were then not the prerogative of man. Girls and boys were required to undergo "upanayanam" ceremonies in order to undertake Vedic studies.'

Anthropologist Arthur F. Ide[53] says in his book *Women Before History Written* that pre-historic women were originally taken by force, out of desire or lust. Humankind was the product of evolution. Give civilized man time to gather all his machines about him, and he will no doubt easily breathe savage, but if you would see still more equal contest, set them together naked and unarmed.

In this book by Arthur F. Ide, Michel Peissel has found that the Minaro community constituted a living museum of life in the days of the stone age man. The 'stone age women' or 'stone age persons' were a matriarchal people. Women made the laws and enforced them. In general, life was pastoral with the women being in charge of daily routine. Deities mostly were women and female goddess predominated. When pre-historic males were at war or on the hunt, women not only tended the homes, but like early historic women, were also powerful, resolute, determined, interested, crafty, cunning, insightful, adventurous, resourceful, experimentative and indigenous.

Anjali Bhave,[54] in her book *Of Women Caste: The Experience in Rural India,* opines that the Indian caste system has a rigid hierarchical form of the four-fold typology of *Varna* (castes): *Brahmin, Kshatriya, Vaishya* and *Sudra*. In all earlier studies on villages of India, one wonders if women were at all important to the village structure and systems of social interaction. Dwelling on the peculiar blending of *Brahmin* and Victorian prescription on the appropriate behaviour of women in society, and their implications for women across all castes and classes, it has been speculated that social and religious identities in colonial times may have become more caste-bound than they were in pre-colonial India. Gender relations emerged as a powerful new means for the colonial hegemony itself. Bhave has described how gender roles in India embodied in space. She found that space contains a clue to behaviour and is instrumental in communicating social norms. She points to the cultural practices of lumping together women and *Sudras*, that is, the untouchables, who are often jointly referred to as prime pollutants – the former temporarily on account of menstruation, and the latter permanently because of their lowly caste and occupational status. As caste-perpetuated lineage-based structures grow, high value is accorded to those who maintain the lineage by producing sons. Women, like other underprivileged groups, present a challenge because of the total dominance of the repressive structures.

Sujata Gothaskar[55] has, in her book *Struggles of Women at Work*, discussed about women activists involved in trade unions and of organizations of women in the informal sectors of the economy in India. Women's participation in ongoing struggles is influenced by the diffuse boundaries between women's work and leisure, paid and unpaid work and work and non-work relations.

The status of women in any nation portrays the progress of that particular nation. Although the Indian woman has come a long way in her cultural level from the Vedic period to the present status of achieving economic independence in the twenty-first century, yet due to many social, religious, cultural and political demands on her, she is still bound by the shackles of certain traditions and rituals, which distort her image to all around her.

From the Vedic period uptil now, the ideal woman is portrayed as home-loving, caring, concerned for the welfare of her husband and children, supportive, helping men to achieve their ambitions, not having any desire of her own, or even a sacrificing figure. She would accept her role as daughter, wife and mother in the male-dominated society without a whisper, but at the same time, be very feminine, pretty and patient. This kind of image has been implanted in the minds of the society by the Vedas, and religious leaders, and now continued in the present-day mass media and even the small screen.

Sushila Agarwal,[56] in *Status of Women,* brings out clearly the changing nature of the status of women and traces its specific characteristics. The problems of the status of women involve equality between men and women. Women, throughout the world, have been considered the 'second sex' or the 'inferior sex'. Equality and status are closely associated with power. Changing status involves the sharing of power on an equal footing with men in decision-making and its implementation at all levels. The societal value framework plays an important role in determining the changing status of power equations and hence, the status of women involves the distribution and redistribution of power.

In the global context, the women of the Third World require a different treatment, a different perception. Nelly P. Stromquist[57] in the book *Women in the Third World: An Encyclopedia of Contemporary Issues* has capably argued why we should make a distinction, and in what respects? Women are obviously not a homogeneous group and differences emerge in terms of social class, ethnicity, religious affiliation, and age. Consequently, they face a variety of conditions. Women in Lagos, as a group, have very little in common with women in San Francisco. And, within countries themselves, differences may be enormous. Wealthy women living in splendid isolation and in the luxury that affords them many servants on most counts cannot be compared with the women working as maids and food vendors in the streets of developing countries. At the same time, there is also a commonality of experiences and interests among women. Similar sexuality issues tend to be faced by women regardless of social class and wealth. Men's control over women's bodies, restrictions about abortions, the fear and reality of rape and sexual harassment, restricted social expectations about fields of study and employment are but a few of these commonalties.

Jyoti Mitra[58] has recorded after detailed studies, in *Women and Society: Equality and Empowerment,* that equality of women is necessary as a basic condition for social, economic and political development of a nation, as well as for an improvement in employment opportunities. Society owes a special responsibility to women because of their childbearing capability. The housewife's contribution should be admitted as economically and socially productive and contributing to national savings and development. Marriage and motherhood should not become a disability in women's fulfilling their roles.

The issues of women and development, women and poverty, and women and agriculture were basically non-issues until Easter Boserup[59] came up with her landmark study *Women's Role in Economic Development,* on data from Africa, Asia, etc. Arriving a few years ahead of the International Women's Year in 1975, which began with an unprecedented international conference to discuss the status of women around the world, Boserup's study proved to be a catalytic factor in opening up the field of women and development to critical inquiry. She traced the marked decline in women's economic status under colonial and post-colonial periods. She contended that biases, prejudices and misunderstandings, related to women's labour force participation, had eroded the household economic base, thus contributing to an overall increase in poverty. Integrating women into the process of socio-economic development was of vital importance in achieving overall development. There was a sharp decline in labour force participation of women in India, particularly in agriculture, and the corresponding rise in female unemployment over several decades up to 1971. Women usually work longer hours at more tedious, low-skilled and underpaid jobs. Women are best supplementary providers.

Amit Kumar Gupta[60] draws a correlation between the status of women in India and the world's economic order and does not believe in looking at the Indian women's position in isolation in his book *Women and Society: The Developmental Perspective*. The differences in cultural background, political perspective and attitude towards the problems of women created many obstacles within women's groups. The women in our country are oppressed not only because of their class and sex, but also because of the way in which our country is linked to the international economic order. We recognize the strong need for an autonomous women's movement as part of a strategy which aims at these social changes.

Veena Majumdar[61] pointed out in her book, *Emergence of Women's Questions in India and the Role of Women,* that even within the problems of women, those of the upper and middle classes received maximum attention. Social and religious leaders confined their efforts to evil social practices which were prevalent among the upper classes.

Even enfranchisement of women in India is only for the middle class. So, she saw the problems of women basically as economically dependent problems. She also said: 'Unless the economic and social utility of women in the eyes of their family and nation by opportunities to take part in social and economically productive roles is recognized, the national neglect of women will continue.'

Krishna Ahuja Patel[62], in her book *Women and Sustainable Development: An International Dimension,* emphasizes on the need to recognize women's work in monetary terms. Woman's work in isolation of other factors neither brought her fair and equal wages nor the added status that it was supposed to bring. Just as the status of women does not by itself go up simply because they are co-breadwinners with their husbands, it also does not automatically diminish simply because they are unable, for complex reasons, to play that role. Their role within the family as rearers of children, and as wives and mothers, forces them to give up or reduce their economically productive role out of home, and to that extent they do not emerge from their unequal condition or periodically return to it. In treating woman as an industrial worker, we tend to overlook the other and more vital aspect of identity. In practically all societies, women are deeply involved in bringing up the family, and therefore, relating themselves in a complex fashion as a member of family, than do men. The problem of women thus compels us to consider them against the background of a network of social relationships, attitudes, practices, and a manner in which all these constrain and prevent them from enjoying a fair measure of social inequality.

UN[63] publication *Too Young to Die*: *Genes or Gender* strongly advocates the role of education as the critical factor in improving the health of the girl child, or adult women and generally elevating her status. It is stated that in both the developing and developed countries, more males than females are born. There are strong links between a woman's education, her reproductive behaviour and the survival of her children. Does the education of a mother bring about a relative improvement in health and survival of her sons and daughters?

Sonia Bathala's[64] book *Women, Democracy and the Media* places the blame for the source of discrimination squarely on the family. Various practices which put women in a subordinate position and which have an impact on gender relations by and large remain unquestioned at both the societal and state levels. This also shows the interlocking nature of social and political patriarchal forces. At the society level, female children are largely unwelcome. Family is the foremost institution which denies fundamental rights to girls in the form of restricted movements, association, education, career opportunities, right to property, right to work, etc. Girls are largely not encouraged to enter any other profession except marriage. Thus, they play good daughters-in-law, wives, mothers, as a part of their *dharma* or in the name of cooperation or for fear of criticism or to seek a protective environment. It might be because they get accustomed to a life of dependence and security in the early years of life and hence internalize it. Family is the foundation of a social order which keeps women in place. Outside the family comes the civil society, that is, a social space comprising the wider neighbourhood or community. The community guards the family norms and even promotes them further by remaining silent on various critical events happening in its vicinity and within its knowledge and thus maintains the social consensus. It avoids interference in the 'private sphere' and in practices like domestic violence, dowry harassment, bride-burning, female foeticide or denial of various fundamental rights to women, etc. thus rendering them as a 'natural phenomenon'.

Margaret Hall[65] talks of the changing values in a world of change in her essay on 'Patriarchal Values' in the book *Women and Identity*. She says: 'Patriarchal values are pervasive throughout most of this world system of values. The institutionalized subordination of women to men is enormously resistant to change, given the status quo of those who benefit from it. The rise of more egalitarian values in some relatively small areas also is vulnerable to every political cross world. While homogenization of lifestyles has diluted traditional modes throughout the world system, in many instances distinctive and powerful traditional influences have been revived to cope with the political instability of economic materialism. In Middle Eastern societies, for example, long established traditions have been revived to buttress religious values in the midst of economic wealth.'

Noam Chomsky[66] in the book *Liberating Theory* has written with conviction and clarity that 'in spite of many different societies, there has been a remarkable continuity regarding a few important features of most kinship systems of which we have any knowledge. One critical kind of domination of man over woman, patriarchy, or male supremacy, has appeared as a key feature of most kinship system to date'. Patriarchy is the name for any kinship system in which the role divisions between gender groups grant fewer duties and more benefits from kinship activity to men than women.

The book *Platform for Action: Fourth World Conference on Women 1995 (UN 1996)*[67] records: 'Education and training for women has always been an essential tool for achieving the goals of equality, development and peace. Non-discriminatory education benefits both girls and boys and thus contributes to more equal relationships between women and men. Equality of access to attainment of educational qualifications is necessary, if more women are to become agents of change. Literacy of women is an important key to improving health, nutrition and education in the family and to empowering women to participate in decision-making in society. Investing in formal and non-formal education and training for girls and women brings with it high social and economic returns. Discrimination in the girl's access to education persists in many areas, owing to customary attitudes, early marriage and educational materials, sexual harassment and lack of accessible schooling facilities.'

In their edited book *Changing Status and Role of Women in Indian Society*, C. Chakrapani and S. Vijay Kumar[68] have made an extensive and multidisciplinary effort to examine the changes in the status and role of women in the Indian society. Such a study needs to take into account the varied roles women are called upon to play in their lives. The editors, therefore, have done well to bring together scholars from different disciplines to share their rich empirical experiences under five broad sections: Women and Development, Health and Education, Economic Activity, Political Participation and Women and Victimization.

The book *Women & Indian Society: Options and Constraints* by Andal N.[69] deserves a special mention here. In this work, the author has attempted to reflect the thinking of sociologists as they charted the trajectory of the early feminist movement, and commented on their goals and strategies. The chapters deal with the world's women and how they negotiated their living in different areas of activity like politics, commerce, education, media, health or the law and much else. This book is about women's identity, the pressures of culture route, and the hard choices that women specially have to make to retain their identity.

Efforts have also been made to scan available relevant secondary data and to assimilate all interesting and informative studies regarding the status of women to form the base for this study.

The Problem

The influence of structure and culture of a society on the lives of its members, more specifically the female sex, can hardly be overemphasized.

Diversity is found in Rajasthan as we move across from bigger cities to remote villages and enter obscure tribal habitats. The status of women has to be examined with relevance to the typical socio-cultural domain in each strata, which constitutes the pattern of marriage, rites and rituals, structure of family and socialization, issues of hierarchy and level of education.

Women's health, fertility and mortality are also closely linked with their status and while examining them, this study also gauges the nature and quality of modern health care services in tribal, rural and urban segments with specific reference to their concept of health, nutrition pattern, prevalent diseases, ethno-medical practices and also maternity and child care practices.

Political participation of women is an important determinant of their inclusion in mainstream development process. This also acts as an enabler for their empowerment. To gauge this important aspect, an attempt made to enquire into their initiative and inclination to participate in the political process.

An attempt will be made to assess and recognize the value of women's contribution to household economy both indirectly by way of unpaid labour in household and agricultural fields and also directly by earning from employment outside.

Fast-growing industrialization and urbanization, coupled with contemporary electronic revolution in the context of globalization, are influencing every walk of life. Modernization of society is taking place at a fast pace and women are also exposed to contemporary modernizing processes due to the impact of mass media. Educated urban women have started to shun inhibition in debating issues of female body and sexuality. To what extent this awareness has filtered down to the rural and tribal women deserves to be studied.

Leisure forms an essential part of our life and rejuvenates from the monotony of work and meeting the biological needs. Though the social structure and culture of a society has a direct concomitance to the patterns of leisure, it apparently seems that leisure has predominantly remained a prerogative of males as it is they who have all the freedom to use leisure as they like. It does not imply that women have no leisure, but what is important is the extent of freedom they enjoy for using their leisure time since freedom is an essential component of leisure. As such, the question of freedom vis-à-vis leisure has direct relevance to the status of women.

Therefore, it is proposed that all the aforesaid problematic issues which in varying degrees are related to women's overall status be studied in an overall context of the three major segments of women – tribal, rural and urban. This would bring to fore not only a holistic but also a comparative picture of the status of women belonging to all the major sections of our society.

Objectives

The major objectives of the present research are:

- To understand the relative position of tribal, rural and urban respondents within their socio-cultural domain.
- To explore issues related to health and maternity of women across these segments.
- To study the extent of political participation exhibited by respondents and the consequent empowerment it entails.
- To examine the effects of financial independence on the overall status of women and draw a comparison between working and non-working respondents.
- To probe sensitive issues such as gender, body and sexuality and analyse trends emerging across various segments.
- To gain insights regarding the extent and utilization of leisure.

Universe and Methodology

Since this study is focussed on a comparative study of women in the tribal, rural and urban society of Rajasthan, it is imperative that a sample fraction be included from all these segments in the overall sample of the study.

Since the major tribal groups of the region (from where we have taken the urban and the rural sample fraction) are said to have undergone major changes because of urban influences, it was thought proper that only such a tribal group be included in the study which has least urban exposure. The Garasias not only fulfilled this criterion but since they are also the least studied tribal group in the state of Rajasthan, it was thought proper that they constitute the tribal sample fraction of the study.

Garasia: The Tribal Community

Garasias constitute the third largest tribal group of Rajasthan after Meenas and Bhils, and inhabit Abu Road and Pindwara tehsils of Sirohi district, Kotra, Gogunda and Kherwara tehsils of Udaipur district and Bali and Desuri tehsils of Pali district. Their total population as per the

1991 census is 1,48,179 and this has distribution of 60,462 in Abu Road and 53,909 in Pindwara tehsil of Rajasthan.

The origin of Garasia has been a matter of conjecture by historians. The problem has become complicated on account of some historians confusing Girasia tribals with Grasya chieftains. Col James Tod came in contact with some Grasya chieftains of Mewar and wrote that a Grasya chieftain was one who held land (*gras*) by grant (*patta*) of the prince for which he performed service with specified quotas at home and abroad, renewable at every lapse[70]. Thus, a Grasya Jagirdar has perspective rights on land. He considered 'Grasya' to be derived from 'Gras', meaning subsistence.

Different scholars have used different spellings such as Grasia, Girasiya, Girrasia, Girresseya, Grasya, Girasia for the Garasias.

The word 'Girasia' originated around the thirteenth century. There is no earlier mention of the word in literature or inscriptions. The literal and etymological meaning of the word 'Girasia' can be understood if we remember that it is derived from denoting a forest-dwelling people. The Persian word 'Groh'[71] has led to the derivative Girahia, which has become Girasia. It only suggests that the Garasias had a 'tribal' character and inhabited the area where they are found. Their tribal character goes against their having originated by a mixture of different castes, as Erskine postulated.[72]

The forest-dwelling tribes like Bhils and Nishads were not under the control of Aryans as the Sudras[73] were. The word 'Nishad' of the '*Vajsaneyi Samhita*', according to law, is explained by commentator Mahendra to mean a 'Bhil'.[74] Not only this but in Yaka's *Nirukta,* the Nishads have been distinguished from the four *varnas*. In other words, these bow and arrow using, forest-living non-Aryan tribal Bhils, Nishads or for that matter any other tribe can safely be said to be of the same stock. According to Weber, these tribals were settled aboriginals. The socio-economic conditions, religious practices, mythology, internal *adakhs* (sub-clan), physical appearance, dress and other habits of the Garasias are very similar to that of the Bhils. It is because of the similarity that Lt Col Eriskine allied them with Bhils.[75] Historically, the Garasias may be called Bhils (using the word in a generic sense) though now they do not like to be called as such because the word is now used in a specific sense. In this sense, they claim to rank higher than Bhils.

According to oral history, the Chauhan Rajputs of Jalore when defeated at the hands of Alla-ud-Din Khilji (1,368 A.D.) fled to Bhil-infested hilly terrain. They overpowered the local Bhils and to pacify them also parted with some subsistence in their favour. These Bhils – *gras* holders – later on came to be known as Garasias and formed an endogamous community. It is also suggested that they are descendants of a Bhil girl and Rajput prince. Their origin is in Sirohi district. Their bardic account and folk songs link them with medieval Rajput history.

Sociologists and anthropologists are of the opinion that tribals do not leave their habitation even in modern times when better amenities and facilities are available. It goes to show that the tribals, Garasias in this context, are original inhabitants of the region in which they are found today. This is a sufficient denial to the explanation given by Tod, which confuses the origin of the Garasia with the word 'Gras', meaning a mouthful. The origin of the word has no economic overtones. It is a description of their habitat. His theory is of Garasias having been the descendants of Rajputs or Bhils and not Garasias. The social organization and customs of the Garasias, besides differences in physique and colour, reveal that they are fundamentally different from the Rajputs. They have the systems of Kawara Natra living as husband and wife without marriage, Raj-Baji (elopement), Khaichana (marriage by force), Ata-Sata (exchange), Natra (widow remarriage), which the Rajputs do not have. They are animists whereas the Rajputs are the followers of Hinduism. They are basically a bow and arrow using tribe while the Rajputs used swords and spears.[76]

The Garasias are divided into three endogamous territorial divisions, viz., Moti Niyat (caste), Nanki Niyat and Nichli Niyat. They are further sub-divided into as many as 28 exogamous, totemic clans or *adakhs* such as Parmar, Solanki, Raidara, Rathore, Bansia, etc. 'Phalia' or hamlet is generally inhabited by members of common lineage.

The Garasia society is patrilocal, patrilineal, kin-based and segmented. They mostly live in a nuclear family. Monogamy is preferred but polygamy is not abandoned in case of no issues. They cremate their dead. Rituals of marriage and death are almost like those of upper-caste Hindus. The Garasias have deep belief in various deities such as Dharamraj, Thakurji, Hawlo, Ganeshji, Kalaji-Goraji, Chamunda, Abu, Sitla and Amba Mata. Bhakar Baosi is a very powerful deity and hence very much dreaded. Bhopa is the traditional priest-cum-medicine man. Devra and Matadham are the sacred centres of the village. Garasias observe festivals like Akha Teej, Holi, Diwali, Navratri, Rakshabandhan, Dussehra, etc. They have a rich tradition of folk tales and folk songs.

The Garasia language is an admixture of Marwari, Bhili and Gujarati. Their dialect is known as Nyar-ki-Boli or Nyar dialect. one of the characteristic features of this dialect is the pronunciation of 's' as 'h'. The traditional male apparel is *safa* or *potiyu*, i.e. turban, the colour of which depends on age; red for young and white for aged, white *kurta, angarkhi* and *dhoti*. Traditional women attire is very colourful and comprises *gherdar ghagra, julki* and *odni*. Both the sexes are fond of using silver ornaments. Tattooing is very popular among women.

Map 1 *Location Map of Area of Study (Tribal) Sirohi District*

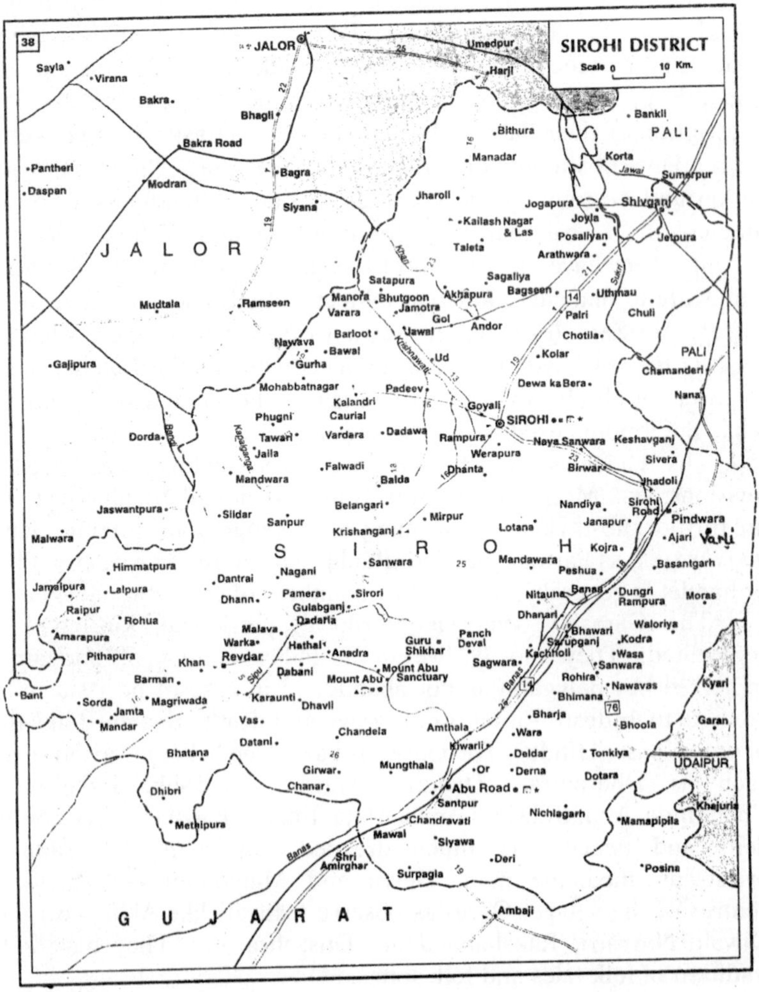

They are non-vegetarian. Their staple food is maize, *jawar*, rice and wheat. *Rab* or *rabdi* is the most popular food. *Churma, lapsi, malpua,* etc. are ceremonial food. Drinking of liquor is linked with their tradition. They normally brew liquor for consumption on community occasions like marriages and festivals.

The Garasias are settled agriculturists and also collect minor forest produce. Animal husbandry and wage-earning are also prevalent. *Halmo* and *helaru* are traditional systems of cooperative and economic activity prevalent in the society.

The Garasias are classified as a Scheduled Tribe, which identifies them in state administration documents as a socially disadvantaged community. They live in the marginally productive region of Sirohi and have little access to services and resources. All these indicators point to their being caught in what Chambers et al., call 'the deprivation trap' and its five interrelated clusters of disadvantage, i.e. physical, weakness, isolation, vulnerability and powerlessness.[77]

Varli village is situated 5 km interior on eastern side of Pindwara tehsil of Sirohi district and was chosen as our universe of study. Out of a total of 166 households, all were Garasias except for a single house wherein a Jogi family lived. Their living conditions are illustrative of acute poverty as majority of houses were temporary structures and we could find only four permanent houses in the entire village. Many houses had a small temple-like structure in their courtyard in which a small idol, usually of an ancestor, is seated, which is called *Bomyaji* in their local dialect and is worshipped.

Basic infrastructural facilities, such as roads, school and health centre, are lacking. We could find pathways created due to continuous movement of carts and carriages. There does exist a primary school running in two small rooms by a boy who had completed education till eighth class. Close to the school is a government-installed handpump for drawing water. In the middle of the village lie three shrines or *Devara* and this was the place for people to gather and discuss as well. Proper health care is not available and the sub-centre can take care of minor ailments only. People rush to the primary health centre at Pindwara for getting relief from prolonged illness. Water is a scarce resource as many handpumps are non-functional and women fetch water from wells situated within the village.

At the village level, there exists strong group cohesion on the basis of kinship. Originally, villages were organized on a clan basis though today one can find people of different clans living in a single village.

Such village-level organizations were meant to provide security and ensure well-being of clan members. Conflicts within the village between members of different clans were settled through village panchayats.

Villages are further sub-divided into *phalis* (streets) on the basis of *adakhs* (clan). Garasias of different *gotras* live in separate *phalis* and indicate their *adakh* as part of their name to maintain their social identity. A person is related to all those bearing the same *adakh* name and this practice enables them to enforce the exogamous injunctions at the time of marital contacts.

The Rural Community

In the spirit of taking the rural sample fraction from the same cultural region as urban, it was deemed proper that a village from within the district of Jaipur be chosen for the purpose of study. Other important considerations were to zero down on a multi-caste village which is in the interior and having least urban influence. Dangarwara village, located 58 km from Jaipur towards south, in Jamuva Ramgarh Panchayat Samiti, seemed to justify the above criterion. It is situated on a *pucca* road connecting Andhi and Jaipur and is bounded by Shekhawala (towards north), Phutala and Jagatsar (towards west), Samor (towards south) and Ramjipura (towards east) villages. Out of a total of 221 families residing in this village, 76 belonged to upper castes, 57 to Scheduled Castes, 21 to Scheduled Tribes and 67 to OBCs. Further microscopic examination revealed that Brahmins, Rajputs and Banias were pre-dominant upper castes whereas Meenas were the only Scheduled Tribe. Various Scheduled Castes lived in Dangarwara included Mahavar, Khatik, Raigar, Bairwa, Harijan, Balai, Dhanka, Koli and Dhobi. Families belonging to OBCs included Nai, Kumhar, Mehra, Mali, Muslims, Kir, Darji, Gusai, Rana, Sunar, Luhar, Khati, etc.

Members of a similar caste usually reside adjacent to one another in the same *gali* (street) or if their members are larger, in a single ward. (unit of a few streets adjacent to one another). A street is named after the class numerically dominant in it. Minor castes such as Sunar, Khati, Rana, etc. live on streets with a mixed population as they do not have their own streets. As per norms, untouchables and lower-caste families reside on the village outskirts and the central part is occupied by higher caste families. However, in recent years, this caste-based settlement pattern has been changed. Each caste has its own panchayat which deals with cases arising out of deviation from accepted norms of behaviour.

In terms of infrastructure, Dangarwara village is electrified and sources of water are tubewells, wells and a river pond. However, all tubewells are not functional and womenfolk have to travel several kilometres to fetch water. The village can boast of a middle school, an ayurvedic consultant, post office and a village panchayat building where all meetings take place. Although there is an allopathic government doctor, several private practitioners also perform in the village. Building of a primary health centre was under construction during the course of study. There were several temples and Hinduism

Map 2 *Location Map of Area of Study (Urban and Rural) Jaipur District*

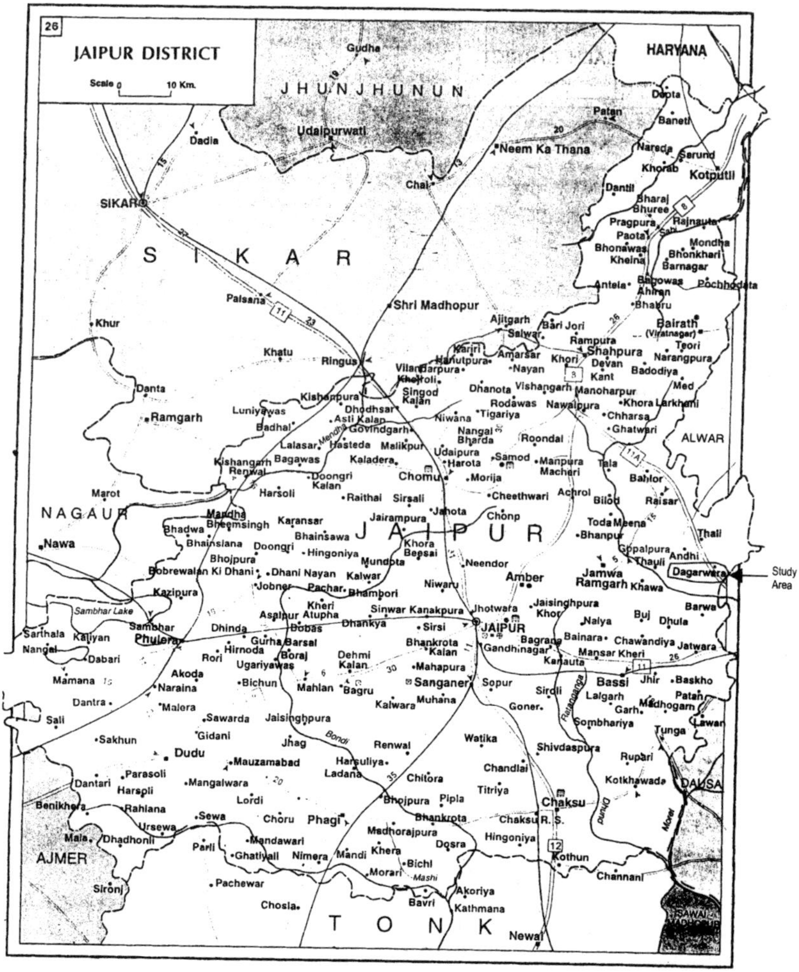

was the predominant religion in the studied village. People celebrated festivals like Diwali, Holi, Rakshabandhan, Dussehra, Akha Teej, Shitla Ashtami, Janmashtami, Shivratri, Ganesh Chaturthi, Teej, Gangaur, Basant Panchami, Id, Mohharam, etc. In Dangarwara village, there were temples of various popular deities such as Shivji, Gopalji, Hanumanji, Devji, Sita Ramji, Bhomiyaji, Bharavji and so on.

Dangarwara is primarily an agricultural village and occupations of the working population have been categorized into the following groups:

- Primary activities such as agriculture and allied activities, that is, forestry, plantation, mining and quarrying, etc.
- Industrial activities such as cottage industries, manufacturing, construction, etc.
- Trade and commerce.
- Transport, storage and communication.
- Services.

There is no regular market place in the village. However, a few shops exist, of which some deal in general household goods. We also came across a cycle repair shop, shops selling and repairing watches, selling clothes and two tea-stalls within this village.

The Urban Community

As far as the urban sample was concerned, Jaipur seemed as the most appropriate choice being the capital of Rajasthan and the fastest-growing urban conglomerate having all sorts of modernizing influences on its populace, particularly women. The foundation stone of Jaipur was laid on 18 November 1727 A.D. by Surya Vanshi Kachhawa, the ruler of Dhundar or Amber, Sawai Jai Singh II.

It was, indeed, for first time that a city of this size was built in India from a blueprint and rigidly followed the rules of Shilpa Shastra. Out of nine sectors, seven were planned for the exclusive use of the people, that is, for their houses, market places and entertainment. Master builders under the expert supervision of Vidhyadhar Bhattacharya transformed this dream into reality by end of 1733 – within six years of laying of the foundation stone. Jaipur was meticulously planned with wide roads and an underground drainage system. Two sectors on the north were reserved for royal places, observatory, offices, etc. The principal road running from east to west and joining Suraj Pol with Chand Pol was 2 miles and 40 yards in length and 111 feet wide and on this, six to seven carriages could be driven abreast.

There were three roads running from south to north and when they intersected the main street, they formed three spacious 'Chaupads' which not only imparted openness to the busiest part of town, but also formed the nucleic of all aesthetic, cultural, entertaining and leisurely activities of people.

Jaipur today has the largest population amongst the cities of Rajasthan. According to the 2001 census, out of 23,24,319 residents, the city has 12,39,711 males and 10,84,608 females.

The Sample

Our sample size included a total of 280 ever married respondents, out of whom 120 respondents were from urban society and 80 each from the tribal and rural society. The term 'ever married' denotes women who have been married once but are not necessarily married presently (that is, at the time of research). As the universe was big and widespread and it was difficult to decide which element was more critical, we used Stratified Probability sampling to divide our targeted population into various subgroups or strata (tribal, rural and urban women). Our sampling technique ensured that there was proper representation from each strata and we could also observe the relationship between our subgroups.

Efforts have been made to make the urban sample fraction as representative as possible by including women from all the three defined sectors, that is, formal, informal and household. We sampled 40 respondents each from these sectors to provide proper representation to diverse backgrounds of each sub-class. Formal sector respondents were well-educated and usually professionally qualified and working in the organized sector with a fixed monthly income. They included doctors, engineers, bank employees, teachers, government officers, etc. Informal sector respondents were usually uneducated and worked to support their families and included lady tailors, women involved in cottage industries such as handicrafts, jems, jewellery, tie and dye, etc. maid servants and vendors selling vegetables. Household sector respondents comprised housewives who were confined within the four walls of the house and did not work for earning.

Out of 165 Garasia households in Varli village, we selected 80 respondents from different *phalis* (streets) and varied *gotras* to provide wholesome representation to the entire population. Out of 221 respondents of Dangarwara village, we provided proper representation to 80 respondents by including respondents of different castes and age-groups and education levels to provide an overview.

The Methodology

A multipronged methodological approach was imperative as the profile and education level of respondents showed great diversity. While a questionnaire-cum-schedule was sufficient to collect data from urban women, among their rural counterparts, we resorted to intensive interviews besides a questionnaire-cum-schedule, supplemented by focussed group interviews and quasi-participant observations while interacting with tribal respondents. A leisurological approach was used to probe deeper to understand various facets of their life in a holistic manner by sharing their leisure and free time.

My being a woman researcher helped immensely as it provided easy and greater access to the tribal and rural respondents. On numerous occasions, when we interviewed women, their husbands were also present and chipped in with valuable information by reinforcing, contradicting and adding, which provided an insight into their thinking pattern and behaviour towards their wives.

Apart from fieldwork, we studied published and unpublished government and other documentary materials to increase the gravity and quality of the study.

Notes

1. Andal, N., 2002. *Women and Indian Society: Options and Constraints*, Jaipur: Rawat Publications, pp. 52–53.
2. Upadhyay, H.C., 1991. *Status of Women in India*, (Vol. I), New Delhi: Anmol Publications, p. 63.
3. Andal, N., op. cit., p. 53.
4. Stalin, 1978, 'Anarchism or Socialism', in *Women and Communism*, Calcutta: New Book Centre, p. 9.
5. Ibid.
6. Engles, 1978. 'Origin of Family', in *Women and Communism*, Calcutta: New Book Centre, p. 11.
7. Ibid., p. 16.
8. Ibid., pp. 10–11.
9. 'Conclusions of All India Conference on Women', 1976. *Social Scientist*, Vol. 4, No. 6, February, p. 57.
10. Thapar, Romila., 1975. 'Looking Back in History', in Devaki Jain (ed.), *Indian Women*, New Delhi: Ministry of Information and Broadcasting, Government of India. p. 5.
11. Ibid., p. 7.

12. Upadhyay, H.C., op. cit., p. 2.
13. Ibid.
14. Kuppuswamy, 1972. *Social Change in India*, Delhi: Vikas, p. 178.
15. Ibid.
16. Ibid.
17. Kuppuswamy, op. cit., p. 180.
18. Gupta, A.R., 1976. *Women in Hindu Society*, Delhi: Jyotsana Prakashan, p. 178.
19. Murli Manohar, K., V. Shoba, 1981. *The Status of Women in India : Some Trends and Issues*, Department of Public Administration, Kakatiya University, p.6.
20. Desai, Neera, 1957. *Women in Modern India*, Bombay: Vora & Co. Publishing Pvt. ltd., p. 74.
21. Gandhi, M.K., 1942. *Women and Social Injustice*, Ahmedabad: Navjivan, p. 132.
22. Chandrakala, P. Hate, 1969. *Changing Status of Women in Post Independent India*, Bombay: Allied Publishers Pvt. Ltd., pp. 113–134.
23. Gandhi, M.K., 1925. *Young India*, February 9.
24. Gandhi, M.K., 1942. *Women and Social Injustice*, p. 12.
25. Omvedt, Gail, 1977. 'Women and Rural Revolt in India', *Social Scientist*, Vol. 6, Nos. 1 and 2, August and September, pp. 3–18 and 21–40.
26. Everet, Jane Mason, 1979. *Women and Social Change in India*, New Delhi: Heritage Publishers.
27. Upadhyay, H.C., op. cit., p. 64.
28. Sapru, R.K., 1989. *Women and Development,* New Delhi: Ashish.
29. India, 1975. Ministry of Education and Social Welfare, *Towards Equality: Report of the Committee on the Status of Women in India.* Delhi, p. 7.
30. Ibid.
31. Srinivas, M.N., 1998. *Village, Caste, Gender and Method: Essays in Indian Social Anthropology*, New Delhi: Oxford University Press, p. 157.
32. Ibid.
33. Gupta, A.R., 1976. op. cit., p. 19.
34. Bhasin, Kamla and Nighat, Said Khan, 1986. *Some Questions on Feminism and Its Irrelevance in South Asia*, New Delhi: Raj Press, pp. 3–4.
35. Rao, Nina, 1985. 'The Woman Question: Perspective for Today', *Social Scientist*, Vol. 149–50, October–November, pp. 3–10.
36. Offen, K., 1992. 'Defining Feminism: A Comparative Historical Approach', in G. Book and S. Jove (eds), *Beyond Equality and Difference*, London and New York: Routledge, pp. 69–88.

37. Jaggar, A.J., 1983. *Feminist Politics and Human Nature*, Sussex: Harvester.
38. Moi, Toril, 1989. 'Feminist, Female, Feminine', in Catherine Belsey and June Moore (eds), *The Feminist Reader: Essays in Gender and the Politics of Literary Criticism*, London: Macmillan, p. 117–132.
39. Kemp, Sandra and Judith, Squires, 1997. 'Introduction', in Sandra Kemp and Judith Squires (eds), *Feminisms*, New York: Oxford University Press, pp. 3–12.
40. Jayawardena, Kumai, 1986. *Feminism and Nationalism in the Third World*, Zed Printers.
41. Schlesinger, P. (et al.), 1992. *Women Viewing Violence*, London BFI.
42. Andal, N. op. cit. p. 163.
43. Evans, Mary, 1997. *Introducing Contemporary Thought*, Cambridge: Polity Press.
44. Andal, N., op. cit. p. 1634
45. Waylen, Georgina, 1996. *Gender in Third World Politics*, Buckingham: Open University Press.
46. Hall, C. Margaret, 1990. *Women and Identity*, Washington: Hemisphere Publishing Corporation.
47. Sethi, Rajmohini, 1999. *Globalisation, Culture and Women's Development*, Jaipur: Rawat Publications.
48. Thapar, Romila, 1975. 'Looking Back in History', in Devaki Jain (ed.), *Indian Women*, New Delhi: Ministry of Information and Broadcasting, Government of India.
49. Mehrotra, Nilika, 2000. 'Perceiving Feminism: Some Local Responses', *Sociological Bulletin*, Vol. 5., No. 1, March.
50. Bhasin, Kamla and Nighat, Said Khan, 1986. op. cit., p. 4.
51. Ibid., pp. 4–5
52. Kosambi, D.D., 1991. 'Historical Perspective of Women', in H.C. Upadhyay (ed.), *Status of Women in India*, Vol. I, New Delhi: Anmol Publications.
53. Ide, Arthur Frederick, 1985. *Women Before History Was Written*, Dallas: Monument Press.
54. Bhave, Anjali, 1995. *Of Women Caste: The Experience in Rural India*, Calcutta: Stree Publications.
55. Gathaskar, Sujata, 1992. *Struggles of Women at Work*, Delhi: Vikas Publishing House.
56. Agarwal, Sushila, 1988. *Status of Women*, Jaipur: Rawat Publications.
57. Stromquist, Nelly P. (ed.), 1998. *Women in the Third World: An Encyclopedia of Contemporary Issues*, New York: Harland Publishing Inc.
58. Mitra, Jyoti, 1997. *Women and Society: Equality and Empowerment*, New Delhi: Kanishka Publishers.

59. Boserup, Ester, 1970. *Women's Role in Economic Development,* New York: St. Martin Press.
60. Gupta, Amit Kumar, 1986. *Women and Society: The Developmental Perspective,* New Delhi: Criterion Publication.
61. Majumdar, Veena, 1985. *Emergence of Women's Questions in India and the Role of Women,* New Delhi: Centre for Women's Development Studies.
62. Patel-Ahooja, Krishna, 1995. *Women and Sustainable Development: An International Dimension,* New Delhi: Ashish Publishing House.
63. U.N., 1998. *Too Young to Die: Genes or Gender,* New York: U.N.
64. Bathala, Sonia, 1998. *Women, Democracy and the Media,* New York: Sage Publications.
65. Hall, C. Margaret, 1990. 'Patriarchal Values', in Margaret, C. Hall (ed.), *Women and Identity,* Washington: Hemisphere Publishing Co.
66. Chomsky, Noam (et al.), 1986. *Liberating Theory,* Boston: South End Press.
67. U.N., 1996. *Platform for Action and Beijing Declaration Fourth World Conference on Women,* New York, U.N. Dept. for Public Information.
68. Chakrapani, C. and S. Vijay Kumar, 1994. *Changing Status and Role of Women in Indian Society,* New Delhi: M.D. Publications.
69. Andal, N., 2002. *Women and Indian Society: Options and Constraints,* Jaipur: Rawat Publications.
70. James, Col. Tod, 1920. *Annals and Antiquities of Rajasthan or the Central and Western Rajput States of India,* edited by William Crooke, Oxford: Oxford University Press.
71. They lived in groups and still follow the principles of 'Giroh' (group cohesion and unity). Bajrang Lal Lohia in his book *Rajasthan-ki-Jatiya,* p. 152.
72. Lt. Col. Erskine, 1910. *Gazetteer of Sirohi,* Ajmer: Scottish Mission, p. 255.
73. Macdonell and Keith, *Vedic Index,* Vol. I, 453.
74. Law, B.C., *Ancient Indian Tribes,* Vol. II, p. 61.
75. Erskine, 1910. op. cit., p. 255.
76. Meharda, B.L., 1985. *History and Culture of the Girasias,* Jaipur: Adi Prakashan, p. 12.
77. Chambers, R., N.C., Saxena and T. Shah, 1989. *To the Hands of the Poor: Water and Trees,* London: Intermediate Technology Publications, p. 10.

2 Status of Women and the Socio-Cultural Domains

Sociologists and anthropologists have expressed varying views regarding social status. According to Linton,[1] 'a status is a position in a particular pattern. It is, thus, quite correct to speak of each individual as having many statuses, since each individual participates in the expression of a number of patterns. However, unless the term is qualified, the status of any individual means the sum total of all the statuses which he occupies. It represents his position with relation to the total society.' Linton perceives role as a dynamic component of status. Thus, the role an individual plays or does not play may lead to changes in status. According to *Zaniecki*,[2] 'a person who is needed by a social circle and whose self possesses the qualities required for the role for which he is needed has a definite social status.' To Merton,[3] social status has been understood in terms of the 'degree to which a person possesses the qualities or attributes which are considered available in a particular society and performs his roles accordingly'. Giddens[4] looks at status as the 'social honour or prestige which a particular group is accorded by other member of a society'. Giddens also feels that this status or privilege may be positive or negative.

The above discussion leads us to the fact that it is not sufficient if a single criterion is taken into consideration for defining the concept of 'social status'. We need to have a wider vision and consider the entire set of indicators to determine the social status of an individual.

While sex refers to the anatomical differences governed by pre-programmed biological constituents, gender concerns the psychological and socio-cultural differences between male and female governed purely by foreordained codes of moral conduct and strictures laid down by society. While the former is important from the point of procreation and survival of the species, the latter greatly impinges the status of women, relegating them to the second best category after men. 'Many authors hold that there are inbuilt differences of behaviour between women and men that appear in one or other guise in all cultures. Others are unimpressed by this argument.'[5] Moreover, to consider the universal trait of male domination over female in terms of biological factors is erroneous. Countering the biological determinism of sexual difference, one should locate gender not as a natural category, emptied of culture and history, but as a context-specific social construct defined by existing power relations and social practices.[6] In other words, to understand gender relations, one must examine the various cultural traits mediated through structural and ideological forces that determine power relations. In fact, this social construction of relations of power-based social life signifies the situation of inequalities of power relations or the dominance and subordination.[7] This is generally true of all societies and more specifically in patriarchal societies with their deep-rooted normative orientations of patrilocal residence, patrilineal descent and patrilineal inheritance and succession which reinforce the centrality of male and expulsion of female to the periphery. Gender inequalities are found in the way families socialize their children and arrange and conduct marriages and the ways in which economic and political institutions overtly or covertly deny opportunities for women's empowerment.[8]

Hence, it is all the more important to understand the socio-cultural processes through which womanhood is constructed.

'The structure of anything consists of the stable relationships among its parts; moreover, the term 'part' itself implies a 'certain degree of stability'. Since a social system is composed of the interrelated acts of the people, its structure must be sought in some degree of regularity or recurrence in these acts.'[9]

Social structure is the pattern of interrelated statuses and roles found in a society or other group at a particular time and constituting a relatively stable set of social relations. It is the original pattern of the interrelated rights and obligations of persons and groups in a system of interaction as analysed in terms of statuses, roles, social norms, and social institutions. The term 'social organization' is sometimes used synonymously with social structure.[10]

Forte[11] believes that the term 'social organization' can be applied to any ordered arrangement of distinguishable whole, that is, to institutions, groups, situations, processes, social positions; but Evans-Pritchard restricts the term to the relationships between groups.

'Social phenomenon constitutes a distinct class of natural phenomenon. They are all, in one way or another, connected with the existence of social structures, either being implied in or resulting for them. Social structures are just as real as are individual organisms. The social phenomenon which we observe in any human society are not the immediate results of the nature of individual human beings, but are the result of the social structure by which they are united.'[12]

Redcliffe-Brown[13] considers all the social relations of a person with others as a part of a social structure; and he includes in the social structure the differentiations of individuals and of classes by their social roles. He says: 'In the study of the social structure, the concrete reality with which we are concerned is the set of actually existing relations, at a given moment of time, which links together certain human beings.'

Beteille[14] states: 'There is some advantage in viewing the social structure as a set of relations between groups of persons having a high degree of consistency and constancy. One can then identify these groups, define their boundaries and specify their mutual positions.'

The term 'social structure' has been used interchangeably with social organization in social anthropology and has been used particularly in the analysis of kinship and political and legal institutions of primitive societies.[15]

But Firth[16] explicitly distinguishes between the two terms. According to him, 'a social organization is concerned with the choices and decisions included in the actual social relations (the working arrangements of society), while social structures refers to the more fundamental social relations which give a society its basic form and which sets limits to the courses of action organizationally possible.'

Lucy Mair[17] says that the word 'structure' is the central concept in the large part of the work done in social anthropology. She adds that the society is thought of not as the culture but as an orderly arrangement of parts, which has to be detected and explained. It consists in relationships between persons which are regulated by common body or recognized rights and obligations.

Social and cultural structure has been defined as an ordered arrangement of relationship between members of a given social group and their way of life and the structure and culture of a society influences the lives of its members, particularly the women.

Society of Rajasthan is characterized by a variety of socio-religious perceptions, practices and institutions resulting in a cultural cauldron, the like of which is rarely seen anywhere else. In addition to the disparate caste system, established practices such as joint family, dowry, arranged marriage, untouchability, male dominance and their privileges and specific rituals from before one's birth to long after one's death give the social process in Rajasthan a uniqueness of its own, which leads to the argument whether all that has been followed is worth persisting with.

India, in the last six decades or so, has experienced vital changes in almost every aspect of her life. The processes of industrialization, urbanization and secularization have sharpened the pace of modernization process. It has brought about politico-economic, socio-psychological and cultural changes in the life patterns and attitudes of the people of this country, especially among the urban population.

The profound social changes that India has witnessed in the last decades have affected women much more than men. The changed socio-economic conditions have widened opportunities with new avenues to express and assert their quality. This, along with the newly-granted politico-legal privileges, is liable to affect their feelings, thoughts and ways of looking at vital issues of life.

The socio-economic emancipation of women in India has brought in its turn changes in their status and outlook. This change in their lives has also affected their views and behaviour patterns with regard to every field of individual and social activity.

In this chapter, an effort has been made to examine the status of women in their socio-cultural domain. The socio-cultural domain includes the pattern of marriage, rites and rituals, structure of family, violence against women, socialization, religion, etc.

Socio-Economic Profile of the Respondents

Age Group

We made a comparative study regarding the age pattern of the respondents and the comparative data is tabulated in Table 2.1.

Table 2.1 *Age Group-Wise Distribution of Respondents*

Age (in years)	*Tribal N=80*	*Rural N=80*	*Urban*				*Total N=280*
			Household N=40	*Informal N=40*	*Formal N=40*	*Sub-Total N=120*	
15–20	2(2.5)	9(11.2)	—	1(2.5)	—	1(0.8)	12(4.3)
21–30	30(37.5)	31(38.8)	17(42.5)	17(42.5)	6(15.0)	40(33.4)	101(36.0)
31–40	37(46.3)	32(40.0)	12(30.0)	16(40.0)	27(67.5)	55(45.8)	124(44.3)
Above 40	11(13.8)	8(10.0)	11(27.5)	6(15.0)	7(17.5)	24(20.0)	43(15.4)
Total	80(100)	80(100)	40(100)	40(100)	40(100)	120(100)	280(100)

Figures in parentheses indicate percentages.

The distribution of age pattern indicates early marriage and motherhood in tribal, rural and even urban household and informal sectors. In contrast, most of urban formal women got married late in life since their priorities regarding education and career were to be satisfied first.

Monthly Family Income

We tried to determine the economic status of family by asking respondents regarding their monthly income. Results are tabulated in Table 2.2:

Table 2.2 *Monthly Family Income*

Monthly Income (in ₹)	*Tribal N=80*	*Rural N=80*	*Urban*				*Total N=280*
			Household N=40	*Informal N=40*	*Formal N=40*	*Sub-Total N=120*	
Less than1,000	13(16.2)	8(10.0)	—	1(2.5)	—	1(0.8)	22(7.9)
1,000–4,999	63(78.8)	63(78.8)	4(10.0)	38(95.0)	1(2.5)	43(35.8)	169(60.3)
5,000–9,999	4(5.0)	7(8.7)	20(50.0)	1(2.5)	4(10.0)	25(20.8)	36(12.9)
10,000–19,999	—	2(2.5)	12(30.0)	—	24(60.0)	36(30.0)	38(13.6)
20,000 and above	—	—	4(10.0)	—	11(27.5)	15(12.5)	15(5.4)
Total	80(100)	80(100)	40(100)	40(100)	40(100)	120(100)	280(100)

Figures in parentheses indicate percentages.

Majority of respondents (60.3%) belonged to such families which had a monthly income between ₹ 1,000–4,999. These included 95% of urban informal sector, 10% of the urban household sector, and about 79% each of rural and tribal respondents. Only 2.5% formal urban sector respondents were found in this bracket. Similarly, 13% of total respondents confirmed earning between ₹ 5,000–9,999. These included 10% of the formal urban sector, 2.5% of the informal urban sector and one-half (50%) of the household sector respondents. Besides, 8.7% of rural and 5% of tribal respondents were also included in this class.

Almost a similar proportion (13.6%) of total respondents informed earning between ₹ 10,000–19,999. Within the urban community, majority (60%) of the formal sector respondents, 30% of the household sector and 2.5% of the rural respondents belong to this affluent section. A total of 8% of the total respondents earn less than ₹ 1,000 per month. These included 2.5% of informal sector, 10% of rural and 16.2% of tribal respondents. In sharp contrast, nearly 5% of total respondents admitted earning even more than ₹ 20,000 per month. These included more than one-fourth (27.5%) of the formal urban sector and one-tenth (10%) of household sector respondents.

Caste-Wise Distribution

While studying the profile of respondents, we categorized them into various castes as shown in Table 2.3.

Within the urban community, majority of (59.2%) respondents belonged to upper castes, nearly one-fourth (24.2%) to middle castes and 13.3% to lower castes. Major constituents of upper castes were Brahmins, Rajputs, Jains, Banias and Punjabis. Middle castes were dominated by Sindhis and Yadavs, while Bairwas, Harijans, Raigars and Kolis belonged to lower castes. Only 3.3% respondents belonged to other communities and religions such as Muslim and could not be categorized on the basis of above. In the formal sector, majority (90%) were from the upper castes. This trend was similar to the household sector where 80% of respondents belonged to the upper castes, and of the remaining 17.5% to the middle castes and 2.5% to the lower castes. This ratio was turned upside down wherein urban informal sector 45% respondents were from middle castes, 37.5% from lower castes and 10% from other castes. Only 7.5% of urban informal sector respondents belonged to upper castes.

Table 2.3 *Caste-Wise Distribution*

Category	*Tribal N=80*	*Rural N=80*	*Urban*				*Total N=280*
			Household N=40	*Informal N=40*	*Formal N=40*	*Sub-Total N=120*	
Upper Castes	80(100.0)	30(37.5)	32(80.0)	3(7.5)	36(90.0)	71(59.2)	181(64.6)
Middle Castes	—	28(35.0)	7(17.5)	18(45.0)	4(10.0)	29(24.2)	57(20.4)
Lower Castes	—	21(26.3)	1(2.5)	15(37.5)	—	16(13.3)	37(13.2)
Others	—	1(1.2)	—	4(10.0)	—	4(3.3)	5(1.8)
Total	80(100)	80(100)	40(100)	40(100)	40(100)	120(100)	280(100)

Figures in parentheses indicate percentages.

In the rural community, 37.5% respondents came from the upper castes, 35% from the middle castes and more than one-fourth (26.3%) respondents came from lower castes. While Brahmins, Rajputs and Banias constituted upper caste rurals, Kumhars, Suthars, Nais, Sunars, Lohars, Khatis, Meenas, Malis and Dhobis fell amongst middle castes. Lower castes amongst rural comprised Harijans, Raigars, Kolis and Dhankas. In a singular instance, we came across a Muslim respondent.

The prevailing perception and norms of caste-wise segregation have some relevance in tribal society. However, in our course of study, 100% of respondents belonged to upper castes.

Educational Status

Education and socialization are interlinked processes and imply inculcation of norms, values, attitudes, morals and different skills, status, etc. As a matter of fact, its importance as the prime initiator of change is too obvious to be dilated upon at length. Simultaneously, it is an established fact that the rate and level of literacy progressively decreases in the rural communities as compared to their urban counterparts. The situation gets further worsened sex-wise from male to female. An attempt to plot the education level of respondents from illiterate at one end and professionally/technically educated at the other led to the results which are compiled in Table 2.4.

It is interesting to note that 37% of urban household sector women were technically/professionally or highly qualified. In the urban formal sector, a large number of respondents (75%) were technically/professionally qualified. This was reflective in their forward-looking attitude and economic self-reliant status.

Table 2.4 *Educational Status*

Level of Education	*Tribal N=80*	*Rural N=80*	*Urban*				*Total N=280*
			Household N=40	*Informal N=40*	*Formal N=40*	*Sub-Total N=120*	
Illiterate	80(100.0)	52(65.0)	—	20(50.0)	—	20(16.7)	152(54.3)
Literate	—	9(11.3)	—	5(12.5)	—	5(4.2)	14(5.0)
Primary	—	10(12.5)	6(15.0)	8(20.0)	—	14(11.7)	24(8.6)
Middle	—	9(11.3)	5(12.5)	3(7.5)	—	8(6.7)	17(6.1)

Cont'd...

...Cont'd

Higher Sec./ Senior Sec.	—	—	4(10.0)	2(5.0)	2(5.0)	8(6.7)	8(2.8)
Graduate	—	—	11(27.5)	2(5.0)	8(20.0)	21(17.5)	21(7.5)
Technical/ Professional or Higher	—	—	14(35.0)	—	30(75.0)	44(36.3)	44(15.7)
Total	80(100)	80(100)	40(100)	40(100)	40(100)	120(100)	280(100)

Figures in parentheses indicate percentages.

In the rural community, on the contrary, majority (65%) of the respondents were illiterate. Of the balance, more than one-tenth (11.3%) had reached up to secondary level education, while 12.5% were primary educated and other 11.3% respondents barely literate. All tribal respondents were found illiterate and this was responsible for their low status and insecurity.

The general picture of female literacy in Rajasthan is quite depressing but lower literacy rates amongst SC/ST females are quite alarming, notwithstanding higher rates among a few tribes.

Types of Families

Joint family system has been traditionally an integral part of Indian society and it is also predominantly present in both tribal and rural societies. Hence, it is worthwhile to observe the scenario in this respect. Data collected in this regard is presented in Table 2.5.

Table 2.5 *Family Pattern*

Type	*Tribal N=80*	*Rural N=80*	*Urban*				*Total N=280*
			Household N=40	*Informal N=40*	*Formal N=40*	*Sub-Total N=120*	
Nuclear	64(80.0)	35(43.8)	21(52.5)	21(52.5)	25(62.5)	67(55.8)	166(59.3)
Joint	16(20.0)	45(56.2)	19(47.5)	19(47.5)	15(37.5)	53(44.2)	114(40.7)
Total	80(100)	80(100)	40(100)	40(100)	40(100)	120(100)	280(100)

Figures in parentheses indicate percentages.

It is clear from the table that nearly 60% of total respondents were living in a nuclear set-up. It is interesting to note that a high majority (80%) of tribal respondents opted for nuclear families, followed by nearly 56% of urban respondents and further reduced proportion of 44% respondents in the rural set-up. Urban society has witnessed a sharp degradation of the joint family culture and couples seek more privacy and minimal interference from even blood relatives. This has propagated a sharp increase in the nuclear set-up. Another reason is a transferable job in the urban community due to which children after marriage may be forced to live far away from parents.

As stated above, only 44% of respondents in the rural community were living in nuclear families and 56% in joint families. Lack of exposure, easy lifestyles and interdependency among relatives besides economy of scale in agriculture are major reasons for cohesion among various family members. They realize that division of family assets such as land, cattle, house, etc. will lead to less productivity and more hardship.

In sharp contrast, majority of the tribal respondents (80%) were living in nuclear families. The family pattern amongst the Garasias is nuclear where a person constructs a new hut for himself and his wife. The wife does not have to live in a joint family or face too many restrictions. The new hut is, however, near the huts of his brothers and other clan men. On getting married, a son is given his share of land to cultivate and earn revenue for his house. These separate nuclear families cooperate with each other with regard to all activities regarding cultivation, i.e. sharing well water, oxens to harness to fields and collective labour in fields. This is an interesting mix combining benefits of both nuclear and joint family systems. Households are separate regarding daily production, consumption of food and distribution of income within various members. Secondly, the labour of the wives regarding household activities is limited to individual families. Outside the household, they represent a collective joint family wherever such efforts are required. Even if the male member is away from the village, his brother would prepare the field in his absence and families take full care of each other during illness, etc.

Even in rare cases where one comes across joint families, the following trends may be observed:

- Adult married brothers never lived under one roof.
- Elderly parents lived with the younger son and in such cases, younger son was entitled to a proportionally higher share in land and other resources.
- Multiple wives of singular husband lived under one roof in total harmony and cooperation. Polygamous marriage is considered a

matter of social prestige and successful, powerful and wealthy Garasia males solemnize many marriages and even provide independent living units for each of their wives.

Marriage

Marriage is an important institution in Indian society. All individuals are expected to enter into a marital union and establish their families. While there is much variation amongst different groups regarding marriage customs and beliefs, the institution of marriage itself is common to all. Marriage is an essential socio-religious duty for all Hindus. It is a sacrament, and among the 'twice-born' castes, religious considerations are especially prominent in making marriage obligatory.[18]

Marriage among tribals, on the contrary, is a contract and there is no sanctity attached to it. Tribals value the social recognition accorded to a union between a man and a woman. Marriage also provides legitimacy to children. In a tribal society, social parentage is very important and hence marriage as a form of recognizing parents is given great value. This phenomenon of marriage has been a matter of great interest among anthropologists and the position in regard to respondents of the present study is given in Table 2.6.

Table 2.6 *Types of Marriage*

Type	*Tribal N=80*	*Rural N=80*	*Urban*				*Total N=280*
			Household N=40	*Informal N=40*	*Formal N=40*	*Sub-Total N=120*	
Arranged	10(12.5)	80(100.0)	39(97.5)	37(92.5)	34(85.0)	110(91.7)	200(71.4)
Love Marriage	63(78.7)	—	1(2.5)	3(7.5)	6(15.0)	10(8.3)	73(26.1)
Nata	7(8.8)	—	—	—	—	—	7(2.5)
Total	80(100)	80(100)	40(100)	40(100)	40(100)	120(100)	280(280)

Figures in parentheses indicate percentages.

Types of Marriage

As expected, as in overall Indian context, the predominant mode remains arranged marriage. In totality, 71.5% respondents said they had gone in for an arranged marriage. The performance of marriage, decision regarding the choice of mate, its date and time, etc. are decided by the male head of the family in consultation with other members. Cent per cent marriages in the rural community were arranged marriages and this reduced to nearly 92% in case of urban respondents. Within urban community, in formal sector, we had 85% instances of arranged marriage, which increased to 92.5% in informal sector and 97.5% in the urban household sector. In sharp contrast, only 12.5% of tribal respondents acknowledged going in for such a marriage.

More than one-fourth (26%) of the total respondents got attracted mutually, which culminated in love marriage. In the urban community, 15% of the formal sector, 7.5% of the informal sector and 2.5% of the household sector respondents were in this category. It is interesting to note that more than three-fourth (78.7%) of tribal respondents went in for a love marriage. Besides, we also came across 8.8% of tribal respondents who went in for remarriage (referred to as *nata*) due to the death of husband or incompatibility between husband and wife.

In the popular practice among Hindus, 'marriage' (*shadi*) is the term used to describe the social and ritualized celebrations of a man bringing his wife away from natal home to live with him. It involves an intricate and elaborate religious ceremony at the house of girl after the payment of dowry. The marriage is usually consecrated by a Brahmin priest and sanctions the entry of a girl into sexual and reproductive relations with a man of the appropriate affinal group.

The Garasia *shadi* also involves long rituals over a span of three to seven days. The marriage ceremony among the Garasias is similar to the non-Garasias in terms of the symbolic meanings of the various rituals performed like *Hagai* (*sagai*, engagement) and *Peethi Chadhana* (the application of turmeric paste). Both the bride and groom remain tinged by the yellow paste of the turmeric for several days, even after the paste has been washed off. In North Indian Hindu marriages, turmeric is regarded as pure and auspicious and is used especially at marriages.[19]

Mata Manana ceremonies before and after the *Peethi* include worshipping of the clan mother, who is invited to bless the occasion. Although the nature of ceremonies such as *Peravana* (clothing by mother's brother), *Manda* (*Mandap*), *Phera* (making circles around the holy fire) is similar to Hindu rituals, these ceremonies are administered by any responsible village elder and dependency on a Brahmin for performing these ceremonies is not compulsory. Marriage is considered an important and social celebration and much expenditure is incurred. The Garasia marriage follows the rules of tribal endogamy and village and clan exogamy. A person is prohibited from marrying in his father's (i.e. his own) clan.

Marriage by elopement is a popular form of marriage among the Garasias.[20] This is a traditional way of selecting a wife among the Garasias. Elopement (*Khichaha*) may be either with the consent of two parties or without consent. Selection of a life-partner is the free choice of both the boys and girls. Originally, life-partners were selected by choice and understanding at the village area, market, fairs, marriage ceremonies and forest in which girls were freely allowed to participate by their parents. Garasia people allow their youngsters some amount of freedom in mixing freely with the opposite sex prior to marriage. Among Garasias, there is a complete absence of restrictions on the mobility of girls till their marriage. A young woman can elope with a person of her choice or even force herself upon him, and this union may be socially accepted when the brideprice is settled.

So long as young men and women do not violate the rules and norms related to exogamy in relation to clan endogamy in choosing the life-partner, free mixing between sex is not questionable. These meetings provide opportunities to both the boys and girls for proper and suitable selection of a life-partner. Pre-marital relationship is not considered objectionable among Garasias.

Elopement is pre-planned and needs a long preparation. This has been accepted as the most convenient method of marriage because it is based on the consent of both the parties. It is more economical than arranged marriages and suitable for Garasia parents who are economically not well-off. No religious or marriage rites are performed. After the payment or settlement of *dapa*, the couple is allowed to live like husband and wife and social sanctity is given to such a marriage.

A Garasia marriage has a striking similarity to a traditional North Indian Hindu wedding. There are elaborate rituals and ceremonies with feast spread over several days. However, Garasia marriage takes place after the couple have lived together for several years and often even after birth of their children. In essence, a Garasia marriage does not indicate the starting of a couple's conjugal relationship as in traditional marriage.

Nata means the remarriage of a divorcee, abducted or eloped woman. There is a provision for divorce and remarriage among the Garasias as amongst other tribal groups. Widows are not degraded and are free to marry. Many times, a married woman enters into a relationship with another man and this relationship is also known as *nata*. This relationship is given social sanction only after the second husband pays a compensation amount known as *dava* (literally, challenge) as decided by the village panchayat to the previous husband of the woman. This amount is more than the *dapa* by at least one-and-a-half times, while in case of widow remarriage, the brideprice or *dapa* is lower than in an ordinary case.

In a rural set-up, occurrence of *nata* is there amongst lower castes. However, we did not come across any such case during the course of the present study. The kind of taboos or rigid restrictions governing marriage that are prevalent in non-tribal societies are generally absent in tribal society.

Marriage and Dowry/Brideprice (Dapa)

The custom of dowry is another feature of Indian society in which the bride's parents give gifts and cash to the boy's family at the time of marriage. In the last 50 or 60 years, it has become coercive. '... dowry, in due course, became the deciding factor in the marriage market among several communities in India.'[21] Dowry has become a social evil and has also led to the emergence of various social, economic, psychological and ethical problems in the society. As a result of modernization, it is hoped that people would also reframe their ideas in this direction.

In contrast, the system of dowry has never existed in tribal context. Tribal society believes in the concept of brideprice (*dapa*), which is paid by the groom to the family of his would-be wife. Traditionally, it was in kind, that is gifts, animals, etc. But, now, it has an added dimension of giving cash also. To evaluate the level of existence of such systems, we asked our respondents regarding dowry/*dapa* given or received by their parents during their marriage. Results are presented in Table 2.7.

Within the urban community, the amount of dowry was significantly higher in the formal and household sectors as compared to their counterparts in the informal sector. Likewise, in the urban household sector, 22.5% respondents said they gave a nominal dowry of ₹ 2,500. For another 17.5% respondents, this was between ₹ 2,500–4,999 and for 15%, the amount stretched up to ₹ 50,000. Only in 5% cases, more than ₹ 50,000 was spent on dowry. However, 40% of the household and 20% of the formal sector respondents could not elaborate on this topic. In sharp contrast, more than half (52.5%) of the respondents in the urban informal sector gave normal dowry up to ₹ 2,500, whereas 47.5% respondents did not elaborate on this topic.

Table 2.7 *Expenditure on Dowry/Brideprice*

Expenditure (in ₹)	*Tribal N=80*	*Rural N=80*	*Urban*				*Total N=280*
			Household N=40	*Informal N=40*	*Formal N=40*	*Sub-Total N=120*	
None	3(3.7)	—	1(2.5)	1(2.5)	1(2.5)	3(2.5)	6(2.1)
Less than 500	8(10.0)	8(10.0)	2(5.0)	3(7.5)	1(2.5)	6(5.0)	22(7.9)
500–999	13(16.3)	15(18.8)	2(5.0)	8(20.0)	3(7.5)	13(10.9)	41(14.6)
1,000–2,499	38(47.5)	8(10.0)	4(10.0)	9(22.5)	2(5.0)	15(12.5)	61(21.8)
2,500–4,999	15(18.8)	10(12.5)	7(17.5)	—	—	7(5.8)	32(11.4)
5,000–9,999	3(3.7)	10(12.5)	—	—	—	—	13(4.6)
10,000–24,999	—	4(5.0)	—	—	5(12.5)	5(4.1)	9(3.2)
25,000–49,999	—	6(7.5)	6(15.0)	—	15(37.5)	21(17.5)	27(9.6)
50,000 and above	—	2(2.5)	2(5.0)	—	5(12.5)	7(5.8)	9(3.2)
NR/DK	—	17(21.3)	16(40.0)	19(47.5)	8(20.0)	43(35.8)	60(21.4)
Total	80(100)	80(100)	40(100)	40(100)	40(100)	120(100)	280(100)

Figures in parentheses indicate percentages.

The amount of dowry in rural areas is proportionately much higher in upper-caste educated elite such as Brahmin, Bania, etc. It is surprising to note that in all cases of Meena community, the relevance of brideprice was conveniently ignored. In the last few decades, the Meenas have also adopted certain features and customs of the traditional Hindu marriage and consequently now much expenditure is incurred on the pomp and show. Now, an educated Meena boy demands high dowry for an uneducated girl. The introduction of dowry and other pompous features is the result of their growing contacts with the upper caste Hindus and the process of acculturation. Today, the girl's parents are cajoled, coaxed and coerced into spending more than their means. This trauma continues even after marriage.

Even in the tribal community, the greed and materialistic attitude is on the rise. Most of our older respondents recalled how in their case minimal amount of *dapa* was paid. However, in younger generation, the brideprice has risen significantly higher. Consent of both parties is essential in a Garasia marriage, whether it is an arranged one or by elopement. The Garasia marriage is legalized after paying *dapa*, which differs from person to person depending on the social status of the parents of the bride and groom.

The payment of brideprice is an important aspect of the Garasia marriage. A girl is considered an essential working member of the household and her loss, which the parental family suffers, is compensated by the payment of brideprice. Personal appearance and physical beauty have little relevance to the brideprice. The brideprice is higher for a girl who is thrifty, strong, hardworking and knows the act of home management. A girl who is clean, properly dressed, strong and works properly at home and at field, is more wanted than others.

In general, the women of India face a lot of problems to get a suitable match because of the dowry system. Here, the women are considered life-long liabilities and dowry provides compensation for accepting a girl who would be the future burden for the groom's family. Babu Garasia told this researcher that the Garasia men consider their wives to be good, gentle and hardworking. More brideprice was paid for younger as opposed to older women and within the same generation for those who were more physically fit and reproductive. Similarly, in both brideprice and dowry cases among Garasias, the movement of wives not only facilitates inheritance in the form of flow of money or goods, but it also redistributes rights between the natal and affinal male-headed households. Women, in other castes, strengthen their claim on the immovable property in favour of their brothers. Garasia women strengthen their husband's household with their labour, children and food. They also strengthen their brother's household by providing brideprice and transferring their consumption needs.[22]

The dominance of wife-takers over wife-givers is ensured right from the time of negotiation of marriage. The father of a bride has a status lower than that of the father of a groom. The members of the bride's family are expected to be subordinate to the groom's family members. Otherwise, they may run the risk of cancellation of the marriage.

There is no difference between the '*gharatis*' and the '*baratis*' in Garasia society. Food is usually offered and whatever it is, a *barati* has to accept it without any fuss. The last-minute tensions generally faced in non-tribal marriages are totally absent here.

Expenditure on Marriage

Marriage is regarded as the most important institution in Indian context. Parents try to fulfil their ambition by getting their daughter married according to the best of their resources. We asked our respondents regarding the expenditure incurred on their marriage.

In a Garasia marriage, the items a bride brings to her husband's house include a *vadku* (metal plate), *lota* (a small metal drinking pot), the clothes she wears, and the few pieces of cheap jewellery acquired as gifts or purchased over the years. Sometimes, the bride may also be 'gifted' her favourite goat or calf, if she belongs to a richer family. At her in-laws' house, the bride is presented silver jewellery which she can wear but which remains the property of the husband and his sons.

In a nutshell, it can be inferred that for rural and urban upper-caste inhabitants, marriage is the culmination of life-long desires and ambitions. Such feelings are reflected in pomp and show and heavy expenditure on weddings is incurred by the girls' parents in arranged marriages. However, among the Garasias, instances of arranged marriage are rare as it involves social customs, feasts, etc. resulting in higher expenditure, which most of them cannot afford. Hence, they have conveniently adopted live-in relationships.

Age at Marriage

We plotted the age of respondents at the time of marriage and the results are displayed in Table 2.8.

Table 2.8 *Age at Marriage*

Age (in years)	*Tribal N=80*	*Rural N=80*	*Urban*				*Total N=280*
			Household N=40	*Informal N=40*	*Formal N=40*	*Sub-Total N=120*	
Less than 14	4(5.0)	36(45.0)	2(5.0)	8(20.0)	—	10(8.3)	50(17.8)
14–16	31(38.7)	30(37.5)	5(12.5)	12(30.0)	1(2.5)	18(15.0)	79(28.2)
17–19	30(37.5)	10(12.5)	10(25.0)	11(27.5)	2(5.0)	23(19.1)	63(22.5)
20–22	14(17.5)	4(5.0)	14(35.0)	6(15.0)	8(20.0)	28(23.3)	46(16.4)
23–25	1(1.2)	—	9(22.5)	2(5.0)	22(55.0)	33(27.5)	34(12.1)
26 & above	—	—	—	1(2.5)	7(17.5)	8(6.7)	8(2.8)
Total	80(100)	80(100)	40(100)	40(100)	40(100)	120(100)	280(100)

Figures in parentheses indicate percentages.

Age at the time of marriage is an important indicator and reflects the attitude of parents as well as society towards the girl child. In an urban formal set-up, parents usually do not discriminate between boy and girl and their endeavour is towards providing a conducive environment for study and overall personality development. As a consequence, good school conduction, higher/professional education and a settled earning life are given more importance before marriage.

In the urban household sector, the family could be financially well-off but at the same time, we also came across instances where parents were seen as orthodox and conservative in outlook toward their girl child and in many cases after routine schooling or at best after graduation, they were married off.

Though the outlook was similar in the urban informal sector, things became complicated due to lack of resources and acute poverty. A girl child is considered a liability and efforts are made to get her married off at the earliest. Due to the orthodox outlook, lack of education and exposure, poverty is most significantly observed in the rural community where 45% of respondents were married off before 14 years of age.

In the tribal community, girls get married just after attaining puberty. Thus, 76% of cases of marriage are between 14–19 years of age. A girl child before marriage is free from restriction and can roam independently with friends. After marriage, her life is burdened with the daily grind of domestic chores, besides having a suspicious husband who does not allow her to venture out.

We also studied the age difference between the husband and the wife and results are presented in Table 2.9.

Table 2.9 *Age Difference between Husband and Wife*

Difference (in years)	*Tribal N=80*	*Rural N=80*	*Urban*				*Total N=280*
			Household N=40	*Informal N=40*	*Formal N=40*	*Sub-Total N=120*	
Less than 2	10(12.5)	20(25.0)	8(20.0)	6(15.0)	12(30.0)	26(21.7)	56(20.0)
2–4	30(37.5)	25(31.2)	15(37.5)	12(30.0)	14(35.0)	41(34.2)	96(34.3)
4–6	12(15.0)	10(12.5)	15(37.5)	13(32.5)	13(32.5)	41(34.2)	63(22.5)
6–8	15(18.7)	5(6.3)	2(5.0)	2(5.0)	1(2.5)	5(4.1)	25(8.9)
8–10	9(11.3)	5(6.3)	—	5(12.5)	—	5(4.1)	19(6.8)
More than 10	4(5.0)	15(18.7)	—	2(5.0)	—	2(1.7)	21(7.5)
Total	80(100)	80(100)	40(100)	40(100)	40(100)	120(100)	280(100)

Figures in parentheses indicate percentages.

In more than one-third (34.3%) cases, there was an age difference from 2 to 4 years between the husband and the wife. Trends in rural and tribal communities were similar and 31.2% and 37.5% of respondents, respectively, had above age difference. However, nearly one-fourth (22.5%) of the total respondents had a gap of 4–6 years. This proportion drops to 12.5% and 15% among the rural and tribal people, respectively.

In 20% cases, this gap was less than two years. In the urban community, this included 30% of the formal sector, 15% of the informal sector and 20% of the household sector respondents. Proportion of such respondents was 25% in rural and 12.5% in tribal society. In 9% cases, this gap was between 6 and 8 years of age. In urban society, we came across 5% such respondents, both in formal and household sectors, and only 2.5% in informal sector. Percentage of such respondents rose marginally to 6.3% in rural and significantly to 18.7% in tribal community. For 7% respondents, this gap was increased and remained between 8 and 10 years.

In 7.5% cases, the age difference between the husband and the wife was even more than 10 years. In the urban community, again, this was limited to 5% respondents of the informal sector while this proportion was much higher at 18.7% among rural respondents and dropped down 5% with regard to tribal respondents. In the tribal community, there were a few cases where husbands have two or three wives and the age difference was bound to increase.

Transition and Adjustments in Married Life

To find out the transition from living with parents to living with husband/in-laws, the respondents were quizzed regarding specific areas where they faced resistance from their family after marriage. Nearly 27% did not face any restriction from their in-laws/husband. In the urban sample, such respondents included 50% from the formal sector respondents, 12.5% from informal and 37.5% from the household sector. Besides, 18.8% of the rural and 25% of the tribal respondents also shared their viewpoint.

Respondents who were restricted not to visit anywhere (e.g. temple, river for bathing, relative's house, friends, market, etc.) were 13.7% of the total sample size. Such restrictions were more pronounced both in tribal (25%) and rural (18.7%) communities and were limited to only 5% of the urban informal sector respondents. Similarly, respondents who were not permitted to move out alone for work constituted 7.5% of the total. In the urban society, such restrictions were faced by 2.5% of the formal sector respondents, 10% by the informal sector respondents and again 2.5% by the household sector respondents. A total of 6.2% and 12.5% of rural and tribal respondents, respectively, also acknowledged facing such restrictions.

Respondents questioned on returning late from work formed 6.8% of the total. In the urban society, 10% of the formal sector respondents had faced this situation and 12.5% of the rural and 6.2% of the tribal respondents also agreed with them. It was also observed that 4% of the total respondents, wanted to study further but were not allowed to do so after marriage.

Among urban household sector respondents who wanted to take up a job but could not due to family pressure, the figure was15% in totality. Such cases constituted 2.1% among total respondents.

One-tenth of urban formal sector respondents (1.5% of total) held a grudge that they were not allowed to pursue and participate in sports and dramatics. Another 3.6% wanted to take up membership of various organizations, but were not allowed to do so. In the urban community, 5% of formal and 10% of household sector respondents were in this category. It is interesting to note that 10.5% of total respondents faced restrictions on such trivial issues such as talking to neighbours.

Carefree and unburdened life of a young Garasia girl changes orbit after marriage. In the husband's home, she is besieged with expectations from all family members as well as village elders of *huhara* (affinal village). It is imperative to follow certain norms in her daily life and interaction with blood relatives of husband. She covers her face before certain categories of male affinal members. These include *hahur* (husband's father), *jeth* (elder brother of husband), and *jamai* (elder and younger sisters-in-law's husbands). This concept of *laaj kadhana* (veil) is a token of respect and shame. However, a married woman is not expected to observe *laaj* in front of *hahu* (husband's mother), *devrani* (husband's younger brother's wife) and *nanad* (husband's sister). She is made to realize that her husband's lineage is superior to her parents. A Garasia *vehu* (bride) cannot think of sitting on a cot in proximity of Garasia menfolk. Such actions would indicate that she considers her own lineage (fathers, brothers) as superior to her husband. Such behaviour is unexpected of a Garasia *vehu*. She is also not allowed to eat food cooked by her mother-in-law, sister-in-law or their children. She has to cook her own food and is not allowed to use utensils used by other family members in the husband's house for eating. She brings her own *vadku* (brass plate) and *lota* (water vessel) from *piyar* (natal home) at the time of marriage and uses these throughout her life. However, her husband and children can eat in her vessels and enjoy food cooked by her mother-in-law and sister-in-law, etc. She is expected to maintain decorum and respect and she does not go to houses of husband's relatives unless desired by womenfolk there. Wives are also not free to move in the village unless there is a pressing need or urgency. Due to all this, they are unable to form working groups with other Garasia women.

There is a striking similarity in the overall condition of women in the tribal and rural context. In the village, women of the Rajput caste usually remain indoors and do not work in the fields. Another manifestation of female seclusion is *ghunghat* (veil to cover the face) worn by women of all castes. It is mandatory for a young daughter-in-law to cover her face in the presence of all seniors in the conjugal household, the neighbourhood and even in the village, unless the elderly man is a natal kin. She does not speak directly even with elderly women until several years of her marriage. She nods her head or clicks her tongue to convey short responses. She may communicate directly only after bearing two to three children while still observing *ghunghat*. It is only after becoming a mother-in-law and a grandmother that she can remove her *ghunghat*, and that too before senior women. However, we did not come across any demanding customs in the rural context which are prevalent in tribal society, where women face no restriction in eating food cooked by mother-in-law, sister-in-law and their children.

Discrimination Faced by Girl Child

Socialization turns the child to a useful member of the society and gives him maturity. The child's socialization has always taken place within an institutional framework and has been controlled through institutional channels.[23] Carter Hodding Jr.[24], a journalist and philosopher, stated two goals of socialization process. These are two lasting bequests that should be given to children. One is the roots, the other is wings. Conventional sex-differentiated socialization practice tends to encourage the development of roots in girls and also minimizes the importance of wings. For boys, the pattern is reversed. These roots/wings are acquired through the process of socialization by agents such as parents, teachers, peers and the mass media. The girl child picks up parental values and integrates them into her personality. The parent-daughter relationship is characterized by close supervision and protection. Even in the first year of life, sex-differentiated parental interactions with infants have been observed that girls get less of physical attention from parents. Mothers are more responsive and attentive to their sons than to their daughters, particularly during feeding hours.[25] Boys are given a greater variety of toys, girls are given fewer toys. Girls are expected to play more proximally in their homes, and allowed few independent excursions into neighbourhood. They are accompanied either by their parents or elder brothers if they want to visit a friend. Not much emphasis is given to the achievement of daughters. They are not only forced to be nurturant, obedient and responsible, but also discouraged from being aggressive. Interpersonal orientation, compromise and general welfare are also expected of daughters.

In order to find out the discriminatory attitudes of parents towards the girl child and her specific problems, which is responsible for her inferior status, the respondents were asked whether they had any such feeling. The responses have been exhibited in Table 2.10a.

Table 2.10a *Discrimination Faced*

Feeling of discrimination	*Tribal N=80*	*Rural N=80*	*Urban*				*Total N=280*
			Household N=40	*Informal N=40*	*Formal N=40*	*Sub-Total N=120*	
Yes	4(5.0)	62(77.5)	10(25.0)	19(47.5)	5(12.5)	34(28.4)	100(35.7)
No	65(81.3)	17(21.3)	28(70.0)	20(50.0)	31(77.5)	79(65.8)	161(57.5)
NR/DK	11(13.7)	—	—	—	—	—	11(3.9)
NA	—	1(1.2)	2(5.0)	1(2.5)	4(10.0)	7(5.8)	8(2.9)
Total	80(100)	80(100)	40(100)	40(100)	40(100)	120(100)	280(100)

Figures in parentheses indicate percentages.

Majority (57.5%) of the total respondents denied facing any discrimination between them and their brothers during their upbringing. Within the urban community, 77.5% of the formal sector respondents, 50% of the informal sector respondents and 70% of the household sector respondents were in this category. This proportion increased to 81% in tribal respondents. In contrast to the overall trend, only 21% of the rural respondents denied facing discrimination while more than three-fourths (77%) respondents acknowledged facing some or other sort of discrimination during their upbringing by parents. It is important to note that although the tribal girl child is less privileged and pampered, but the realization of discrimination does not set in as the overall environment makes her feel that this is quite normal and accepted norm. For 100 respondents who acknowledged facing discrimination, we probed further as to the reasons for their feeling so. Results are tabulated in Table 2.10b.

Table 2.10b *Nature of Discrimination*

Nature	*Tribal N=4*	*Rural N=62*	*Urban*				*Total N=100*
			Household N=10	*Informal N=19*	*Formal N=5*	*Sub-Total N=34*	
Domestic work performed by girls	—	20 (32.3)	2 (20.0)	6 (31.6)	2 (40.0)	10 (29.4)	30 (30.0)
Education for boys	4 (100.0)	10 (16.1)	1 (10.0)	3 (15.7)	—	4 (14.7)	18 (18.0)
Boys were fed better	—	15 (24.2)	2 (20.0)	3 (15.7)	—	5 (14.7)	20 (20.0)
Boys had more freedom	—	2 (3.2)	3 (30.0)	3 (15.7)	—	6 (17.6)	8 (8.0)
Demands of boys were easily fulfilled	—	8 (12.9)	—	2 (10.5)	—	2 (5.8))	10 (10.0)
Dressing pattern for girls	—	2 (3.2)	2 (5.0)	1 (5.3)	3 (60.0)	6 (14.7)	8 (8.0)
Excess medical facilities	—	5 (8.1)	—	1 (5.3)	—	1 (2.9)	6 (6.0)
Total	4 (100)	62 (100)	10 (100)	19 (100)	5 (100)	34 (100)	100 (100)

Figures in parentheses indicate percentages.

Nearly one-third (30%) felt discrimination since they did all domestic work. They included 40% of the formal sector respondents and 20% each of informal and household sector respondents. Remaining one-third of respondents all hailed from the rural background. However, none of the tribal respondents cited this reason.

Respondents who felt discriminated against as they were deprived of education constituted 18% in totality. This view was omnipresent amongst all tribal respondents. Moreover, girls' involvement in household chores also keeps them away from school, the other reasons being illness, looking after siblings, poverty and parental apathy. In rural areas, the distance of the school is also an important factor. Parents do not send their daughters to study in schools located at far-off places for security reasons.

Another 20% respondents felt that boys were fed better. This view had no takers in the tribal community and urban formal sector. However, it emerged from 24.2% respondents from rural, 20% from the urban household sector and 15.7% from the urban informal sector.

As the size of family in the rural area is quite large, milk, fruits and sweets are offered specially to the sons. Similarly, 10% of the total respondents felt that demands of boys were not only treated preferentially, but also more easily fulfilled. Such respondents included 10% from the urban informal sector and 13% from the rural areas.

Respondents who felt discrimination in limiting dressing options were 8% and another 6% felt discrimination regarding access to medical facilities. This included a single case from the urban informal sector and 8% cases from rural community.

We observe a strong gender bias in Garasia community where birth of a son leads to great joy as he is considered to represent the family lineage. Birth of a daughter is welcome only after a son as she brings brideprice for the family, uplifting their economic status.

Garasia girls certainly enjoy more freedom than their counterparts among other communities. They can roam about freely, visit markets and forest with their friends (boys and girls), cut jokes with men and are usually free to select their life-partner. Such a meeting can also involve varying degrees of physical interaction. So, the girls have as much freedom as the boys in choosing their life-partner and no one can be forced to marry against her wishes. All unmarried girls are very careful about their personal hygiene.

Girls in upper and middle class urban and rural communities are treated a *paraya dhan* (other's property). Her interaction with male counterparts in viewed with suspicion and she is expected to lead a simple life so that she can be given away by her father to the groom in a pure state in the ceremony of 'kanyadaan' (literally, the given of a girl virgin). In the Garasia case and also among some other lower castes, in contrast, virginity is not a criterion.

Perception of Women's Status

The Indian Constitution provides equal status to both men and women. According to Article 14 of the Constitution, the state shall not deny to any person equality before the law or the equal protection of the laws within the territory of India. Equal opportunities and facilities are available to all. But, in reality, all women do not enjoy this equality of status.

During the study, questions were asked about women's views on the concept of equality between men and women. The respondents were asked whether their status is same as that of men in the family. Table 2.11 presents an analysis of the responses.

As many as 90% of the respondents expressed the status of women to be lower/inferior as compared to men in their family. Within the urban community (76.7%), 40% of formal sector respondents, 100% of informal sector, 90% of household sector and 100% of rural and tribal respondents were in this category. Only exception prevailed in the urban formal set-up, where 58% respondents regarded women's status as equal to men folk in their family. Only 7.5% of the household sector women agreed with them. 2.5% of formal and household sector respondents did not elaborate further on this subject.

Table 2.11 *Status of Woman in Family*

Status of woman in family	*Tribal N=80*	*Rural N=80*	*Urban*				*Total N=280*
			Household N=40	*Informal N=40*	*Formal N=40*	*Sub-Total N=120*	
Equal	—	—	3(7.5)	—	23 (57.5)	26(21.7)	26(9.3)
Inferior status than men	80 (100.0)	80 (100.0)	36 (90.0)	40 (100.0)	16 (40.0)	92 (76.7)	252 (90.0)
N.R.	—	—	1(2.5)	—	1(2.5)	2(1.6)	2(0.7)
Total	80(100)	80(100)	40(100)	40(100)	40(100)	120(100)	280(100)

Figures in parentheses indicate percentages.

We also asked respondents the kind of status their husband accorded to them. Majority of the total respondents said their husbands considered themselves superior. Within the urban community, this feeling emerged from 12.5% of the formal sector respondents, 80% of the household sector respondents and 100% of the informal sector respondents. Besides, 97.5% and 100% of their rural and tribal counterparts also agreed with them. However, the concept of equal status was confined to husbands of 80% of respondents in urban formal and 10% in urban household sectors.

Violence against Women

In India, no comprehensive data is available covering aspects of domestic violence; however, according to various indicators, atrocities and violence against women are on the rise. The United Nations (1994) defined violence against women as 'any act of gender-based violence that results in or is likely to result in physical, sexual or psychological harm or suffering to women, including threat of such acts, coercion or arbitrary deprivation of liberty whether occurring in public or private life'.[26]

Women may be subjected to psychological violence like verbal abuse, nagging, taunting, confinement and deprivation of financial or personal resources at one end while men may physically assault, rape or even burn women in the other extreme. Once she is caught in this vicious circle of violence (psychological and physical), she lives in a constant state of fear, anxiety and insecurity. We asked our respondents if they had any difference of opinion with their husbands which led to quarrelling. Results show that a significant majority (69%) of total respondents acknowledge such quarrels in their married life while this proportion was much higher (nearly 80% average) in urban sub-sections. However, it reduced to 62.5% in rural and 56% in tribal settings.

A vast proportion (35%) of respondents said their husbands blew their lid off by shouting. In the urban context, 28% respondents of formal sector, 30% of informal sector and 25% of household sector also admitted the same. Proportion of such respondents increases to 48% and 36% in rural and tribal communities, respectively.

Respondents who hesitantly admitted the shameful aspect of domestic violence where their husbands expressed their anger by severely beating them up were 21% in totality. Within urban community, there was no prevalence of such incidence in formal sector while one-third (33.3%) respondents in informal sector complained of domestic violence. This proportion drops to 6.3% in household sector and again rose to 28% and 29% in rural and tribal communities, respectively. Prevalence of such incidence was, however, limited to lower and a few middle castes in rural community since their husbands earned low wages or were unemployed. Their frustrations led them to drinking which culminated in quarrels and domestic violence.

Respondents who resorted to passing sarcastic remarks to express their anger constituted 13.5% in totality. In urban society, this situation is faced by about 22% respondents in formal sector, 15.2% in informal sector and 37.5% in household sector. Only 4% of rural respondents agreed with them while we did not find any respondent in the tribal community acknowledging such incidence.

Likewise, respondents who faced mild domestic violence in such a situation formed 10% in totality. Within the urban community, 3.1% of the formal sector and 15.2% of informal sector respondents fell in this category. In addition, 16% of rural and 13.3% of urban household sector respondents also agreed with them.

Respondents who said their husbands frowned and went into a shell to express their anger comprised 7.3% of total sample. In the urban set-up, formal sector and household sector women were more exposed to this situation (18.8% and 15.6%, respectively), while only 3% women in informal sector and 45% in the rural areas faced this situation.

Husbands of 5.2% of respondents became non-communicative to express their anger. In urban community, 15.6% each of formal and household sector respondents face this situation. Another one-tenth (9.4%) of the urban formal (1.6% of the total) sector respondents said that their husbands walked out from the house to express their displeasure whenever they felt angry.

The above trends illustrate that in urban formal society, men are well-educated, financially well-off and hence resort to more dignified and harmless means of expressing their anguish such as sarcasm, silence (becoming non-communicative) or withdrawing from the situation. However, incidents of domestic violence are more pronounced in the household sector (6.3%) as compared to formal sector. In total contrast, respondents of urban informal sector are at the receiving end and at times become punching bags on which frustrations of their husbands find vent. Such frustrations, due to low earnings, lack of resources and hard lifestyle, are also present in rural and tribal society where incidents of heavy domestic violence have increased significantly.

In continuation, since it was logical for respondents to feel pain and anguish, they were asked as to how they expressed such feelings. Results are tabulated in Table 2.12.

Table 2.12 *Ways of Expressing Anger by Respondents*

Ways	*Tribal N=45*	*Rural N=50*	*Urban*				*Total N=192*
			Household N=32	*Informal N=33*	*Formal N=32*	*Sub-Total N=97*	
Frowning	2(4.4)	—	4(12.5)	2(6.0)	5(15.6)	11(11.3)	13(6.8)
Shouting	10(22.2)	16(32.0)	5(15.6)	7(21.2)	5(15.6)	17(17.5)	43(22.4)
Sarcastic remarks	—	1(2.0)	1(3.1)	1(3.0)	5(15.6)	7(7.2)	8(4.1)
Abusing	1(2.2)	2(4.0)	—	1(3.0)	—	1(1.0)	4(2.1)
Beating	—	—	—	1(3.0)	—	1(1.0)	1(0.5)

Cont'd...

...Cont'd

Others:							
Squabble	—	—	1(3.1)	2(6.1)	1(3.1)	4(4.1)	4(2.1)
Not preparing food	1(2.2)	3(6.0)	—	—	1(3.1)	1(1.0)	5(2.6)
Not eating food	2(4.4)	2(4.0)	6(18.7)	5(15.2)	—	11(11.3)	15(7.8)
Beating up children	3(6.6)	7(14.0)	—	4(12.1)	1(3.1)	5(5.1)	15(7.8)
Going out	—	3(6.0)	2(6.2)	—	4(12.5)	6(6.2)	9(4.6)
Going to parents	24(53.3)	3(6.0)	—	—	—	—	27(14.0)
Tolerating	2(4.4)	9(18.0)	7(21.8)	7(21.2)	3(9.3)	17(17.5)	28(14.6)
Silence	—	4(8.0)	6(18.7)	3(9.1)	5(15.6)	14(14.4)	18(9.4)
Total	45(100)	50(100)	32(100)	33(100)	32(100)	97(100)	192(100)

Figures in parentheses indicate percentages.

Respondents who had the guts to retaliate by shouting at their husbands were 22.4% in totality. Within urban community, 15.6% of the formal sector respondents, 21.2% of the informal sector respondents and 15.6% of the household respondents belonged to this category. The proportion rose appreciably to 32% and 22.2% in rural and tribal communities, respectively.

Tolerance, suffering in silence and allowing their anguish to cool down was the only option for 14.7% of respondents in such a situation. In the urban set-up, this included 9.3% of the formal, 21.2% of informal and 2.2% of the household sector respondents. Apart from the above, 18% of rural and 4.4% of tribal respondents were also in the same mould.

Respondents who adopted the time-tested and traditional method of rushing back to their parents' home constituted another 14% of total. Such incidents were confined to 6% of rural and 53.3% of tribal respondents and had no relevance in the urban community. In such cases, since it became difficult for them to continue the usual comfortable life with their husbands in their absence, they would come to their parents in a reconciliatory move.

Silence and non-communication with husband were modes of expressing displeasure and anguish by 9.4% of total respondents. In the urban community, 15.6% of formal, 9.1% of informal and 18.7% of household sector respondents were included in this category. Only 8% of the rural women also adopted the above modes of expressing their sorrow.

Respondents who expressed their anguish by beating up children were 8% in total. This expresses the lack of confidence in confronting a situation head-on and giving vent to frustration on their children. In the urban community, such respondents included 3.1% from the formal and 12.1% from the informal sector. None of the household sector women resorted to such practices. The corresponding proportion increased to 14% in rural and 6.6% in the tribal community.

From the above discussion, it emerges that urban formal sector respondents were more expressive and did not resort to practices like not eating food, beating up children or tolerating as compared to other respondents. They did not avoid the situation by running off to their parents as compared to their rural and tribal counterparts. Informal sector respondents, contrarily, gave vent to their feelings by shouting, squabbling, not eating food, beating up children and tolerating in silence. These trends were quite common with tribal and rural respondents. Rural women also resorted to abusing, not preparing and eating food to express their anguish. In tribal community, respondents resorted to all of above, but majority rushed off to their parents to escape from the situation.

In such a situation of tension and turmoil between the husband and the wife, we also attempted to analyse the role of family members and their disposition in such situations. Results show that in cases of more than one-fourth (26.6%) of the total respondents, the family members remained passive and non-interfering. Amongst urban respondents, 25% in the formal sector, 18% in the informal sector and 31.3% in the household sector were included in this category. The corresponding proportion of such respondents was 30% in rural and 26.6% in tribal communities, respectively.

Respondents who acknowledged intervention of their in-laws to diffuse this situation were 22.4% in totality. In the urban community, about 12% of respondents in all categories of urban and rural communities endorsed the above viewpoint. Cases of in-laws' intervention increased in a significant way to 55.6% in the tribal community. Another 22.9% of total respondents said that their in-laws' generally favour their husbands. In urban society, 19% of formal, 36% of informal and another 19% of household sector women blamed their in-laws to be biased and tilting towards their husbands and endorsing their viewpoint, even if it was not justified. The proportion of such respondents increased to 40% in rural society.

Intervention by children to diffuse this unpleasant situation was acknowledged by 16% of respondents. In urban society, 25% each of formal and household sector women admitted intervention by their children. This proportion dropped to 18% in urban informal and 16% in rural contexts. However, this had no relevance in tribal society, where the children remained aloof from the quarrels of their parents.

The number of formal and household sector respondents in urban society who found favour with their in-laws during such moments of difference of opinion with their husbands stood at 12.5%. However, this did not have any percolation in any other sub-section studied by us.

We were also interested in finding out the mechanism and final outcome of this conflict.

Diffusion of this situation occurred by intervention of others in case of 36% of respondents. Within the urban community, 12.5% of formal sector and 15% of informal sector respondents also held the above view. This proportion increased to 30% in rural and included all the tribal respondents as well. In such a delicate situation, a Garasia wife is counselled by her in-laws/parents and subsequently by elders/prominent people of the village, who try to convince her to adjust and accommodate with her husband's family and in spite of all of their efforts, if she still is unwilling to go back to her husband, then an amicable solution of separation is arrived at. In such a case, she can marry another Garasia male after she repays one-and-a-half times the *dapa* to her earlier husband.

Nearly one-third (30%) of respondents admitted that they compromised due to societal and family pressures. In urban society, 25% of formal sector, 45.4% of informal sector and 31.3% of household sector respondents confirmed to above. This compromising attitude was also reflected by half of the rural respondents. It is pertinent to note that none of the tribal respondents had such a compromising attitude.

It is interesting to note that only 11.4% of the total respondents had patience, mental level and overall conducive environment to resolve their differences by mutual discussion. However, such instances were limited to 31.3% of urban formal and 37.5% of household sector respondents.

We also asked our respondents if this mutual conflict dragged on and led towards a situation of divorce/separation. Responses reveal that while 95% of the total respondents outrightly denied facing this situation, the remaining 5% acknowledged that their daily conflicts and quarrels made the situation unpleasant and they were thinking on the lines of divorce. In the urban community, such instances were limited to only 5% in cases of formal sector respondents, which increased significantly to 15% amongst the informal sector respondents. Little more than 6% of rural and 2.5% of tribal respondents also faced such a prolonged unpleasant situation. However, we did not find any such woman in the urban household sector.

Both the respondents in urban formal sector were not willing to drag on this unpleasantness and, thus, they went in for divorce. In urban informal sector and rural context, divorce was avoided and such an unpleasant situation was diffused due to compromise by either side, tolerance exhibited by wife due to societal and family pressure or intervention by family elders. For the tribal respondents, such an unpleasant situation culminated in divorce.

The data is reflective of the mindset and overall situation of women in urban, rural and tribal societies. In the urban (formal sector) and tribal societies, women are found to be more decisive and courageous and are willing to contemplate even bold steps such as divorce/separation to get out of their daily turmoil and enhance the quality of their life. In rural and urban (household and informal sectors) societies, women think of divorce/separation as a blot on their character and feel that their life would be even more insecure after this. This makes them compromising, adjusting and tolerant to diffuse any confronting situation which can lead to taking daring steps.

In Garasia society, a woman is considered as an outsider in her husband's home and this status works to her advantage when she wants to separate. She does not have any right in the husband's property and has no right/obligation to bring up her children in such cases. Even when her husband dies, she becomes free to plan her future life and her children are looked after by her in-laws/brother(s) of her husband. She is rather encouraged to leave the deceased husband's household and plan her life with another Garasia male. This situation becomes complex if she is well passed her reproductive age and in such cases, she can only fall back upon her brother.

Religion and Worship

People in India are in general religious. 'Religion is the air we breathe in India.'[27] It is assumed that as the primary core of morality and ethics, religion is necessary in life. Religion is apparently practised by going to places of worship, praying at home, observing fast, etc. However, in the wake of the development of science and technology, religious practices are undergoing a change. For instance, modern man has developed his own ideals, values and standards which are different from those of the older generation.'[28] People now do not observe religious practices as strictly as before. In this regard, we asked our respondents regarding their religious beliefs and practices. The results are shows in Table 2.13a:

Table 2.13a *Religious Beliefs*

Response	*Tribal N=80*	*Rural N=80*	*Urban*				*Total N=280*
			Household N=40	*Informal N=40*	*Formal N=40*	*Sub-Total N=120*	
Yes	80(100.0)	73(91.3)	30(75.0)	32(80.0)	37(92.5)	99(82.5)	252(90.0)
No	—	7(8.7)	10(25.0)	8(20.0)	3(7.5)	21(17.5)	28(10.0)
Total	80(100)	80(100)	40(100)	40(100)	40(100)	120(100)	280(100)

Figures in parentheses indicate percentages.

Majority (90%) of the total respondents expressed their belief in specific Gods/Goddesses. In the urban community, such respondents included 92.5% in the formal sector, 80% in the informal sector and 75% in the household sector. It is generally believed that household sector women are more religious in nature and educated, and urban formal sector women are less attached to religious sentiments.

In similar vein, 91.2% of rural and 100% of tribal respondents also expressed immense faith in spiritualism and regarded every happening (good or bad) as God's will.

Table 2.13b *Expression of Religious Feelings*

Feelings	*Tribal N=80*	*Rural N=73*	*Urban*				*Total N=252*
			Household N=30	*Informal N=32*	*Formal N=37*	*Sub-Total N=99*	
Going regularly to temple	—	2(2.7)	—	2(6.3)	2(5.4)	4(4.0)	6(2.4)
Praying	—	13(17.8)	20(66.7)	15(46.8)	30(81.1)	65(65.7)	78(30.9)
Fasting	—	54(73.9)	10(33.3)	13(40.6)	5(13.5)	28(28.2)	82(32.5)
Special offering	80 (100.0)	4(5.5)	—	2(6.3)	—	2(2.0)	86(34.2)
Total	80 (100)	73(100)	30(100)	32(100)	37(100)	99(100)	252(100)

Figures in parentheses indicate percentages.

In response to the query as to how they express their feelings towards their deities, it was observed as shown in Table 2.13b, that within the urban community a large majority of (81%) respondents in the formal sector prayed regularly at home and 13.5% observed fasts to appease their deities, while only 5.4% regularly visited temple. Comparing this with the urban household sector, we found two-thirds women praying regularly and one-third keeping fasts. It is surprising to note that none of the household sector women visited temple regularly. In the urban informal sector 47% respondents pray regularly while 41% respondents keep fasts. We also came across 6.2% cases where respondents went regularly to temple and another 6.2% cases where they made special offerings to appease their Gods.

Moving over to rural section, we noticed majority (74%) women keeping a fast, and only 18% praying to express their religious feelings. A total of 27% respondents visited the temple regularly while 5.4% made special offerings on special occasions. The untouchables, of course, participate in temple rituals from a distance.

In the tribal community, however, women do not have the time and energy to resort to praying, fasting or going regularly to the temple. But, this does not mean that they are not religious. On the contrary, they are deeply God-fearing and make special offerings on festive occasions. According to tribal norms, a woman cannot go to a temple without her husband. A married woman, praying all alone in a temple or making certain offerings, is regarded with suspicion and considered a witch. Hence, tribal women normally express their religious feelings by performing religious acts along with their husbands and clan members on special occasions.

Married Garasia women are not allowed to cook and eat in a religious feast. It is interesting to note that while they prepare the daily meal, for such special occasions the cooking and distribution of food remains the prime responsibility of Garasia men. The sisters and daughters of Garasia men are unable to assume the position of ritual authority but they are allowed to cook and eat in mass events such as a feast. All this indicates that even after marriage, a Garasia wife is considered an outsider in her husband's clan. Daughters and sisters are regarded as belonging to their parents' lineage and they cannot homogenize with their husband's family and clan even after marriage. The situation is totally reversed in rural and urban communities where daughters are considered as *paraya dhan* and from early childhood they are made to realize that their real home is their husband's home.

After marriage, even in the husband's family, they are expected to blend in all activities and remain the central point for all activities.

Garasia women do not play any significant role during religious rituals at the family or community level. In fact, they are not allowed to even enter the place and only male members can officiate again. This is in total contrast to the norms of rural and urban societies where no religious activity can be performed in the absence of a wife *(ardhangini)*.

Sociocultural milieu of Rajasthan showcases great diversity as we move from the developing and modern urban city of Jaipur to the remote villages and even obscure tribal destinations. In our patriarchal society, gender inequality is widely prevalent and illustrative in the ways families socialize with their children, arrange and conduct their marriage. Gender inequalities also resonate when economic and political institutions overtly or covertly deny opportunities for women empowerment.

As a thumb rule, family remains the circle of concern and influence for Indian women and generally they are not eager to break away from the orbit of family and grab power. Even so-called liberated, educated and economically self-reliant women of urban formal sector have their strings attached to family since our society does not provide or recognize any other alternative to family. This has essentially led to her bearing the dual responsibility of household and outside work.

Effect of exposure and mass media is limited to urban cities like Jaipur and in villages and tribal areas, women are still subjugated and dependent upon menfolk due to illiteracy and lack of exposure.

Women belonging to the formal urban set-up were well-educated, financially self-sufficient and were not subjugated by the prevalent male bias in our patriarchal society system. While early marriage and motherhood is widely prevalent in tribal, rural and even urban informal and household sectors, most of the urban formal sector women accorded greater priority to education and career over marriage. Hectic pace of life, self-centred outlook and transferable jobs have degraded joint family culture in the urban community, and more couples have opted for nuclear families. Lack of exposure, easy lifestyle, interdependency amongst relatives, besides economy of scale in farming, have nurtured the joint family system in the rural bylanes of Rajasthan.

It is interesting to note that majority of the tribal respondents were living in nuclear families. After marriage, the bridegroom constructs a new hut for himself and his wife, in proximity to huts of his brothers and other clan members. He also gets his share of land to cultivate and provide for his family. Thus, his wife does not face restrictions and workload of the joint family system as is widely prevalent in villages. Although tribal households are separate as regards daily production, consumption of food, distribution of income and labour of wives regarding household activities, yet they represent collective units for sharing oxen, well water, cultivation or other outside tasks. Thus, it represents an interesting mix of nuclear and joint family.

Notes

1. Linton, R., 1936. *The Study of Man,* Appleton Century-Crafts.
2. Zaniecki, F., 1940. *The Social Role of the Man of Knowledge,* Columbia: Columbia University Press.
3. Merton, R.K., 1976. *Sociological Ambivalence and Other Essays,* New York: Free Press.
4. Giddens, A., 1993. *Sociology,* Cambridge: Polity Press.
5. Ibid.
6. Anandhi, S. and A. Roychoudhary, 1994. 'Construction of Gender', *Social Action,* 44(2): 1.
7. Scott, James C., 1986. *'Weapons of the Weak: Everyday Forms of Peasant Resistance',* New Haven Connecticut: Yale University Press.
8. Indira, R. and V. Shanti, 1997. 'Gender Dynamics in the Context of a Tribal Society: The Case of Jenukuruba', in *Georgepfeffer* and Deepak Kumar Behra (eds), *Contemporary Society and Tribal Studies,* Vol. I, New Delhi: Concept Publishing Company, pp. 168–79.
9. Johnson, M. Harry, 1962. Sociology: *A Systematic Introduction,* London: Routledge and Kegan Paul Ltd., p. 48.
10. Scott, William, P., 1997. *Dictionary of Sociology,* New Delhi: Goyalsaab, p. 395.
11. Meyer, Fortes, 1970. *Time and Social Structure and Other Essays,* University of London: The Athlone Press, p. 3.
12. Radcliffe-Brown, A.R., reprinted 1971. *Structure and Function in Primitive Society,* Cohen and West Ltd., Roadway House. pp. 190–191.
13. Ibid., p. 192.
14. Beteille, Andre, 1969. *Castes: Old and New,* Bombay: Asia Publishing House, p. 3.
15. Fortes, M., 1953. 'The Structure of Unilineal Descent Groups', *American Anthropologist,* Vol. IV, No. 1, p. 21.
16. Quoted from Duncan Mitchell (ed.), 1968. *A Dictionary of Sociology,* London: Routledge & Kegan Paul, p. 186.

17. Mair, Lucy, 1972. *An Introduction to Social Anthropology*, Oxford: Clarendon Press, p.10.

18. Srinivas, M.N., 1991. *Indian Social Structure,* Delhi: Hindustan Publishing Corporation, pp. 47–48.

19. Khare, R.S., 1972. 'Hierarchy and Hypergamy: Some Interrelated Aspects among the Kanya-Kubja Brahmans', *American Anthropology,* 74.

20. *Marwar Raj ki Mardumshumari*, Vol. I, p. 132.

21. Thomas, P., 1964. *Indian Women Through the Ages,* Bombay: Asia Publishing House, p. 53.

22. Unnithan Kumar, Maya, 1997. *Identity, Gender and Poverty,* Oxford: Berghahn Books, p. 200.

23. Davis, Kingsley, 1964. *Human Society,* New York: Macmillan p. 215.

24. Hodding, Carter. Jr., 1984. Cited in Jeanve H. Block in, *Sex Role Identity and Ego Development*, Jossey Bass Publishers, p. 10.

25. Rheingfold, H.L. and K.V. Cook 1975. 'The Contents of Boys and Girls Rooms as an Index of Parents Behaviour', *Child Development,* 46, pp. 459–63.

26. United Nations, 1994. Declaration on the Elimination of Violence Against Women, *U.N.,* Resolution No. A/Res/48/104.

27. Cormack, M., 1961. *She Who Rides a Peacock*, Bombay: Asia Publishing House, p. 119.

28. Kaur, Inderjeet, 1983. *Status of Hindu Women in India,* Allahabad: Chugh Publications, p. 66.

3 Health, Maternity and Fertility

The World Health Organization[1] has defined health as 'a state of complete physical, mental and social well-being and not merely the absence of disease or infirmity'. Health development and health maintenance depend upon the quality of health care, which involves self-care and care by the family, the community and the health care system. Health care is a much wider concept, which includes preventive, promotive and rehabilitative aspects in addition to the curative aspect which the 'medical care' is usually connected with.[2]

Gilbert Lewis[3] has stated in the paper 'Sickness in New Guinea' that 'illness and health are as closely contrasted forces as general concepts but we sometimes find it hard to draw a strict line and say which side a particular case falls. Health and illness indicate either end or continuum'.

Agreeing with Jaspers, Lewis[4] has cited disease as an unwanted and harmful factor in life and has tried to explain illness as related to the capacity for performance. In order to explain the basic meaning of illness, he has also taken the support of Charot[5], a nineteenth century neurologist, who observed that 'there is a particular moment between health and sickness when everything depends on the person, a borderline between discomfort and comfort which is accepted and the decision "I am ill" is taken'.

Acceding to the definition of WHO, Lewis[6] finally stressed that 'health in the positive sense is an ideal approached but never attained'. According to Murray[7], 'health is a personal matter. For an outsider to claim or suggest that he/she knows better about the inside of another is to claim magical powers, and this no one wants to do'.

Health, defined broadly as a feeling of physical, mental and spiritual well-being, is often juxtaposed to its definition as absence of disease and infirmity. However, in reality, the relationship between the well-being and absence of disease is very complex. People's perception of their health, illness and its causes is based on many factors such as social, economic, cultural and environmental. From a strictly scientific point of view, one may assume that those who live in poverty and degraded living environment, and are also involved in occupations which are hazardous to health, should necessarily have a lower feeling of well-being and, thus, complain more of ill-health and illness. However, studies have shown that this is not necessarily so. The rich and well-placed strata complained of illness more often than the poorer strata or that people in the under-developed states in India reported less morbidity than those in the developed states.[8]

There are no straightforward explanations for the process by which an individual's social position is reflected in his/her health status. Even our bodily experiences are coloured by our perception of our social role and the definition of that state in culture. Thus, a state which can clinically be defined as 'illness' may not be experienced so by the woman for whom it may be a natural part of being a woman. Conversely, a clinician may refuse to accept a complaint made by her because it cannot be medically established.

Therefore, any investigation into the health of people necessarily encounters the problem of understanding how health and illness are perceived and understood by people. A strictly medical approach to identify diseases among people, and a strictly sociological approach of accepting non-prompted answers given by people on their health and illness, would not provide the necessary answers. For instance, a number of studies done in the last one decade on women's reproductive health have found that while there is less reporting of reproductive illness by women in surveys, on clinical examination a very large number of them were found suffering from disease.[9]

Concepts of Health, Illness and Disease

Health is a function not only of medical care, but also of the overall integrated development of society – cultural, economic, educational, social and political. Each of these aspects has a deep influence on health, which in turn influences all these aspects. Hence, it is not possible to raise the health status and quality of life of people unless such efforts are integrated with the wider efforts to bring about the overall transformation of a society. Good health and good society go together.[10]

The disease denotes the condition of the human body in which something has gone wrong and has upset the normal functioning of the body, including the mind. There is a continuum from a predisposition or premonition of illness which may or may not be experienced or noticed even by the individual concerned, to a definite condition of illness manifested by signs or symptoms and impairment of body functions. This continuum may further extend from mild sickness to severe sickness and death or recovery from sickness back to a debilitated condition and later to a normal condition.

There is a difference between disease and illness or sickness. While 'disease' refers to a medical conception of pathological abnormality which is indicated by a set of signs and symptoms, 'Illness', on the other hand, refers primarily to a person's subjective experience of ill-health and is indicated by the person's feeling of pains, discomfort and the like.[11]

Disease is invariably used in a fairly limited and scientific sense. *The Oxford Dictionary* defines it as a condition of body, or of some part or organ of the body, in which its functions are disturbed or dearranged – a morbid physical condition. Illness, on the other hand, is defined much more loosely as the quality or condition of being ill (in various senses). These senses are listed as:

(i) Bad moral quality, condition or character.
(ii) Unpleasantness, disagreeableness, troublesomeness, hurtfulness, noxiousness, badness.
(iii) Bad or unhealthy condition of body, the condition of being ill, disease, ailment, sickness.

So, it can be seen that with disease the focus is objective, and is seen in terms of the specific impaired state, whereas with illness the focus is more on the subjective and diffused consequences of the disease process. To say that a person is ill implies that the consequences of such a state transcend the mere by biological and physical consequences of organic malfunction and affect his/her whole social life in important ways.[12]

Illness is a social rather than biological state. It is a social reality that is distinct from (and on occasion virtually independent of) physical reality and medicine creates the social role of illness; the behaviour of the 'sick' varies from one culture to another, very often independently of disease and constitutes a reality in itself, as does the behaviour of the healer vary from culture to culture. It is the analysis of what David Mechanic terms 'illness behaviour' of the patient along with the analysis of 'diagnosis behaviour' and 'treatment behaviour' of the physician or healer.[13]

Evidently, an important aspect of women's health is the strain put on the women's body by actual reproduction and the resultant short-term and life-long health problems. However, studies on sexual or maternal health are not sufficient to understand how women's health condition changes after they enter into marriage and motherhood. These do not imply merely the responsibility of meeting the partner's sexual needs and the biological reproduction of children. Regardless of the other economic roles that they may perform, women in all societies undertake the responsibilities of 'reproductive labour'. We must define it as a 'work relationship'[14] into which women enter as wives and mothers. Women must undertake all the tasks that are necessary for the sustenance of their household. How burdensome this role becomes depends on many factors, including the resources available to the household, the expected number of children they must bear and raise, the number of dependents and sex-wise and age-wise division of work within the household.

In general, as reproductive labour is seldom transferred to male members of the household, adult women in the household are often the sole members of the family to undertake this 'reproductive labour'.[15]

The social pattern of health beliefs and health behaviour is another principal area of sociological concern in public health. The social processes which affect the values and beliefs of entire societies as well as the behaviour of individuals are important in all areas of public health. Past and present beliefs affect both consumers and providers in the recognition of illness, the seeking of care and treatment, and the evaluation of outcome. Much of social science theory has been formulated and manipulated to account for the way individuals perceive and act on illness, for example, the concepts of labelling, role, deviance and stigma.[16]

Thus, the beliefs systems significantly affect the practices of health care and treatment. The cumulative experiences are socially transmitted and get institutionalized gradually.

In this chapter, the belief system of the people of the three studied communities – tribal, rural and urban – has been explored. Various aspects of health and disease, such as causation of various diseases, spread of disease, prevention of disease, modern medicine, food and nutrition, pregnancy, childbirth, childcare and family planning and the like have been studied and findings presented.

Beliefs Regarding Health and Its Related Aspects

There are many beliefs regarding health and its related aspects prevailing in both tribal and rural communities. In the Garasia community, the concept of health is directly related to the working capacity of Garasia. Men who can do manual labour for 4–5 hours are considered fit and healthy.

On the question of health, they distinguish a person of good physique (fatty) from a person of bad physique *(kamzor)*.

Likewise, illness for Garasias is the abnormal state of feeling unwell. A person who is confined to bed or takes rest because of the lack of normal capacity to work is considered ill. So, a suffering person stops his/her routine activities as he/she cannot perform them due to illness. They do not think it to be caused by the neglect of body. According to them, disease is the symbol of unhappiness, tragedy, fear, sufferings, expenditure and end of life.

Causes of Illness

According to most Garasias, sickness occurs to some extent as a result of supernatural power, but there are other factors too, such as environmental. In their opinion, minor ailments like cough, mild fever, cold and insect bite (snake, scorpion) are normally caused by their living conditions. On account of their living in forested areas, which are full of vegetation, seasonal infections and communicable diseases are treated by herbs, but prolonged and uncontrollable diseases are always attributed to the *veer* (spirits). These diseases or ailments are considered to have been caused by displeasure of a *veer*. The Garasias identify specific diseases with specific *veers*. The Garasias' belief in different kinds of Gods, spirits and *veers* has been sustained mainly because they are related with the health and happiness of the people.

During the study, it was observed that villagers have a belief that health is the result of absence of illness or injury in the body. They consider a person healthy when he or she remains free from any type of illness.

Illness for them, as stated earlier, is the abnormal state of feeling unwell. Thus, the normalcy of a person's physique is associated with the performance of accepted and expected roles.

There is another viewpoint too: sickness, according to most villagers, occurs to some extent as a result of indulgence in *pap* (sin) and *dosh* (faulty) that accrues to a person on account of disobedience of the laws of nature and religion. One has to suffer with sickness not only for the *pap* and *dosh* committed now or in the recent past, but also for those committed in the remote past, in earlier lives, and the degree of sickness which depends upon the accumulated extent of his sinfulness.

The villagers are of the view that one's sinful acts bring illness not only upon that particular person but upon the members of family and community also. Therefore, as a community treatment and cure of prolonged sickness, tribals prescribe several acts of appeasing Gods through prayers, vows, invocations and holy bath.

Villagers ascribe diseases like leprosy, tuberculosis, jaundice, paralysis and blindness to past sinfulness and violation of religious norms. They also believe that the causes of certain diseases like asthma *sookha rog*, fevers like malaria, typhoid, skin diseases and heat stroke are natural and physical.

General Categorization of Diseases

Diseases, which are a disorder of both body and mind, are classified into the following three categories: (i) natural diseases, (ii) supernatural diseases, and (iii) magical diseases.

Natural Diseases

They, it is felt, are caused by disobedience of natural laws. Such diseases are the logical consequence of the violation of certain natural or physical norms. Tribals have reported a number of physical or natural causes of diseases which operate directly on the organism to produce illness. Some such causes are as follows:

Haap Khayo (Snake Bite), *Visu Khayo* (Scorpion Bite), *Kutro Khayo* (Dog Bite): Due to the forest area nearby, many snake and scorpion bite cases occur every year during the rainy season.

Taa Aayo (Fever-Malaria): This occurs due to unhygenic conditions and lack of an efficient drainage system, which causes accumulation of stagnant water in ditches in and around the Garasias' hutments or fields. These standing water spots breed mosquitoes that spread malaria.

Gombara (Boils), *Sanda* (Wound), *Ghagar* (Eczema): These are caused by physical forces such as their unhygienic way of living.

Dama (Asthma): This is caused due to excessive smoking.

Hoo Lagna (Heat Stroke): In May and June, there is scorching heat and vegetation is low. Such extreme weather conditions sometimes cause heat stroke.

According to the opinions expressed by a majority of villagers, gastro-intestinal diseases like worm infection, diarrhoea and cholera occur because of physical factors.

On the contrary, the data collected in this regard in urban areas indicates that most of the above mentioned diseases are caused by natural or environmental factors.

Supernatural Diseases

They are caused by supernatural powers or causative agents such as evil spirits, wrath of deities, etc.

Evil spirits: According to a generally accepted notion, an evil is an immaterial, non-divine being of fairly independent existence associated with a particular disease.[17]

The tribals are usually very much conscious of their religion (animism). Belief in supernatural beings occupies an essential part in their society and culture. The Garasias are, in no way, an exception to it and they have installed a number of deities in different parts of the village to obtain security from the dangers of natural calamities like droughts, floods, etc. as well as diseases, epidemics, etc. They believe that human life is governed by the natural forces like wind, sun, moon, rain etc. and also some supernatural or unseen powers living in the nature. Moreover, they also take it for granted that human life is insecure and unseen powers guide the human beings in every walk of life. According to them, dissatisfaction of the deities causes sickness or disease among the human beings as well as domestic animals.

Besides the deities, it is also believed that the ancestral as well as other spirits known as *veers* may also cause similar afflictions by casting their evil eye on people. In the Garasia society, a number of such evil spirits are known to cause harm.

Garasias believe that certain diseases such as locking of jaw, headache, bleeding from vital organs, burning sensation, prolonged fever, etc. are caused by evil spirits. These spirits attack persons of all ages. Some other bodily defects caused by spirits are general weakness, paralysis, and mental and physical weaknesses.

Garasias consider *veers* to be most powerful due to their mobility and invisibility and they can be either male or female spirits. Depending upon the type of spirits, different methods for appeasement are prevalent.

Similarly, disease is also said to have occurred due to an evil eye or negligence of proper worship of the spirits. So, Garasias associate specific diseases to specific *veers*. In such cases, 'Devala' is called instantly and requested to speak and advise *veers* whose propitiation is needed. In the Garasia society, *veers* are contacted and controlled by the Devala, being a physician as well as magician. Garasias also take a recourse to religious treatments such as prayers, offerings to Gods and spirits and visiting Bhopa. Devala offers charms and *jhad-phoonk* (amulets) for redemption of a person from the ill-effect of evil spirits.

The rural community assigns the permanent abode of evil spirits to an old peepal tree. It is a common belief that a person passing under the peepal tree after sunset and before sunrise might run the risk of being invaded by evil spirits. Lactating mothers and breast-feeding children get intruded by such spirits, specially at and after sunset.

The symptoms of invasion by evil spirits include consumption of excessive food or a sudden rise in hunger or excessive laughing or weeping without sufficient provocation, or keeping sick for long, or the general feeling of resignation and lethargy or sudden reduction in weight and energy.

Wrath of deities: It is a common belief among the rural people that certain diseases like chicken pox, small pox, leprosy and tuberculosis are caused by the wrath of deities. Garasias also attribute these diseases to their local deities, notably Bhairu Baba and Shitla Mata. They also worship Pubuji and Tejaji for a cure of these diseases.

Goddess Shitla is considered a powerful deity by Garasias because of her connection with illness, especially fever caused by chicken pox or small pox. According to Sodari, (Garasia women) in chicken pox pray to the Goddess: *'Shitla Mata hàmare gair pavana banke aati hai* (Goddess Shitla comes to stay as our guest)'. Garasias also believe that the disease has to be treated with care and reverence for fear that it would worsen if the visiting deity is displeased.

Though small pox has been eradicated from the world, it still persists in Rajasthan. It was observed during the present study that a large number of urban people also believed and worshipped the Goddess Shitla in order to save their children from eruptive fevers like chicken pox and measles.

Magical Diseases

According to Garasias, magical diseases are caused by the intervention of human beings possessed with magical or supernatural powers such as sorcerers and witches. The effect of an evil eye is the most common conviction prevalent among them. Some individuals get possessed with magical powers that cause a negative and harmful impact on the people of the other community, particularly children and women. The most common practice is the *maili veddya* (black magic), which is used for causing bad effects like disaster and illness on chosen objects (a person or animal). Hence, Garasias were reluctant in providing any information regarding various magical practices. They did not entertain any direct queries regarding the nature or origin of such magical practices because as they felt, this would reduce effectiveness or even annoy the spirit of magic, leading to misery and disease. The Garasia expert confides the details of *mantras* only in his disciples and does not speak loudly even while performing a *pooja* ceremony. Although magic is primarily used for curative purposes, it may also be used to protect from the harmful intentions of malevolent spirits.

Garasias invite *'mooth'* when they are jealous or have serious differences with someone. It is also said if an evil eye watches with appreciation a person wearing a fine dress, eating good food, living happily or looking healthy, such a person is adversely affected by *mooth*. *Mooth* has been derived from the word *'moothi'*. It is believed that in order to cause death or sickness of a person, or an enemy, a Garasia takes up in a *moothi* (closed fist) charm magic and sends it to the direction of the person to whom he wants to cause a disease. This act is only performed by Devala. Garasias also believe that a *mooth* can fly from one place to another and lead to blood vomiting. The victim becomes motionless or feels a burning sensation in some bodily organ or the whole body. It is also believed to lead to giddiness, trembling and weakness in body.

Witch, or in Garasia language a *dakan*, is supposed to possess mysterious supernatural powers of casting an evil eye with disastrous results to the victim. Among Garasias, women are experts in black magic. Magic is quickly and easily acquired and retained for longer by women. According to them, the woman who knows black magic and always lives in isolation is considered a witch. She does not sleep at night but always wants to attend fairs and festivals, so she can perform magic quietly. Magical power of witchcraft is concentrated in her eyes and spit. It is believed that eyes of a witch are so powerful that as soon as she looks at any person, he/she feels some sort of trouble. Many Garasias talked about the presence of a witch in the form of a village woman. If a person starts feeling a loss of appetite and sometimes falls unconscious and gets a state of mental disease, he is assumed to be affected by a witch.

As a means of sufficient caution against the envy of an evil eye, Garasias take preventive measures by making a black spot on the forehead of every child. This spot is marked with *kajal* (collyrium), which they also use in their eyes. The belief is that the evil eye shall be distracted by this black spot and the impact of his envy or glare on the child shall be reduced. When a child suffers from sickness, the Garasia keeps a big *rota* (*chapati*) of flour paste on one of the village crossings to get relief. Magically-charmed white stones are also kept on the roof of the huts to ward off the curve and evil eyes to dissolve the ill-effects of witches. Garasia women wear black threads in the lower part of their legs as protection against harm caused through magic.

Like tribals, rural and urban people also believe that the effect of an evil eye is the most common conviction prevalent among them. They also accept that children and women are prone to this harm. If a person possessed with these powers passes an uncalled-for remark on a child about his/her being beautiful or intelligent, the child either falls ill or starts losing health for no physical reason. So, they also take preventive measures by marking a spot of *kajal* on the child's forehead.

However, unlike the Garasias, rural and urban people do not believe in witchcraft, but *mooth* practices are also present among rural people to harm or cause sickness to the enemy. According to villagers, a person can either die or suffer from paralysis, haemorrhage or bleeding in any organ due to *kaman*, also called *mooth*. *Kaman* is used by throwing cereals on the enemy after preparing it with charm in order to produce disease.

Treatment Behaviour

Each society is found to develop some kind of value system within its own ethnoscience for the concept of treatment of disease. There are some universal perceptions of health and disease where all the human societies possess some common consideration and at the same time there are also some social perceptions, though the concept and treatment of diseases are different in all three societies, i.e. tribal, rural and urban. Besides the unique socio-cultural systems and perceptions, environmental factors or conditions are also responsible for health and disease, so the treatment behaviour is also different.

Keeping in view the most basic issues in the study of health and disease, this section has been designed to delineate the concept of illness as explained by the people, the classification of diseases, home remedies, herbal, magical and medicinal treatments, and role of specialists. Due attention has also been paid to discuss the diagnosis of the diseases, including the techniques of detection by specialists as well as the common man. Ethno-medical beliefs and practices are influenced by culture. The relationship between human sickness, treatment, healing medicines and the rest of culture in a society is intimate. The concept of disease, classification of disease, procedure of diagnosis and therapy are all influenced by culture. They do not, of course, cover the whole range of misfortune a community may face over a long period of time and in general sense. To a large extent, treatment procedures and medicines offered are traditional, which fall under the category of ethno-medicines. Ethno-medicines is a sum-field of medical anthropology that deals with the study of traditional medical systems. In the case of Garasias, it was found that the community, in its treatment behaviour towards the sick, depends to a great extent on these traditional medicines. The traditional methods of treatment among the Garasias can be discussed in two different categories. As has been discussed earlier, their basic concept of disease or illness is explained by magico-religious beliefs. But, the first and foremost type of treatment is herbal treatment and the second is magico-religious. Minor ailments like cough, mild fever, cold, insect or animal bites, skin diseases, etc. are treated by herbal methods but prolonged and uncontrollable diseases are always attributed to the *veers* (spirits).

Treatment by Herbal Medicines

Herbal treatment is practised among the Garasias as a popular method of dealing with diseases. For some common diseases like cold, cough, mild fever, minor cuts, wounds, insect or animal bites, etc. they take herbal medicines directly as per the advice of the Bhopa. Bhopa also administers some enchanted herbal medicines to the patients. Some common diseases in the Garasia society and their herbal medicines may be seen in Chart 2.

Chart 2 *Common Diseases in Garasia Society and their Indigenous (Herbal) Medicines*

Local name of the diseases	*English equivalent*	*Indigenous medicines*
Taap	Fever	Root of *sillutti* and *adusa* is used
Dama	Asthma	Root of *hathan* juice is applied
Nakor	Epistaxis	Juice of *nadaru* is applied on the forehead
Gombara	Boil	Leaves of black *dhatura, gilor, bhuabri, kasubaro*
Ghagar	Eczema	Gum of *doom, dod* and leaves of wild fig
Masa	Piles	Roots of *kantor* and bark of *areetha*
Kharjavo	Treatment of wound	Leaves of *Korji,* opium and *lahsun*
Kutara Khayo	Dog bite	Bark of *arlua, tutar,* dry *galka, arka* milk, *neem* leaves
Haap Khayo	Snake bite	The roots of *nag-vel. akor, kankodi, amina, vidrekhs, dhatura-akda* and *kher*
Visu Khayo	Scorpion bite	Roots of *labua, auk, khakhara* and *akda* and *toohar* milk

Illiteracy, malnutrition, ignorance and unhygienic conditions are some of the common causes of diseases among Garasias. On account of their living in forested areas, which are full of vegetation, seasonal infections and communicable diseases are frequent in this region.

Magico-religious Treatment

(i) *Deities for prevention of diseases:* According to Garasias, the main male deity Bhairu and the two female deities, Kuldevi (clan mother) and Shitla Mata (pox goddess), are considered strong and powerful, having *veers* or accompanying spirits, who can be male or female. Garasias often blame these spirits for illness and ailments. They also attribute a few diseases to a particular deity; for instance, epidemic diseases like cholera, small pox, etc. are attributed to Shitla Mata, who is represented by a pockmarked stone-set under a tree. Thus, in an effort to avert these diseases, they regularly worship the deity. Kuldevi, also known as Mata, is worshipped and her blessings are sought for enhancing fertility. A major part of marriage ceremonies also includes worship of the Kuldevi/Mata.

Bhairu is considered powerful because of his association with destruction. According to some Garasias, Bhairu was the protector of Lord Shiva's wife.

Thus, the Garasias have great belief in supernatural powers of Gods, Goddesses, *Baosi* (ancestors) and *veers* (spirits) who think of their welfare and fulfil their desires. They generally pledge to the deity and such an act of pledging is called *'manauti'* or *'bolma'*. All those persons who have asked for *manauti* give offerings after the fulfilment of *manauti*. Sacrificial offerings to the Gods and Goddesses depend on the nature of pantheon *'maili'* or 'Ujli', which is preferred and determined in advance. The quantity of these offerings also differs from God to God and *Baosi* to *Baosi*. The *ujli* offerings consist of *matar, churma*, jaggery, *ghooghri*, coconut, grains, fruits and flowers, whereas the *maili* offerings include blood, liquor and animals like goat and hens. The blood of animals is also poured on the deity and mutton is cooked and distributed to all the community members. It is believed by the Garasias that if such *bolma* or *manauti* is made from the core of one's heart, it positively gets fulfilled by the grace of the deity. On the other hand, if after the fulfilment of a *bloma*, the person does not abide by the promise he made to the deity and does not offer what he pledged, he commits one of the greatest sins and is subjected to sufferings and misery. Some of the deities in this category are: Amba Mata, Bhairuji,

Shitla Mata and Badi Mata, Chamunda Mata, Asapuri, Bhakhar Baosi (Mountain Deity), Phulera Mata, etc.

(ii) *Sickness due to veers (spirits)*: Garasias believe that spirits (*veers*) can be both malevolent (Gobru) and benevolent (Bhello). The Gobru spirits (*Bhoot, Bhootani and Chudel*) are invisible malevolent spirits, causing different types of diseases. They believe that young persons whose desires are not fulfilled become ghosts after death. Ghost is controlled through magical performance and can be ordered to spare the victim. The ghost then is corked in an earthen pot or in a bottle and buried deep on the banks of a river. On the other hand, Bhello (benevolent spirits) are the guardian spirits of the Garasia community. They always help their followers, bring prosperity in the family, develop fertility, give happiness and human growth.

Veers (spirits) can be both malevolent and benevolent. According to a Garasia's belief, there are as many as 101 *veers*. As stated earlier, they identify specific diseases with specific *veers*. These *veers* are named for their various effects caused on the organs of the body, so in case of a disease caused by spirit intrusion, Devala (physician-cum-magician) is called to remove the spirits by some rituals. Devala, on account of his role in controlling these *veers*, through certain rituals and sacrifices of goat or hen, invokes the spirit which is finally removed through certain spells from the body of patient. Most often, the Garasia women, in order to prevent their children from the spirit intrusion, accept some magical charms from Bhopas which consist of iron or copper lockets containing some herbal medicines. Some of the most important diseases caused by *veers* and *pooja* (prayer) offered to them have been shown in Chart 3.

Chart 3 Pooja *(Prayers) Offered to Seek Relief from Diseases Believed to be Caused by* Veers *(Spirits)*

Name of veer	*Disease caused*	Pooja *offered*
Angio	Half portion of the body becomes senseless and partly paralysed	Goat and liquor
Agio	Burning sensation in the body	Goat, coconut liquor and handful of six types of grains
Basnio	Difficulty in speaking and breathing	Flesh and liquor
Baltanio	Pains in the legs, arms and different joints	Three coconuts, three lemons, each cut into four pieces thrown in four directions

Cont'd...

...Cont'd

Dantio	Toothache and gum disease	Seven types of grain mixed with seven colours
Kasbio	Person becomes pale, suffers from jaundice	250 gm oil put in the plate and touched seven times from the head towards feet of the patient, seven lemons with jaggery given for seven days
Narsinga	Disturbance of nervous system	Coconut and liquor
Phepadio	In lung and kidney	Hen sacrificed and blood offered
Sulio	Bodyache	Coconut and liquor
Suklio	Emaciates young children	Goat and liquor
Rangito	Bleeding from vital organs, including bleeding with urine and stool	Goat sacrificed, liquor coconut and seven types of grains
Tavanio	Headache, giddiness	Nine pieces of red and white cloth with nine grains and kumkum, egg is put in the broken earthen pot, circled seven times over the head of the patient

Besides these, there are other *veers* such as sajanio, masanio, gothio, antario, dhunio, satilio, kajelio, balio, jalio, amilio, etc. It is believed by the Garasias that almost all *veers* could be influenced by Devala and go to the aimed person and cause the desired effects on his/her body. When such persons do not recover, the Garasias go to Devala or Bhopa to find out the disease.

Traditional Healers in Garasia Community

For the purposes of diagnosis and treatment of diseases, as well as rituals/ceremonies to be performed in this regard, the Garasias have a number of magico-religious specialists in their society. All these specialists are not alike. They have different specializations which they acquire from their parental generations as well as personal practice. In the Garasia society, three types of magico-religious functionaries are found. They are: (i) Bhopa, (ii) Devala, and (iii) Khoont.

Bhopa (Shaman)

Bhopa is the religious head of the society. This position is hereditary and is always occupied by male members. He worships all the surrounding deities and spirits in order to protect the villagers from epidemics and other diseases. The function and role of a Bhopa is manifold. He plays the role of a medicine man, a sorcerer and a priest, as per the needs and requirements of the people. As the priest, he also presides over all the village festivals. Similarly, as a doctor or medicine man, he also prescribes and prepares the herbal medicines for all sorts of common diseases. The Bhopa can himself entice the spirit to enter his body at times when communication is desired. The Bhopa makes specific body movements and sounds when the spirit enters his body. Bhopa is possessed (visited) by the spirits of only one deity. There are three grades of Bhopas:

(i) *Pat Bhopa* – Who can go to the nearest enclosure of the God.
(ii) *Khelio* – Who can enter the place of worship but keeps away from the enclosure.
(iii) *Velio* – Who cannot enter the place of worship.

Devala

Devala is a male sorcerer in the Garasia society. Devala literally means a man who drives away *vala* (danger). He specializes in treating and curing the evil effects of *veers* and spirits. He practises magic and magical rites and worships spirits with whom he is supposed to be having direct links. The Devala removes the ill-effects of spirits with the help of magical spells and charms whereas Bhopa wards off the dangers by worshipping the Gods. Sometimes, the Bhopa works together with the Devala but the Khoont does not accompany or sit next to a Bhopa.

Khoont

Khoont is a ritual expert who is of special importance during the funeral ceremony. The Khoont acquires the knowledge through training and practice. While Bhopas are not paid for their services, the Khoont and the Devala are both paid.

During protracted interaction with the Medical Officer of PHC at Pindwara and members of some Garasia families, it was observed that the community is ignorant and careless about ailments and does not bother about them unless they reach critical levels, posing a threat to life.

When a person falls sick in the Garasia community, he is taken to the Bhopa for herbal treatment for certain specific diseases, as it is the least expensive. The community has intrinsic faith in this treatment. Some who do not respond to this treatment are taken to magico-religious persons. Allopathic doctors are consulted only when the cause of the disease is not understood or disease is at an advanced stage. Although the treatment given by the doctors here is free, but most of the time the medicines prescribed are not available at the PHC dispensary. It is financially prohibitive for the community to purchase such costly medicines from the market. They do not accept modern medicine because they have to spend very little money on the treatment of illness either by Bhopa or Devala, since payment is indirect – in the form of kind or some cash. Traditional medicines do not have to be bought, but are prepared from common plants and animals.

This explains the reason why sometimes people die but do not go to the dispensary.

Treatment Behaviour of Rural People

The rural people, especially women, take home remedies during illness. During the field investigation, it was observed that a person who falls ill in the rural community is never taken to the regular medical dispensary in the initial stages. He or she is treated in the family, particularly by the old woman of the house. The knowledge about the method of treatment of common ailments and the medicines to be administered is transmitted from generation to generation as family legacy. All the medicines for such common treatments are generally available in the family kitchen.

Some of the home remedies are based on the concept that food items have two kinds of impact on the body – hot (*garam*) and cold (*thanda*). Sickness also, according to them, is the result of exposure to either cold or heat. Therefore, if certain items are withdrawn from a sick person's diet, it is believed that he would get automatically cured. If, for example, food items which generate heat are withdrawn from the diet of a person suffering from heat stroke, and some other items that have a cold impact are added, the person will get cured in course of time. We found some interesting ethno-medicines practised in the rural community.

Home medication is generally performed as first aid treatment by the villagers for almost all common diseases except in the case of snake bite. On the other hand, there are many diseases like dog bite, injury, etc. in which villagers depend on home remedies for treatment.

Like tribals, rural people also have an unflinching faith in the powers of their deities. They, therefore, keep them pleased and favourable through various prayers, offerings and devotional activities from time to time so that they are saved from their wrath that may cause sickness and suffering. Shitla Mata is also worshipped by the rural people for prevention of the spread of small pox. Besides, they also worship other deities for the treatment of illness and for fulfilment of specific desires. In fact, cent per cent cases of snake bite in rural

Rajasthan are treated by local faith healers through propitiation of local God Tejaji, who is believed to be a snake-bite curer. Rural people also believed in *mannat* or *manauti* for the treatment of illnesses and for fulfilment of specific desires. Some of the other deities in this category include Ramdeoji, Bheruji, Shitla Mata, Badi Mata, Hanumanji, Tejaji, Narayani Mata, Ganeshji.

Before taking a patient to the hospital for allopathic treatment, most rural people prefer to go to their traditional faith healer first, like Ojha and Bhopa, for the diagnosis of the disease and the treatment takes place through charm *(mantra-tantra)*, *jhad-phoonk*, amulets and magico-religious therapy. In case of chicken pox, measles, hysteria, whooping cough and mental diseases, traditional rituals and ceremonies are performed to treat the patient. With his family members, the patient visits the Ojha or Bhopa who offers some *bhabhoot* (ash), out of which some is to be touched to the forehead and some to be placed on the tongue for being swallowed. This is supposed to relieve the patient from the ill-effects of an evil eye. Sometimes, a *tabeej* (amulet) is given to the patient or *jhad-phoonk* procedure is followed by the Ojha. A *tabeej* is a small sacred device made generally of copper and is worn round the neck or the arm with the help of a black thread. It is believed by rural people that after wearing this sacred device, one becomes totally covered against spirits or evil eyes.

Priests, Ojhas or Pirs hold a respectful position in rural society. People call them with great regard and in times of need they are visited for asking relief. They do not charge any fee at the time of offering a treatment. However, when the patient is cured, they are given items in kind at times such as food, grain or fruit and/or some cash (₹ 5, 11, 21 or 51) or they build a room/expansion of temple in accordance with the seriousness of the patient and the economic condition of the family.

The closest PHC is located at Andhi with one Medical Officer, one compounder and an ANM posted there. Rural people visit this only in the time of acute need, though the frequency of visits and the percentage of villagers visiting it are quite low. Villagers also complain that the medical staff are often absent and even when they are available, they are not sincere to their work. This has considerably reduced the faith of the rural people in government treatment.

In rural areas, there is more prevalence of private medical practitioners. At times, they are not qualified but are popular and consulted more frequently as compared to government doctors. Besides consultation, they also give medicines and are available even at odd hours during emergencies. They go to the patient's house if someone is critical and cannot come to their clinic. Regarding payment of fee, they extend flexibility according to affordability of patients and ask them to pay at ease and on availability. All this has led to a thriving business of private practitioners in rural areas.

In sharp contrast, the quantity and quality of health services are much enhanced in urban areas with PHCs, hospitals (government and private) and options of ayurvedic, unani and homeopathic easily available besides common allopathic treatment. Urban people choose from a wide variety of options depending upon their affordability and personal preference. Besides medical treatment, people also seek relief from traditional/religious methods in case of chronic and critical diseases. In this section, we take a bird's eyeview of the overall health scenario in the percolation of modern health facilities in the tribal and rural belts. We also analyse differences in approach towards treatment between men and women and their likely reasons.

During the course of study, we attempted to find out how male members of the family sought relief during illness. The results are summarized in Table 3.1

Table 3.1 *Source of Treatment Among Males*

Source of Treatment	*Tribal N=80*	*Rural N=80*	*Urban*				*Total N=280*
			Household N=40	*Informal N=40*	*Formal N=40*	*Sub-Total N=120*	
Hospital (government or private)	5 (6.2)	55 (68.7)	40 (100.0)	33 (82.5)	40 (100.0)	113 (94.3)	143 (61.8)
Traditional healer	70 (87.6)	15 (18.8)	—	4 (10.0)	—	4 (3.3)	89 (31.8)
Can't say	5 (6.2)	8 (10.0)	—	3 (7.5)	—	3 (2.5)	16 (5.7)
NR/DK	—	2 (2.5)	—	—	—	—	16 (5.7)
Total	80 (100)	80 (100)	40 (100)	40 (100)	40 (100)	120 (100)	280 (100)

Figures in parentheses indicate percentages.

In totality, 61.8% male members sought relief from government/private hospitals/PHCs. These include allopathic, homeopathic and ayurvedic both in isolation and in combination. In urban community, 94.3% male members preferred private/government hospitals for treatment while all the respondents of the household and the formal sectors went to hospitals. The percentage of such respondents among the informal sectors stood at 82.5%. Most of the male members of the household and formal sectors in the urban community were well-educated and economically well-off and this reflects in their preference of treatment too. Some exceptions exist in the informal sector where 10% respondents sought treatment from traditional healers like Pir, Ojha, etc. due to non-affordability of allopathic treatment.

In the rural community, more than three-fourth respondents (68.7%) sought relief from PHCs/private practitioners. Another 18.8% depended upon traditional healers. An interesting observation during the study of the rural area was that nearly one-third of the male members consulted private practitioners because they could pay for the consultation fee and medicines at ease and or in instalments.

In the tribal community, majority (87.5%) depended on traditional healers such as Bhopa for treatment. This is due to their belief that all ailments are wrath of Gods/Goddesses or due to the effect of evil spirits. Only 6.2% tribal respondents said that their male members sought relief from PHCs. It is clear that under the impact of modernization and diffusion of ideas, some male members of the Garasia community have also started visiting the PHC for allopathic treatment. Only a small number of families took their members to the PHC immediately on sickness without wasting time on faith-healing by traditional healers and the rest only when all other methods of curing the sick became ineffective.

We asked our female respondents as to how they sought relief when they fell ill. Results, as presented in Table 3.2, show that more than one-third (36.4%) sought relief from government hospitals during sickness.

Table 3.2 *Source of Treatment among Females*

Source of treatment	*Tribal N=80*	*Rural N=80*	*Urban*				*Total N=280*
			Household N=40	*Informal N=40*	*Formal N=40*	*Sub-Total N=120*	
Hospital (Government or Private)	—	15 (18.8)	30 (75.0)	17 (42.5)	40 (100.0)	87 (72.5)	102 (36.4)
Traditional healer	60 (75.0)	20 (25.0)	—	2 (5.0)	—	2 (1.7)	82 (29.3)
Take medicine from medical/grocery store	—	2 (2.5)	2 (5.0)	10 (25.0)	—	12 (10.0)	14 (5.0)

Cont'd...

...Cont'd

Household remedy/herbal medicine	—	25 (31.2)	5 (12.5)	2 (5.0)	—	7 (5.8)	32 (11.4)
Nothing/stay at home	20 (25.0)	10 (12.5)	3 (7.5)	5 (12.5)	—	8 (6.7)	38 (20.7)
NR/DK	—	8 (10.0)	—	4 (10.0)	—	4 (3.3)	12 (4.3)
Total	80 (100)	80 (100)	40 (100)	40 (100)	40 (100)	120 (100)	280 (100)

Figures in parentheses indicate percentages.

In the urban community, 72.5% respondents preferred government/private hospitals, while in contrast none of the tribal respondents sought relief from the same. Only 18.8% of rural women went to PHCs/private practitioners. Within the urban community, 100% of formal, 75% of household and 42.5% of informal sector women adopted the above measure during illness.

One-fourth of urban informal sector women took medicine from medical/kirana store without consultation. In contrast, only 5% of household and 2.5% of rural women adopted such self-medication. While 12.5% of household women in urban community took household remedies, only 5% of informal sector women in urban community depended on these remedies. In contrast, 31.2% of rural women still depended upon their household remedies for curing such ailments. Likewise, 12.5% of rural, 7.5% of household and 12.5% of urban informal sector women preferred to take rest and depended on self-healing mechanism of human body for recovery. Three-fourth of tribal women depended on traditional healers for herbal and magico-religious treatment, whereas the remaining one-fourth (25%) preferred to take rest during illness and did not take any medication.

During field investigations in tribal areas, we discovered that women were suffering from goitre, malaria, fever, skin diseases, backache, problems related to their reproductive functions like heavy and painful menstrual flow. Non-availability of lady doctors adds to their woes, since they are reluctant to discuss their gynaecological problems with male doctors.

Similarly, in rural areas, it was noticed that the major ailments were injury, backache, stomach disorders and a variety of diseases related to reproductive functions such as genital tract infection (leucoria or white discharge or 'safed pani'), heavy and painful menstrual flow or postural problems. Such gynaecological problems were more prevalent amongst lower-caste rural women and even medication did not provide permanent relief as symptoms resurfaced when medication was stopped. Frequent and prolonged treatment was financially not possible and hence they suffered in silence. Such repeated problems were reflective of their poor living conditions with almost no regard to self-hygiene. Even when symptoms surfaced, the women refrain from discussing their problems with others. Women often cite embarrassment and shame as reasons for their silence.[18] Even when women visit a health provider, they are reluctant to describe their problems. For example, they simply tell providers that they are suffering from *kamjori* (weakness) or that the provider should feel their wrist to assess their internal problems.[19]

When women feel that their daily lives are being disturbed by gynaecological morbidities, they begin a treatment process by using home remedies and/or follow these with visits to traditional healers, or unqualified private practitioners. In rural Rajasthan, women are generally seen eating foods like water chestnut, which are believed to have strengthening qualities and relieve problems like white discharge and prolapse. Rural women strongly believe that all their problems are rooted in economic vulnerability and the inability to feed themselves, become strong and fight illness.[20]

Cultural norms also play an important role in shaping women's knowledge of the cause of illness. This culturally-based knowledge can be correct and protect women, or it can be incomplete or erroneous and render them more susceptible to infections.

An attempt was, therefore, made to find out if respondents faced any discrimination regarding access to medical treatment. The responses are encapsulated in Table 3.3a.

Table 3.3a *Discrimination Regarding Medical Treatment*

Discrimination	*Tribal N=80*	*Rural N=80*	*Urban*				*Total N=280*
			Household N=40	*Informal N=40*	*Formal N=40*	*Sub-Total N=120*	
Yes	68(85.0)	65(81.0)	15(37.5)	30(75.0)	—	45(37.5)	178(63.6)
No	12(15.0)	15(19.0)	25(62.5)	10(25.0)	40(100.0)	75(62.5)	102(36.4)
Total	80(100)	80(100)	40(100)	40(100)	40(100)	120(100)	280(100)

Figures in parentheses indicate percentages.

The data delineates that nearly two-third (63.6%) respondents acknowledged that they have faced discrimination with regard to medical treatment. On the other hand, 36% respondents could not recollect any such incident. In tribal and rural communities, this situation was even worse wherein 85% and 81% women, respectively, faced discrimination.

Situation is totally reversed in the urban sample wherein a much less percentage (37.5%) of women accepted facing discrimination as compared to the rural and tribal women. Majority (75%) of this is contained in the informal sector which was economically weak, insecure and uneducated. Similarly, 37.5% respondents of the household sector also accepted facing discrimination. Surprisingly, not a single respondent in the formal sector reported such discrimination. This may be attributed to their education level, economic self-reliance and role as the major contributor to family income.

Discrimination regarding treatment by gender is significantly observed among the cases of urban, rural and tribal communities. Male members of the family are given preference over females. In our attempt to probe further the reasons for discrimination, the following viewpoints emerged:

Table 3.3b *Reasons for Discrimination in Medical Treatment*

Reasons	*Tribal N=68*	*Rural N=65*	*Urban*				*Total N=178*
			Household N=15	*Informal N=30*	*Formal N=0*	*Sub-Total N=45*	
Patriarchal norms	10 (14.7)	20 (30.8)	5 (33.3)	8 (26.7)	—	13 (28.9)	43 (24.7)
Financial	—	28 (27.6)	2 (13.3)	12 (40.0)	—	14 (31.1)	32 (17.9)
Location of health centre	19 (27.9)	—	—	—	—	—	19 (10.7)
Hesitation	14 (20.5)	4 (6.2)	—	—	—	—	18 (10.1)
Negligence	—	10 (15.4)	5 (33.3)	—	—	5 (11.1)	15 (8.4)
Non-availability of medical staff	10 (14.7)	8 (12.3)	—	4 (13.3)	—	4 (8.8)	22 (12.3)
Burden of work	15 (20.6)	5 (7.7)	—	4 (13.3)	—	4 (8.8)	24 (13.5)
NR/DK	—	—	3 (20.0)	2 (6.7)	—	5 (11.1)	5 (2.8)
Total	68 (100)	65 (100)	15 (100)	30 (100)	—	45 (100)	178 (100)

Figures in parentheses indicate percentages.

It is evident from Table 3.3b that out of 178 respondents who reported discrimination, nearly one-fourth (24.7%) felt that the roots of such discrimination are embedded in the patriarchal system wherein male members are looked upon as bread-winners, old-age security and carriers of lineage. Hence, every priority is accorded to them in medical treatment. Another 17.9% respondents felt that discrimination arises due to financial reasons and society finds it useless to incur expenses on the medical treatment of women.

In the urban community, the formal sector outrightly denied any discrimination, hence these respondents were not probed further. In the household sector, however, patriarchal norms and self-negligence were major reasons (33.3% each), while nearly 13.3% women also cited financial reasons. In the informal sector, while the proportion of respondents giving patriarchal norms as the reason for discrimination dropped to 26.7%, majority of women cited financial reasons (40%) and burden of their work (13.3%) as the other major reasons for discrimination. Another 13.3% of women did not seek medical attention due to non-availability of lady medical staff because male members of the family do not like such checks-up by the male doctors.

While patriarchal norms were cited as the reason for discrimination by 30.8% of the rural respondents, the proportion in the tribal community of such respondents was much reduced (14.7%). In a similar way, while none of the tribal women mentioned financial reasons, more than one-fourth (27.6%) of rural women held financial reasons as being responsible for discrimination. Tribal women mentioned location of health centre (27.9%), hesitation in approaching medical staff (20.5%), burden of their daily work (20.6%) and non-availability of lady medical staff at PHCs (14.7%) as the other major reasons for this discrimination. Married tribal women cannot go out alone without the consent of their husbands. The PHC is located far away from the village and as such is inaccessible to them. In the rural community also, 15.4% of women did not take medical treatment due to their own negligence/ignorance while 12.3% were perturbed due to non-availability of lady medical staff. Another 7.6% could not find the time from the routine of their chores to seek medical treatment.

Thus, it is clear that good health is severely constrained by women's lack of autonomy to make health care decisions for themselves. Seclusive practices that restrict their mobility and socialization lead them to underplay their own health problems and they suffer in silence. They also lack control over economic resources with which to seek remedy and health care. Financial and opportunity costs further limit women's access to health care. Families spend less time, effort and money seeking health care for women than for men.

The risks of death and diseases are strongly related to socio-economic conditions. In most settings, the poor and disadvantaged are more likely to suffer complications of health. Men justify the central role they play in the health care choices for women. Women have no freedom in such matters but men have all the freedom and power to decide.[21] In some settings, seclusion patterns restrict women from seeking care from male doctors, especially for reproductive health problems.[22] Women's illness ranks low among family priorities, especially when the condition is perceived as non-threatening or self-limiting, thus delaying the decision to seek care.[23]

Maternity and Fertility

Marriage is not defined as a means of satisfying personal needs but as high road of motherhood and the ultimate expression of one's feminity. Motherhood is the visible evidence of a woman's virtue and the source of her strength, all the more so if it produces sons. Of her many roles (e.g. daughter, sister, wife, etc.), maternity is the essential source of respect and prestige on the part of kin and society. In this regard, Kakar[24] observes:

> 'Whether her family is poor or wealthy, whatever her caste, class or region, whether she is a fresh young bride or exhausted by many pregnancies and infancies already, an Indian woman knows that motherhood confers upon her a purpose and identity that nothing else in her culture can. Each infant born and nurtured by her safely into childhood ... is both a certification and redemption.'

Motherhood, thus, constitutes a moral as well as biological project which makes a woman feel useful and 'naturally' competent. *Maternity* health care refers to the health care of expecting and lactating mothers, which generally starts from the act of delivering a child. *Fertility behaviour* refers to the process of bearing and rearing children in the context of the household and the wider society. It covers the process, including institutional mechanisms, leading directly or indirectly to childbirth and other demographic outcomes like child survival and mortality. In this section, we will identify not only the socio-cultural factors influencing fertility but also the institutional mechanisms, i.e. customs, rituals, ceremonies, etc.

Childbirth

A woman's reproductive health status is closely influenced by the age at which she attains motherhood. For that matter, every conception need not necessarily result in motherhood. Abortions, miscarriages, still-births, infant deaths are all direct consequences of early marriage. A woman married early is also likely to conceive early and gets trapped in the vicious circle of conception-motherhood-nursing-more conceptions. In view of these, it is very important to examine the age at which our respondents had their first child.

An enquiry into the age of respondents at the time of first child-birth revealed that more than one-fourth (28.6%) of women were between 20–25 years, another 25.7% between 17–19 years and 19.3% were below 16 years at first childbirth. Only 6% of the respondents were between 26–28 years and 2.5% even more than 28 years at the time of first childbirth. In the urban formal sector, more than two-third respondents (67.5%) experienced motherhood between 23–28 years. Only 15% women had early childbirth when they were between 17–22 years of age. In some cases (12.5%), first childbirth was delayed and took place even after 28 years. This group of women is highly educated, working, economically self-sufficient and a major contributor to family income and, therefore, late childbirth might be due to late marriage and personal and professional pressures.

In sharp contrast, child marriage is more prevalent in the urban informal society and as a consequence, 17.5% women experienced motherhood even before attaining 16 years of age and another 60% between 17–22 years. Besides early marriage, low education, unawareness and inhibition in usage of family planning methods also contributed to the above. Exceptionally, in 15% cases, the first child was born between 23–25 years of age. In the household sector, a large majority (77.5%) of women were between 20–25 years of age at the time of first childbirth. Among the remaining, 7% experienced motherhood between 17–19 years and 5% below 16 years of age.

In the rural community, girls get married in early ages which explains why 43.8% respondents were even less than 16 years old at the time of first childbirth. Another 32.5% gave birth to the first child between 17–19 years and 16.2% between 20–22 years of age. Only in a few isolated cases (7.5%) had women attained age of 23–25 years during first childbirth.

In tribal society, although there is not much prevalence of child marriage, yet the husband wants to burden his wife with family responsibilities at the earliest after marriage. This is reflective of insecurity in their mindset due to prevalence of extra-marital affairs. Majority of the respondents (43.8%) were between 22–24 years and another 35% were between 17–19 years during the first childbirth. Barely 12.5% respondents experienced motherhood before 16 years of age and only in a few isolated cases 8.7% women were between 23–25 years during the first childbirth.

Thus, it can be concluded that in each group women are besieged by a unique socio-cultural environment which may or may not lead to early marriages and early childhood.

We also plotted the gap between marriage and childbirth on a scale from less than a year to more than seven years. Table 3.4 reveals the data obtained in this regard:

Table 3.4 *Gap between Marriage and Birth of First Child*

Gap (years)	*Tribal N=80*	*Rural N=80*	*Urban*				*Total N=280*
			Household N=40	*Informal N=40*	*Formal N=40*	*Sub-Total N=120*	
Less than one year	24(30.0)	8(10.0)	3(7.5)	—	4(10.0)	7(5.8)	39(13.9)
1–2 years	27(33.8)	20(25.0)	25(62.5)	16(40.0)	21(52.5)	62(51.7)	109(38.9)
3–4 years	13(16.3)	14(17.5)	5(12.5)	9(22.5)	8(20.0)	22(18.3)	49(17.5)
4–5 years	8(10.0)	10(12.5)	2(5.0)	2(5.0)	4(10.0)	8(6.7)	26(9.3)
6–7 years	3(3.7)	10(12.5)	—	1(2.5)	—	1(0.8)	14(5.0)
6 and above	4(5.0)	18(22.5)	3(7.5)	9(22.5)	1(2.5)	13(10.8)	35(12.5)
NA	—	—	2(5.0)	3(7.5)	2(5.0)	7(5.8)	7(2.5)
NR	1(1.3)	—	—	—	—	—	1(0.4)
Total	80(100)	80(100)	40(100)	40(100)	40(100)	120(100)	280(100)

Figures in parentheses indicate percentages.

In case of 38.9 per cent respondents, the gap was between 1–2 years and in case of 17.5%, it was 3–4 years. While 14% women gave birth to their first child in less than a year after marriage, in 9.3% cases the gap was up to 4–5 years and in 5% cases, 6–7 years. Surprisingly, for 12.5% of respondents, the birth of a first child took place seven years after marriage. Most of the urban household women experienced early motherhood, that is 7.5% in less than a year and 62% in a gap of 1–2 years after marriage. For 12.5% of urban household women, the gap was 3–4 years and for another 5%, between 4–5 years. And, 7.5% respondents of this sector acknowledged that they had given birth to their first child after seven years of marriage. Likewise, majority of the urban informal sector women (40%) had a gap of 1–2 years and another 22.5% of 3–4 years between marriage and childbirth. Significantly, in case of nearly one-fourth respondents (22.5%), childbirth was delayed by more than seven years of marriage. So far as urban formal women were concerned, they also experienced early motherhood. In 10% cases, it was less than a year and in case of more than half of them (52.5%) between 1–2 years from marriage. This can be explained by the fact that urban formal sector women get married quite late and hence prefer early maternity. Only in isolated cases (2.5%) was childbirth delayed by more than seven years.

Rural women who had reported cases of early childbirth, i.e. in less than a year, were only 10% whereas one-fourth (25%) reported 1–2 years from marriage. Another 42.5% women delivered a child between 3–7 years, and for 22.5% women, maternity was delayed for more than seven years from the date of their marriage.

In tribal society, however, Garasia men do not believe in spacing of children. They believe that early and frequent deliveries will keep their wives fully occupied in domestic chores, ruling out any possibility of extra-marital affairs. For 30% tribal women, the gap was less than a year whereas in 33.8% cases, this was 1–2 years from marriage. Nearly 16% Garasia women experienced motherhood after 3–4 years of marriage. In the tribal community, in only 5% cases, motherhood was delayed by more than seven years.

Thus, it can be stated that women hardly play any role in taking a decision when to have children and it is the prerogative of their husbands to determine the gap between the marriage and childbirth.

We asked our respondents whether their first delivery took place at parents' home or husband's place. While 61% stated their first delivery took place at their husband's home, in the urban setting, more than three-fourth (77.5%) in urban formal sector, more than half (52.5%) in the informal sector and more than two-third (67.5%) in household sector women fell in this category. Besides, an overwhelming majority (82.8%) of rural women were also in this group of respondents. Only 31.2% of tribal women admitted having delivered their first child at the husband's home.

On the other hand, according to 36.4% of the total respondents, their first child was delivered at their parents' home. Mostly tribals

(69%) are included among such respondents. It is convention and tradition among tribals to deliver their first child at the parental home.

As in other tribal groups, it is also customary among Garasias that a married woman should deliver her first child at her *piyar* (natal, parental home) and subsequent deliveries can take place at the in-laws' house. It is believed that a young woman needs great emotional and physical care at the time of the first delivery which she can comfortably get at her *piyar*. In her in-laws' house, she has to observe *laaj kadna* (veil) and cannot directly communicate with elders. Thus, during the later days of the first pregnancy, the pregnant woman is brought to the parents' house and the entire expenses on the process of childbirth are borne by her parents. At the time of the second delivery, the woman can stay with her in-laws but her parents take clothes and sweets for the mother and the child. The expenses of the third and subsequent deliveries are borne entirely by the husband.

The above convention does not have much relevance in rural and urban backgrounds as only 16.2% of rural and 28.3% of urban households had this practice.

Data pertaining to the place of birth, i.e. whether the delivery was conducted at home or hospital, is presented in Table 3.5 and provides an insight into the aspect of maternal safety during childbirth.

Table 3.5 *Place of Delivery*

Place	Tribal N=80	Rural N=80	Urban				Total N=280
			Household N=40	Informal N=40	Formal N=40	Sub-Total N=120	
House	80(100.0)	70(87.5)	7(17.5)	23(57.5)	2(5.0)	32(26.7)	182(65.0)
Hospital	—	10(12.5)	31(77.5)	14(35.0)	36(90.0)	81(67.5)	91(32.5)
NA	—	—	2(5.0)	3(7.5)	2(5.0)	7(5.8)	7(2.5)
Total	80(100)	80(100)	40(100)	40(100)	40(100)	120(100)	280(100)

Figures in parentheses indicate percentages.

It can be seen that in totality, (nearly one-third) 32.5% of respondents got the delivery conducted at hospitals. In the urban community, 90% of formal sector respondents preferred hospitals as compared to nearly three-fourth of the household sector respondents. However, in the urban informal sector, only 35% of respondents could afford to seek the facility of hospitals and among the remaining, 57.5% got the delivery conducted at home. In the rural community, 87.5% women preferred to remain at home for delivery and only 12.5% went to PHC/hospitals for delivery. As regards the tribal community, all deliveries were conducted at home. Though the medical infrastructure in the form of Primary Health Centres and other medical services are expanding in the country, the pace of development is not uniform. The high incidence of deliveries at home in rural and tribal areas is a clear indicator of the low health status of women in the country.

Much of the anxiety associated with pregnancy among urban women does not exist among rural and tribal women. The knowledge about childbearing is derived much early in life through various customs and observations in the household and neighbourhood. It is common for children to observe the birth process among domestic animals like cows, buffaloes and goats. Moreover, young girls assist elderly women and *dai* in conducting deliveries at home and in the process also gain knowledge about childbearing and childbirth much before they themselves attain the age of maturity.

We tried to find out as to who had supervised the delivery conducted at home. Table 3.6 depicts the results:

Table 3.6 *Conduction of Delivery at Home*

Conduction of delivery	*Tribal N=80*	*Rural N=70*	*Urban*				*Total N=182*
			Household N=7	*Informal N=23*	*Formal N=2*	*Sub-Total N=132*	
Household women	4(5.0)	6(8.6)	1(14.3)	3(13.0)	—	4(12.5)	14(7.7)
Dai	76(95.0)	64(91.4)	5(71.4)	19(82.6)	1(50.0)	25(78.1)	165(90.7)
Others	—	—	1(14.3)	1(4.4)	1(50.0)	3(9.4)	3(1.6)
Total	80(100)	70(100)	7(100)	23(100)	2(100)	32(100)	182(100)

Figures in parentheses indicate percentages.

Respondents depending on a *dai* for the first delivery stood at 91%. Besides, 19% women in urban informal and 5% women in urban household sectors, 64% rural and 95% tribal women were also in this category. For 13% of urban informal sector women and 14.3% of urban household sector women, delivery was conducted by household women within the family. A total of 8.6% of rural and 5% of their tribal counterparts also fell in the same category.

In the Garasia community, most of the deliveries are conducted by a *Huhani* (*dai*), who is a socially recognized maternity help from the community itself. For purposes of delivery, she is preferred being one among them, well-acquainted with their habits and family traditions, and possessing the essential experience of conducting deliveries for many years. Another reason why she is preferred to a regular ANM of PHC or sub-centre is that the expenditure is much less. She is always available in the village locality and, unlike an ANM, comes immediately even if called at odd hours. She also performs additional services such as cleaning effluvia and placenta, burying the placenta, cleaning the delivery room and mopping it with mud and cow dung, bathing the baby and giving post-natal massage to the child and the mother. All these services cannot be expected from an ANM. In a large number of families, we also found elderly women conducting deliveries with the help of other women of neighbourhood. *Dai* is called only when a woman is undergoing delivery for the first time or when a complication is apprehended.

Among Garasias, as soon as the labour pains of a pregnant woman start, the family prepares for the arrival of the child. First, they worship 'Gotra Raj' and all the herbs and indigenous medicines are kept ready. Delivery takes place generally in a small room or covered space. The woman takes rest after the delivery in a space which is not frequently used by menfolk. In cases of difficult deliveries, they pray to Baosi (as respect to their ancestors) for not causing any harm or for an easy delivery. After the birth of the child, the *vastuta* (placenta) is cut with the sharp end of an arrow. *Vastuta* is not thrown but buried in the north corner of the house as it is believed that such an act would bring prosperity and good health, both to the mother and the child. Throwing it outside is considered an insult against motherhood.

Heat in the place is provided with the help of a bowl of coal, or burning wood or even bricks heated on fire-heat, which according to them helps in contraction of body muscles that are extended and released in the process of delivery. Certain indigenous medicines are given to the woman for facilitating contraction of muscles. *Dai* or elderly women also apply some pressure on the abdomen for removing any unwanted material from inside. Elderly women of the family also instruct the pregnant woman not to scream or groan labour pains at least to the extent of being audible to the folk. Otherwise, pains shall increase and become intolerable. Pain in child delivery is conditioned partly by the strong influence of cultural training, a matter-of-course perception, and its frequent occurrence (at home) in a society with high fertility. People are accustomed to experiencing and handling child delivery with fear, panic and uncertainty. Unlike in modern society, pregnancy and child delivery are not a major cause for anxiety, expenditure and dependence on medical experience.[25] For the women of tribal and rural communities, labour pains are an inevitable aspect of a desirable and obligatory part of their lifecycle. Pain during childbirth is considered a natural burden and necessary evil that has to be endured. Childbirth might be physically painful but the prestige and high social value attached to motherhood glorifies it.

A pregnant woman's significance for the household, the family and the community is expressed in several ways. The various institutionalized practices during pregnancy and childbirth indicate the high value that the society has placed on procreation. For a woman, pregnancy and childbirth, especially the first childbirth or a son's birth, leads to her status graduation and is accompanied by important rites of passage.[26] The intimate and active participation of the household and other relatives reinforces the woman's emotional and moral make-up. The ritual associated with childbirth periodically converts the obligatory into the desirable. These are what Bernstein[27] calls consensual rituals in-as-much as they function and transmit and reinforce society's central value system. Rituals have a highly condensed and predictable message with extra verbal or indirect meanings. They are a form of 'restricted code'. They evoke organization of sentiments and revivify the social order within the individual. Rituals accord public acclaim to a new mother for her favour to the household. Both the infant and the new mother are assigned a high value during birth associated rituals.

Although the mother suffers physical pain during childbirth, her sufferings are substantially curtailed because relatives, neighbours and the wider community pool their resources. The resources consist essentially of mutual help and sharing provided by people through their physical presence and work at any times. The community resources are the various local beliefs and practices which people have been employing for a long time to ensure successful childbirth.

Self-control in labour during child delivery is constantly encouraged through the prevailing harms. A woman delivering a child while working in the field is applauded and praised as a simple soul. The confidence and self-reliance perpetuate the belief that pregnancy and child delivery are a matter of routine in a woman's life. By the third and subsequent child deliveries, the matter-of-course attitude towards childbirth becomes more marked. By repeated births, mothers acquire sufficient knowledge and courage to deliver babies all alone at home and even in the field.

During the course of the present study, we came across Jomi, a 28-year-old Garasia woman, working fulltime in the field even when her fourth pregnancy was in an advanced stage. She scoffed the idea of going home and taking rest. She had actually delivered her third child while working in the field. That day, she had irregular and bearable pain and she had gone to work. While working, pains suddenly shot up and she cried loudly and her neighbour came for help from a nearby field. As she squatted, the baby was delivered. She cut the umbilical cord with a sickle, took a piece of *odhni* and wrapped the newborn baby and set out for home.

In yet another instance, Hajri delivered her third daughter in the field. Parte, another 26-year-old Garasia woman, also delivered her fourth child while working in the field. When pains started, she rushed home, where she could find no one for help. Here, she delivered her fourth child all alone by herself.

Pre-natal Care

Minimum pre-natal care consists of three tiers. The first level provides basic medical care through first contact workers at home, sub-centres or the PHCs and proper nutritional diet. Level two provides care at small hospitals through doctors and requires a set-up that includes facilities for foetal monitoring. Level three provides sophisticated medical care to the newborn and mothers at large hospitals through specialists.

We tried to find out from our respondents if any special care was taken during their first pregnancy as regards to food, medical check-up and rest.

As many as 46% of the total respondents acknowledged taking special care during the first pregnancy. They, majority (73%) of urban respondents who were also of the same view, included 90% of urban formal, 50% of urban informal and 80% of urban household sector women. Little more than one-third (33.7%) of rural and 17.5% of tribal respondents also took special care during their first delivery. With this, it can be concluded that well-educated and financially well-off women in urban formal and household sectors afford to take special care during pregnancy. This number dropped to 50% in the urban informal sector where respondents were preoccupied with the dual workload of their household as well as their working responsibilities.

In the rural community, non-availability of female medical staff was the main hindrance in regular medical check-ups and vaccination during pregnancy. Hesitation and minimal communication between husband and wife in a joint family system was another reason for lack of care.

In the tribal community, as described earlier, pregnancy is considered a normal and desirable condition for a young and married woman. For most of the period of pregnancy, until a woman went into labour, she performed the normal household chores and social obligations. Fetching water for drinking and cooking from even far-off places, chopping firewood, taking care of older children, if any, cooking for the entire family, and even tending to cattle and goats, are all part of such daily routine. Health workers advise them more rest during pre-natal and post-natal periods but as these women do not live in a joint family set-up and as Garasia men do not ordinarily share the household responsibilities, such advice is not often put into practice. Even no special diet is given to a Garasia pregnant woman. She eats the same food as other women in the family eat. But, her intake is expected to increase. Elderly women in the community advise pregnant women to eat more as 'the one inside also needs foods'. Besides, the nutrition provided to pregnant women and lactating mothers is also not sufficient. Due to their poor economic condition, they cannot afford proteins in the form of pulses. Even fats in the form of ghee or oil are used scarcely and in a very small quantity. Most of the time, they live on *roti* or *bati* of *makka, bajra,* wet chillies, salt and onion. Depending upon the milching animals, they only sometimes get milk. It is obvious that the general nutritive value of such food is very low.

Garasia women are motivated for pre-natal care by lady health workers. The preliminary services are provided to them at their doorstep and they are persuaded to visit the health centre. But, still, they seem hesitant to go. Except in complicated cases, they follow the traditional method of delivery. Most of the Garasia women do not know what these pre-natal medicines are intended for. Most of them think that they are for 'good health' or for 'producing blood'. Some Garasia women believe that these are meant for easy delivery.

The same attitude was found towards pre-natal care among the rural lower caste and poor women. However, in case of upper and some middle caste women, during the last days of pregnancy, they are prohibited from lifting heavy loads. Throughout the period of pregnancy, both rural and tribal women are encouraged by elderly women of the family to grind grain on the handmill (in rural *chakki*, and in tribal *ghatti*), as it is considered to facilitate smooth childbirth. It is a common belief among all the communities in Rajasthan that regular physical activity by pregnant women in their daily routine of life not only facilitates labour but also makes the delivery less painful.

The Garasia community has a plethora of taboos to be followed by pregnant women. Majority of the respondents identified and elaborated taboos as follows:

1. Pregnant women are barred from seeing the new moon as it is believed to lead to eye defects of the baby in womb.
2. During eclipse, a pregnant Garasia woman has to remain standing and sitting as lying down is not permitted.
3. Fire should be put from root head side so that the child remains in the correct position in the mother's womb.
4. Pregnant women do not attend any ceremonies related to death as spirit influences would lead to miscarriage.

Not only the woman, but a prospective father also has to follow some taboos. He does not cut anything which is growing as this is considered inauspicious. He would also avoid driving a nail or sticking a pole in the ground and also avoid eating meat of animal sacrificed to evil spirits.

Some Common Beliefs Related to Childbirth

The Garasia community firmly believes that deliveries during *Shukla Paksha* (bright nights) yield a son while deliveries during *Krishna Paksha* (dark nights) lead to the birth of a daughter. Likewise, if due to extra enlargement of foetus the abdomen of a pregnant woman is extended more than normal, she will give birth to a female child, whereas in case of less enlargement, a male child shall be born. It is also a common faith that if the labour pains start at the abdomen, it is the indication of a female child, and if it starts at the back, the child shall be a boy. If the delivery takes place before the completion of nine months, a male child is born, and if the period is extended beyond this period, the child shall be a girl. The food linkages of a pregnant woman are also an indication of the gender of the forthcoming child. Linkages for sour and salty food indicate a female child while linkages for sweets indicate a male child.

The Garasia community has a strong gender bias in favour of the male child. When a male child is born in the family, they exhibit their pleasure by ringing a *thali* (bronze plate) with the help of a big spoon, so as to let the news spread to the neighbourhood. On the other hand, when a girl is born, they move a *hoopra* (soop) in the air. It creates no sound when moved in the air. This process of announcement of childbirth is also prevalent in rural and urban Rajasthan.

Post-natal Care

Childbirth raises the status of a married woman in her in-laws' house, as she commands more respect in the household when she becomes a mother and her children survive. Papanek[28] observed that a woman's personal worth is related to her fertility performance and she attains the status by being the mother of a number of children, especially sons.

The Delivery Process

The process of delivery of a child in Rajasthan is locally called *jaapaa*: '*jaa*' means 'birth' and '*paa*' means 'to receive'. When a woman is said to be in the state of *jaapaa,* she starts receiving additional care and attention. The new mother is called *jachacha*. A new mother not only gives by the way of childbirth but receives as well. Her gains are both material and symbolic. Her child is her highest reward. So, she receives extraordinary care and attention. However, the maternity period is a special occasion for a woman that provides a break from the daily tiring routine. Special dietary provision is an additional favour usually conferred on this occasion.

We tried to find out from our respondents how soon they got involved in domestic chores after delivery. Responses are tabulated in Table 3.7.

Nearly one-third (31.4%) took a gap of 10–20 days. Apart from 15% of informal and 12.5% of household women in the urban sector, these included 46.2% of rural and 50% of tribal respondents also. This was mainly due to nagging workload and poor economic conditions that they cannot afford to stay away from work for long.

Table 3.7 *Involvement in Domestic Work after Delivery*

Period	*Tribal N=80*	*Rural N=80*	*Urban*				*Total N=280*
			Household N=40	*Informal N=40*	*Formal N=40*	*Sub-Total N=120*	
Less than 10 days	25(31.3)	7(8.8)	2(5.0)	13(32.5)	—	15(12.5)	47(16.8)
10–20 days	40(50.0)	37(46.2)	5(12.5)	6(5.0)	—	11(9.2)	88(31.4)
21–30 days	10(12.5)	5(6.3)	10(25.0)	6(15.0)	7(17.5)	23(19.1)	38(13.6)
31–40 days	5(6.2)	14(17.5)	12(30.0)	10(25.0)	20(50.0)	42(35.0)	61(21.8)
41 & above	—	9(11.2)	8(20.0)	3(7.5)	12(30.0)	23(19.1)	32(11.4)
NR	—	8(10.0)	3(7.5)	2(5.0)	1(2.5)	6(5.0)	14(5.0)
Total	80(100)	80(100)	40(100)	40(100)	40(100)	120(100)	280(100)

Figures in parentheses indicate percentages.

Similarly, another 21.8% took a gap between 31 and 40 days before getting involved in routine activities. Among urban women, these included 50% of formal, 25% of informal and 30% of household sector women. Proportion of such respondents reduced to 17.5% among rural and 6.2% in tribal women. The urban formal sector respondents are educated, financially well-off and give due diligence to maternity by taking rest of at least 30 days and more in 80% cases, while another 17.5% of such respondents take a break of 21 to 30 days. A nearly similar pattern can be observed for urban household sector women where 50% of the respondents took a break of more than 30 days and another 25% between 21 and 30 days. For 12.5% of the respondents, this period was only 10 to 20 days, while in 5% cases the return to daily routine occurs in less than 10 days. In sharp contrast, 37.5% of urban informal sector respondents get involved in their daily schedule in less than 10 days, 15% give a gap of 10 to 20 days and another 15% of 21 to 30 days before getting involved in their usual schedule. One-fourth (25%) of such respondents can afford to rest from 31 to 40 days and another 7.5% even more than 40 days after delivery. Such a trend is reflective of the uneducated status in most cases and compulsions to work and contribute to family income continuously. Another reason can be that they cannot afford to take longer leave from the workplace.

In the rural community, a significant number of respondents (46.2%) get back to the daily grind in 10 to 20 days after delivery. For 8.8% of respondents, this period was even less than 10 days. Likewise, 17.5% of the respondents took a gap of 31 to 40 days, 6.3% between 21 and 31 days and more than one-tenth (11.2%) more than 40 days after delivery. In the rural community, the post-natal period extended between one and two months if the child was a male, whereas it was restricted from 10 days to a month in the case of a female child. This discrimination applied to the dietary provisions and favours as well. On the whole, both the male child and his 'fortunate' mother were cared for and looked after in a better manner than in case of the female child. This difference was further revealed in terms of the nature of festivities and rejoicing following the childbirth. Another reason in the upper caste women is the prevalent norm to abstain from cooking and major household works as they are considered impure till 40 days of childbirth.

In the tribal society, as their lifestyle demands getting involved in household activities at the earliest, 31.3% respondents took less than 10 days and 50% between 10 and 20 days for getting involved in domestic work. Only 12.5% of the respondents took a rest of 21 to 30 days and 6.2% of 31 to 40 days before returning to work.

The special treatment given to a woman becomes more elaborate after the delivery. The rules prescribing the hours and the nature of work and rest as well as consumption of nourished food are to be relaxed for the *japaiti*. Such relaxations are crucial for speedy recovery. The various comforts provided to a woman are unthinkable in normal times.

In all the three communities, i.e. tribal, rural and urban, the *japaiti* is made to rest with the child even during day time, although almost late in her pregnancy, she was made to work. The complete bed rest continues for seven days from the day of delivery, which is supposed to be a period of ritual impurity called *huttak* in tribal and *Sutak* in urban and rural communities. A new mother is prohibited from taking bath for they believe that after the delivery of the child, the body of the mother is in cold state. A cloth is wrapped over the head to protect her from a sudden stroke of air, which they believe could harm her. A sheet is also tightly wrapped round the waist, so that it could help her regain its shape.

In rare cases, the Garasia mothers get a massage from another lady of the house or from a *dai*. A more privileged new mother is given a massage with oil or ghee by a *dai* to relax and bring her back to the normal state. Only a few rural women in Brahmin, Rajput and Bania castes and those of richer households in other castes get this privilege. The majority of other women take the help of close relatives or friends for massaging so as to avoid payment to the *dai*, while some do it themselves.

However, some immediate steps are taken to prevent both the mother and the child from the invasion of evil spirits. The child is marked with a black spot on the forehead, and an arrow or iron piece (in tribal) or knife (rural and urban) is kept near the head of the new-born child, while a black thread is tied around the wrist of the mother as well as the child. Besides this, during the period of *sutak* – a period of five or seven days of ritual impurity – the mother and the child are not allowed any exposure outside. While breastfeeding, the head of the lactating mother and the face of the child should always be covered with *odhni* or clothes in order to avert an evil influence. In *loon-mirch-karna*, some salt and dried red chillies are held inside the closed palm and rotated seven times around the mother and the child. This material is then thrown into the burning fire. It is believed that if it does not produce a pungent smell, the mother and the child are under the spell of an evil spirit.

Diet of Mother

The diet for *jachacha*, in tribal community (i.e. *huavad*) and in rural and urban communities (i.e. *kevaka*), is prepared in *ghee* and is culturally valued as among the best of foods. It is a special reward for the *japaiti*, as it is meant specially for her, and is also served to her in bed. She is treated with special care both in terms of food and rest. It is believed that this preparation has a special medicinal value and helps the woman regain her physical energy after the turmoil of childbirth. She is not allowed excessive liquids, as they believe it would swell and deshape the body. As long as she is on the herbal portion of diet, she is restricted from eating curds or any other eatable made of curds or gram. After the period of *sutak,* however, she is allowed to have semi-solid diet such as *khichri, lapsi, roti* and *dalia*.

In urban and rural communities, this herbal sweet is considered special for women. It was also observed that the *jaapaa* and special diet are not uniform in all castes in rural community. Many poor people belonging to lower and middle castes cannot afford a special diet and care to the same extent as the rich and upper caste can. Their special diet is usually prepared in oil, prescribed for other *japaitis.* Their post-partum rest is also shorter.

Rituals

A *japaiti* is considered ritually impure. This impurity is believed to render things in her household impure too. Therefore, she is secluded and not permitted to move even from her bed during the five or seven days of *sutak* upon childbirth.[29] The new Garasia mother becomes ritually impure for a period of seven days and this period is called '*huttak*', during which this impurity extends to all the members of the household as well. On the seventh day, after giving a ritual bath to the Garasia mother, both the mother and the child are taken to Baosi with five small balls of *churma* and five handfuls of maize. All of Baosis are worshipped on this occasion. During the worship of Baosi, *jaware* are sown and its proper sprouting is believed to indicate that the child will be enjoying his full lifespan. Generally, women take two weeks of full rest but some start their household work even after a week.

However, in urban and rural communities, the ritual bath can be advanced or postponed by a day or two depending on the pressure of work on the new mother and on those attending on her. So, on the fifth or seventh day, after giving the ritual bath to the mother, the women of the house worship Sun (*Surya Pooja*) in which the mother also participates as a mark of purging and freedom from *sutak*. But, the woman's ritual impurity is believed to continue for at least 21 to 40 days. Even after the period of *sutak,* the mother is prohibited from moving out. She is allowed this liberty when the *chuda* is changed. In this ritual, held after a month of the childbirth, the old bangles of the mother, which she was wearing at the time of delivery, are replaced with new ones as a mark of purification.

In the tribal context, there is no difference in rituals as regards to a boy or a girl. However, in the rural society, birth of a son is the sign of social prestige and is celebrated by distribution of sweets. Birth of a son leads to *Kua Poojan* (worshipping the well) after 40 days. A Brahmin astrologer may also be consulted regarding the auspicious time for this occasion. Lower caste/poorer sections also perform this ceremony but without consulting a Brahmin and according to their means.

Unsafe motherhood is still a reality in many parts of India, and this is especially true of rural Rajasthan. Very few women have access to ante-natal care. A large proportion of rural women are victims of the natural depletion syndrome, which leads to a gradual physiological drain on women. Early marriage also has serious consequences on the health status, to the extent of jeopardizing the life of young girls. One of the prime causes for the high maternal mortality rates in the country is early marriage. Anaemia is very severe during pregnancies. Deliveries conducted largely by untrained attendants under unhygenic conditions are also responsible for the high incidence of maternal morality. Limited knowledge of health and nutritional needs during pregnancy and post-natal periods is another contributory factor. Even today, only one in three babies is delivered by trained attendants.[30] During the course of study, therefore, an attempt was made to find out if the family had faced any incident of death of the mother or child during the delivery.

Respondents replying in affirmative stood at 42% and this included within the urban society 12.5% each in formal and household urban sectors and 52.5% in informal sector. In addition, 47.5% of rural and 61.2% of tribal respondents also acknowledged incidents of death of mother or child during delivery.

More than two-fifth (43.2%) of the respondents confirmed that the newborn death was of a baby girl while 41.5% said it was a baby boy. In 15.2% cases, the mother could not survive after pregnancy. In urban formal sector, there were two cases of death of a baby boy and three cases where a newborn girl had expired. These were isolated instances from the total samples. In urban informal sector, in 33.3%, cases, infant mortality was of a baby boy while in 57.7% cases it was baby girl. In 9.3% cases, the mother could not survive after delivery. In urban household sector, there were again stray incidents where in two cases the infant mortality was of a boy and in other two cases of a girl. In a singular instance, the mother could not survive.

In rural community, in 31.6% cases, infant mortality was of a baby boy while in 42.5% cases, it was a baby girl. In 26.3% cases, the mother could not survive after delivery. Moving on to the tribal community, in 53% cases, death occurred of a baby boy whereas in 36.7% cases, it was a baby girl. In 10.2% cases, the mother could not survive.

The data is reflective of the childbearing and rearing practices. Particularly in rural area and in urban informal sectors, the proportion of girl child deaths was significantly higher. Preferential treatment to boys, specially in feeding and medication, partly explains the lower mortality rates of the male child. The above pattern is supported by Khan et al.[31] who gathered evidence indicating discrimination against the daughter in duration of breastfeeding and provision of food and medical care.[32] *Visaria* sums up the subtle discrimination against daughters by mothers, who give priority to sons and husband over daughters and themselves in every respect. Such self-effacement partly contributes to the higher infant mortality of females.[33]

During the study, an attempt was made to plot various reasons for death of mother/child during delivery/post-delivery. Table 3.8 depicts the relevant information:

Table 3.8 *Reasons for Death During Delivery*

Reasons	*Tribal N=49*	*Rural N=38*	*Urban*				*Total N=118*
			Household N=5	*Informal N=21*	*Formal N=31*	*Sub-Total N=31*	
Early delivery	18 (36.8)	8 (21.1)	2 (40.0)	2 (9.5)	—	4(13.0)	30 (25.4)
Complication in delivery	4 (8.1)	8 (21.1)	1 (20.0)	10 (47.6)	3 (60.0)	14 (45.1)	26 (22.0)
Low-birth weight of baby	—	2 (5.2)	2 (40.0)	5 (23.8)	2 (40.0)	9 (29.0)	11 (9.3)

Cont'd...

...Cont'd

Due to religious reason	18 (36.8)	2 (5.2)	—	—	—	—	20 (16.9)
Lack of adequate care	—	12 (31.6)	—	2 (9.5)	—	2 (6.4)	14 (11.9)
Mother's illness/weakness	9 (18.4)	3 (7.8)	—	2 (9.5)	—	2 (6.4)	14 (11.9)
DK	—	3 (7.8)	—	—	—	—	3 (2.5)
Total	49 (100)	38 (100)	5 (100)	21 (100)	5 (100)	31 (100)	118 (100)

Figures in parentheses indicate percentages.

Early delivery was pinpointed as the reason for death of mother/child during delivery by one-fourth (25.4%) of the respondents. Not a single respondent in the urban formal sector cited this reason. However, 22% of the respondents opined that such deaths occurred due to complication in delivery. This view was more strongly prevalent in urban respondents (45.1%) and 21% of their rural counterparts also agreed with them. In tribal areas, the distance and unavailability of public transport are common problems to health care utilization. So, delays and difficulties in accessing appropriate care influence maternal deaths. For certain deaths, parents and other elderly people were unable to give any specification but nearly 17% of the respondents believed that such incidences were the will of God and beyond their control. A total of 5.2% of rural and 36.8% of tribal women also had a similar belief. However, this view had no takers in any section of urban society. Although rural and tribal people offer causes and explanations of deaths, they believe that ultimately death follows God's will.

Nearly 12% of the respondents attributed such instances to lack of inadequate care, which included 9.5% of urban informal and 31.5% of rural respondents. Lack of facilities and unawareness regarding regular check-ups during maternity also lead to such deaths. Rural areas have no access to specialized gynaecologists to handle typical and complicated cases. Another 12% of the respondents feel the reasons lie in mother's weakness/illness, which include 9.1% of urban informal sector, 8% of rural and 8.4% of tribal respondents. These are underprivileged sections of society and right from birth a girl child remains impoverished and undernourished. On growing up, she is overworked in domestic and outside chores, which deteriorates her health. She is not even given special care during and after pregnancy.

Bhatia[34] argues that early fertility and malnutrition increase the possibility of infant deaths, which in turn leads to increased pregnancies at smaller intervals, weaker mothers and more infant deaths. Several other studies also report lower stillbirths and pre-natal mortality rates and higher birth weights among who received ante-natal care.[35] Studies of IIPS explain that three out of four women are delivered at home, usually in unhygienic conditions, and two out of three continue to be delivered by untrained attendants (including *dai*).[36]

Several studies conducted in developing countries have provided conclusive evidence that there exist health risks related to pregnancies which are too closely spaced, which have become too numerous. These risks apply to both the infants and the mothers. We attempted to correlate the relevance of these empirical findings in the present study regarding the number of children and their socio-economic background. Data is presented in Table 3.9.

Table 3.9 *Number of Children*

No. of children/ Type of family	*Nil*	*1–2*	*3–4*	*5–6*	*7–8*	*9+*	*Total Respondents*
No. of families in tribal community	2 (2.5)	17 (21.3)	17 (21.3)	30 (37.5)	9 (11.2)	5 (6.2)	80 (100.0)
No. of families in rural community	—	21 (26.2)	32 (40.0)	20 (25.5)	6 (7.5)	1 (1.2)	80 (100.0)
No. of families in urban household sector	2 (5.0)	13 (32.5)	22 (55.0)	3 (7.5)	—	—	40 (100.0)
No. of families in informal sector	3 (7.5)	10 (25.0)	14 (35.0)	12 (30.0)	1 (2.5)	—	40 (100.0)
No. of families in formal sector	2 (5.0)	34 (85.0)	4 (10.0)	—	—	—	40 (100.0)

Figures in parentheses indicate percentages.

In tribal society, children are considered a gift of God and for most respondents the ideal number of children is at least five. Of 80 respondents, 21.3% had 1–2 children and another 21.3% had 3–4 children but they were not satisfied and were looking forward to have more children. Of the remaining, 37.5% respondents had 5–6 children, another 11.2% had 7–8 children and 6.2% had more than eight children.

Another reason for Garasias to opt for more children could be their hard life, which is labour-oriented, and they want to strengthen their hold over their land and belongings. Deaths also occur in early childhood due to lack of health and proper diet. According to Garasias, the birth of a child is a blessing from heavens and whosoever tries to prevent it by any method commits a sin that shall not be forgiven. A child expected by a married couple should be accepted with all pleasure and without any grudge. Out of 80 respondents of the rural background, 26.2% had 1–2 children while 40% had 3–4 children. For 25% respondents, the number of children was even more than five. The above trend clearly indicates that rural folk tend to opt for more children as majority is illiterate and do not opt for family planning due to lack of cooperation from the husband. Another important factor is societal and family pressure for a male child, which may lead to more number of children.

In the urban household sector, out of 40 respondents, majority (55%) had 3–4 children while 7.5% had more than five children. The remaining 32.5% women had 1–2 children. Even in this group of urban women, although most of the respondents were well-educated and financially well-off, they had a strong desire for a son due to family and societal pressures. This orthodox outlook leads to an increase in family size till their urge for a son is satisfied.

In the urban informal sector, 25% had 1–2 children, 35% had 3–4 children and another 30% more than five children. In 7.5% cases, there were no surviving children. Most informal sector women were uneducated, and dependent on husbands for most decisions. They want more children because an increase in the number of children leads to more working hands and earning members. Parents do aspire that at least one son can be spared for education so that he can end up with a white-collar job and associated prestige. In the urban formal sector, however, an overwhelming majority (85%) of respondents were found satisfied with 1–2 children. Only 10% had 3–4 children. In 5% cases, there were no offsprings. Most women in this section were educated, qualified, economically self-reliant and assertive.

All this reflects and radiates into their personal life as they limit their family and want to provide the best resources for 1–2 children. Educated women tend to have an appreciation of the advantages a small family can bring. The exposure which educated women tend to have regarding modernizing influences helps them to discuss with their spouses the need for having smaller families.

Family Planning and Fertility Control

In 1952, the government adopted family planning as an official programme and the approach was essentially 'clinical' till 1963. It was expected that people would come for advice and services to a few clinics that were opened under the programme.[37] It was only in late 1963 that the approach was modified with the introduction of extension education. With this modification, emphasis was laid on motivating people to accept family planning as well as on promoting services. A full-fledged Department of Family Planning, under the Ministry of Health and Family Planning, was created in 1966 for effective planning and execution of the programme. The important objectives included the desire to spread the knowledge of family planning methods and develop among the people an attitude favourable for adoption of contraceptives.

'Like pure water and like nutrition, food family planning is essential for good health.'[38] This statement brings out the enormous importance of the practice of birth control for a human being in today's world. Scores of women in India are not in a position to control their fertility and as a result have to go through a vicious circle of unwanted conceptions, abortions or child deaths. According to the World Fertility Survey (SFS), some 300 million couples who say they do not want any more children are not practising contraception.[39] Inability of most women to control their fertility is directly related to a situation where they do not have the power to take a decision relating to their own body and life. Factors such as ignorance about safe-sex practices, social attitudes towards childbearing patterns and blind belief in fatalistic values are also responsible for women's helplessness in their nature of fertility-related decisions. Women need intervals between pregnancies. Short intervals between childbirth can be extremely dangerous for overworked and undernourished women, contributing to their becoming victims of the maternal depletion syndrome.

Family Welfare and Population Control

'Family welfare' refers to the welfare of family with a norm of a small family having two children. According to the definition taken up by the World Health Organization (WHO), it is 'a way of thinking and living that is adopted voluntarily upon the basis of knowledge, attitude and responsible decisions by individuals and couples in order to promote health and welfare of the family group and thus contribute effectively to the social development of a country'.

'Population control' implies the control of population through policies intended to decrease the birth rate or growth rate. This depends on three factors – KAP, where 'K' stands for knowledge of methods, 'A' for attitude towards small families and 'P' for the practice of family planning methods.

'K' or knowledge of methods refers to awareness about the methods of contraception, the place of their availability, and the price and quality in which these are available. Garasias live in their secluded world untouched by electricity and media. Some information regarding family planning programmes is available due to personal interaction with an ANM posted at the local sub-centre. Garasia women rarely visit this sub-centre due to their workload, though the means of family planning like pills, condoms, etc. are made available at their doorstep by the ANM.

In rural areas, the most effective source of knowledge is interpersonal communication like friends, neighbours and relatives. Some, however, got knowledge from the radio and TV. In the urban areas, TV and radio are the most effective means of providing knowledge about KAP. The source of availability of contraceptives for rural people is PHC at Aandhi tehsil, which provides pills (Mala-D) and condoms (Nirodh). The doctor and ANM posted at the PHC also provide guidelines about the use of these methods. While family planning methods are available free of cost at the PHC, the quantity of these methods for each time is fixed. Mala-D is provided as a one-month course, while contraceptives for males are available on demand.

'A' or attitude refers to the general acceptability or non-acceptability of family planning methods by a community or group of people. 'P' or practice suggests the actual use of contraceptives in day-to-day life. Knowledge of family planning is almost universal in Rajasthan but the practice of contraception is low. Data pertaining to birth control measures used by the subjects of the present study is presented in this section. A query on usage of family planning methods yielded the following results as summarized in Table 3.10a.

Table 3.10a *Adoption of Family Planning*

Adoption of family planning	*Tribal N=80*	*Rural N=80*	*Urban*				*Total N=280*
			Household N=40	*Informal N=40*	*Formal N=40*	*Sub-Total N=120*	
Yes	30(37.5)	23(28.8)	15(37.5)	14(35.0)	20(50.0)	49(40.8)	102(36.4)
No	50(62.5)	57(71.2)	25(62.5)	26(65.0)	20(50.0)	71(59.1)	178(63.6)
Total	80(100)	80(100)	40(100)	40(100)	40(100)	120(100)	280(100)

Figures in parentheses indicate percentages.

More than one-third (36.4%) of the respondents confirmed having adopted family planning. Among them were 40.8% of urban respondents, 28.8% of rural and 37.5% of tribal women. Amongst urban women, the usage of family planning methods was much more prevalent in formal sub-sector (50%) as compared to 37.5% and 35%, respectively, among their household and informal sector counterparts. Besides, the use of birth control measures was also higher among women with a higher level of education, who were financially well-off and had an exposure to media.

On the choice of options of family planning, our respondents cited various methods which are abridged in Table 3.10b.

Table 3.10b *Family Planning Methods*

Type	*Tribal N=30*	*Rural N=23*	*Urban*				*Total N=102*
			Household N=15	*Informal N=14*	*Formal N=20*	*Sub-Total N=49*	
Oral pills	20(66.7)	2(8.7)	3(20.0)	3(21.4)	5(25.0)	11(22.4)	33(32.3)
Copper-T	2(6.7)	1(4.3)	4(26.7)	4(28.6)	7(35.0)	15(30.6)	18(17.6)
Condom	8(26.6)	3(13.0)	2(13.3)	2(14.3)	4(20.0)	8(16.3)	19(18.6)
Sterilization	—	17(73.9)	5(33.3)	5(35.7)	4(20.0)	14(28.6)	31(30.4)
NR	—	—	1(6.7)	—	—	1(2.0)	1(0.9)
Total	30(100)	23(100)	15(100)	14(100)	20(100)	49(100)	102(100)

Figures in parentheses indicate percentages.

Nearly one-third (32.3%) of the respondents preferred to take oral pills for avoiding unwanted pregnancies. This method was most popular amongst tribal respondents (66.7%) and this popularity diminished to 22.4% amongst urban and only 8.7% amongst rural respondents. Availability of family planning methods was better in tribal than in rural areas. Nearly 17.6% of the respondents used Copper-T. This was most prevalent among urban women where 35% of formal, 28.6% of informal and 26.7% of household respondents adopted it for planning their families. On the contrary, only 4.3% of rural and 6.7% of tribal women had adopted Copper-T. Services in the urban environment are much better for administering Copper-T than tribal and rural contexts and hence it is preferred more in urban areas, where it is a success. Nearly one-fifth (18.6%) of the respondents depended on their husbands to use condoms for family planning. In the urban set-up, these included, 20%

of formal sector, 14.3% of informal sector and 13.3% of household sector women. Moreover, 13% of rural and 26.7% of tribal women also fell in this category. It is surprising to note that the maximum usage of condoms was in the tribal society, even ahead of the urban society. Furthermore, 30.4% of the total respondents preferred sterilization. In all, 20% of formal, 35.7% of informal and 33.3% of household sector women in urban community and a large majority (74%) of rural women constituted this group of respondents.

So, sterilization was the most common method of family planning among illiterates and those with little education in both urban and rural areas. Most of the rural women had undergone sterilization after the birth of five or six children. There were only two cases where sterilization was undergone after the birth of the eighth and tenth child. Thus, the pattern of usage of family planning devices suggests that very little choice is exercised or available in rural areas. For majority of women, the first and the last method of contraception is sterilization. A survey conducted in early 1980s in rural areas of Bihar and Rajasthan indicated that 75% and 85% of respondents, respectively, reported sterilization as the preferred mode of contraception.[40] The use of sterilization is generally higher in rural areas whereas the use of reversible methods is more in urban areas.

Though extensive publicity campaigns are organized from time to time, not all women seem to have the willingness to make use of birth control measures. Acceptance or non-acceptance of contraception is influenced by many factors. We, therefore, asked our respondents to cite the reasons for not adopting family planning.

More than one-fourth (26.4%) of the total respondents did not adopt family planning as they wanted children. They included 30% of urban formal sector women, who felt that their family was not complete as they had only one or no off-spring. About 23% of urban informal women did not adopt family planning because they wanted more children to increase their family size. More offsprings means more working hands to contribute to the family income. A total of 28% of urban household sector women also fell in the same category. However, the major reason for increasing the family size was family and societal pressure for giving birth to a son.

Table 3.10c *Reasons for Not Adopting Family Planning*

Reason	Tribal N=50	Rural N=57	Urban				Total N=178
			Household N=25	Informal N=26	Formal N=20	Sub-Total N=71	
Want children	10(20.0)	18(31.6)	7(28.0)	6(23.0)	6(30.0)	19(26.7)	47(26.4)
Religious reason	16(32.0)	—	2(8.0)	3(11.5)	—	5(7.0)	21(11.8)
Psychological reason	10(20.0)	18(31.5)	6(24.0)	8(30.8)	4(20.0)	18(25.4)	46(25.8)
Reluctance by husband	8(16.0)	5(8.8)	—	4(15.4)	—	4(5.6)	17(9.6)
Using another method	—	—	5(20.0)	—	5(25.0)	10(14.0)	10(5.6)
Not needed	3(6.0)	4(7.0)	2(8.0)	2(7.6)	2(10.0)	6(8.4)	13(7.3)
DK/NR	3(6.0)	8(14.0)	3(12.0)	3(11.6)	3(15.0)	9(12.6)	20(11.2)
Non-availability of contraceptive	—	4(7.0)	—	—	—	—	4(2.2)
Total	50(100)	57(100)	25(100)	26(100)	20(100)	71(100)	178(100)

Figures in parentheses indicate percentages.

A little less than one-third (31.6%) rural women also fell in the above category and wanted more children. For lower caste rural women, the ideal family size was at least four children and the survival rate of infants was also low due to lack of nutrition and proper vaccination. Among upper caste rural women also, the preferred size of family was 2–3 children, of which they yearned for at least two sons. In a similar manner, 20% tribal respondents also expressed their desire for more children as the reason for not adopting family planning. An ideal family size in a tribal society was five children. However, the number of children usually stretches up to 12.

Slightly more than one-fourth (25.8%) of the total respondents quoted psychological reasons for not taking up family planning. In addition to 20% of formal, nearly 31% of informal and 24% of household sector women in urban society, 31.6% of rural and 20% of tribal respondents also agreed with them. The feeling of shame and inhibition in asking for family planning methods is the major roadblock in spreading the usage of family planning. It is pertinent to note that the prevalence of this feeling was not only amongst uneducated tribal and rural communities, but had significant relevance in the urban community also. Rural women acknowledged feeling hesitant in asking for contraceptives from the PHC staff. Moreover, in the tribal context, this feeling is even more enhanced because the use of a contraceptive to prevent childbirth is regarded as a sin, particularly by family elders.

Another 12% of total respondents abstained from family planning due to religious reasons. This feeling was confined to 32% of tribal, 11.5% of urban informal and 8% of urban household sector women. Most of the urban informal sector respondents in the above category were from the Muslim community and thus resisted adopting family planning methods due to religious sentiments. In Garasia community, too, children are considered a gift of God and preventing their birth by any method is regarded a sin of the highest order.

Reluctance by husband in adopting family planning methods also emerged among nearly one-tenth (9.6%) of our respondents. This was restricted to 15.4% of urban informal, 8.8% of rural and 16% of tribal respondents. Garasia men are of suspicious nature and tend to burden and keep their wives occupied in caring for children. They feel this would rule out any possibility of extra-marital affairs. In the urban informal sector and rural community, husbands were, however, not inclined towards methods of family planning due to lack of awareness and misconceptions.

As 7.3% of the total respondents were of higher age group, they did not require any family planning methods. These included within urban set-up 10% formal, 7.6% informal and 8% urban household sector women. Besides, 7% rural and 6% tribal women also fell in this category. For 7% of rural women, the main reason for not choosing family planning was non-availability of contraceptives. Among urban respondents, 25% of formal and 20% of household sectors relied on traditional methods such as periodic abstinence as a measure to control fertility.

It was also observed that family planning methods are not tailor-made to suit the lifestyle of tribal and rural women. Sometimes contraceptives like Mala-D have to be taken with a certain regularity for a particular duration, at a particular time and starting from a particular period. According to Garasias, they feel quite uneasy in following such regularity because they do not live disciplined and time-bounded lives. Women usually forget to take oral pills daily due to their hectic lifestyle and preoccupation with domestic and outside works.

Besides women in the Garasia community, some rural lower caste and poor women also complained that their houses are so small and privacy so limited that it is difficult for them to keep oral pills and condoms away from the reach of children. Tulsi Patel[41] has also observed that there are families where couples do not prefer using condoms because they believe it will create a very embarrassing situation if their children get access to them and blow them as balloons. Health concern is another reason for not taking pills more frequently in rural areas, as it may cause nausea, vomiting and headache. Other reasons for discontinuation of pills were dissatisfaction with the method, side-effects and pregnancy due to its irregular consumption.

With regard to Mala-D and other oral contraceptives, womenfolk nurture a strange belief that with the use of these the body gets weak and the blood turns into water. About IUCD like Copper-T, there is a belief that it leads to excessive bleeding. Three cases from tribal and two from rural set-ups were observed in which women visited PHC for removal of Copper-T because they suffered from excessive bleeding and pain.

Due to certain myths regarding sterilization, Garasia men are apprehensive and do not prefer this minor operation. They feel this would lead to impotence and reduce their physical capacity.

Another reason for avoiding sterilization is that men consider second and third marriages as prestigious and can go in for this at any stage of life. Hence, they do not prefer to incapacitate themselves by sterilization. During the course of the study, no male member of Garasia community admitted having undergone sterilization. Even though some Garasia women were aware of sterilization (tubectomy), they were not receptive towards it. They consider fertility as an important asset and fear their husbands would disown them if they adopted sterilization. Some Garasia women also expressed their apprehension that after sterilization if their husband dies due to any calamity/accident, their future would be doomed. They were also under the misconception that they would need complete rest for a few days after the operation. Since they cannot afford to do so due to their domestic and household responsibilities, they do not prefer to go for it. This is the reason that none of the respondents had undergone sterilization but some were contemplating *doorbeen nasbandi*. Some of the rural women were also worried about the success of the sterilization operation. This emerged from their experience of certain cases at PHC or sterilization camp, where a woman who had undergone tubectomy conceived again.

Thus, people of all the three communities were aware of the family planning programme and some had adopted it in order to restrict the size of their family. Some of the rural and tribal people also wanted to adopt it but improper knowledge about family planning methods creates a hurdle. In rural areas, the services of government medical staff are very poor and doctors are available only in the PHC. Whenever the ANM visits village households, she meets women in a very friendly manner but the presence of other family members, particularly males, poses an obstacle in their frank and free discussion on matters of family planning. All this contributes to their apathy for the use of family planning methods.

Individual variables seem to be having a profound effect on the rate of use of contraceptives. A positive attitude towards contraception is a function of the awareness of the need and then 'type' of measures available. It is important to know the extent to which these measures suit an individual's temperament and value system. Reproductive behaviour also depends on contextual factors such as stay in a nuclear or extended family and the presence or absence of in-laws and other relatives, as they seem to hamper the couple's freedom of choice regarding contraception and size of the family. Some an individual characteristics do seem to have an independent influence upon an individual's behaviour irrespective of the contextual factors.[42]

Attitudes Towards Childlessness

Birth of a child symbolizes the culmination of family and social responsibility. In the Indian context, family is not regarded complete without a child and the husband and wife strongly yearn for it. More specifically, it is not a happy situation for a married woman. In the Garasia community, childless married women are looked down upon and considered having committed sins in the past. All efforts are made to worship deities and if this period prolongs, husbands have the options for going in for a second or even third marriage. In the tribal community, we came across three cases where husbands had remarried since their first marriage could not yield any child. It is important to note that in the tribal context, women are made the scapegoat while in reality the reason of infertility may be the husband. However, the community does not accept so and the curse of infertility is borne by womenfolk.

In the rural set-up, the situation is no better and within lower castes, the husband is free to marry again. In rural upper castes, we did not come across any case of remarriage by the husband due to childlessness. In the urban sector, we came across two households, three informal and again two formal sector couples who did not have any offspring. However, they were persisting with both medical treatment and religious worship to satisfy their craving for a child.

Abortion

Abortion is an important parameter of reproductive behaviour. In various countries, liberalization of abortion laws has led to a sharp decline in the birth rate. In India, abortion laws were liberalized way back in 1972. Findings of an ICMR[43] study in 1989 suggest that the tendency to go in for an abortion is more prevalent amongst well-educated women. This is an obvious implication of pressure to limit the family size and their awareness and easy accessibility to services for terminating unwanted pregnancies. The advent of amniocentesis in mid-1970s was primarily meant to detect genetic disorders in the foetus. Double standards inherent in our social system have led to gross misuse of this technology to determine sex of the foetus. In one of the earliest studies on this subject, Ramanana and Bambawala[44] illustrated that 430 out of 450 women in an urban clinic went in for abortion on discovering that the baby was female.

In sharp contrast, in all the 250 cases where a son was predicted, women carried their pregnancy to term, even at the cost of risks of genetic disorders. Over a period of time, several other authors also highlighted the misuse of amniocentesis for sex selection.[45] In recent years, ultrasound has replaced amniocentesis as the primary sex-determination technique, making it more convenient and readily available.

We asked the respondents if their family had ever resorted to female infanticide. The perception of Garasia women regarding abortion is limited to accidental termination of pregnancy which they call *pani toda* in their local dialect. None of them favoured or induced medical termination of pregnancy for purpose of birth control. This is termed *tabar patakna* in the local language and is prohibited in the Garasia community due to religious reasons and is also socially unacceptable. Similar attitudes were observed in the rural and urban sections. Although they were aware of techniques of sex determination, none of the respondents acknowledged going in for such methods. We came across only two isolated instances in formal urban sector where women resorted to abortion on discovering they were going to give birth to a daughter. In both cases, they had two daughters already and had a strong desire for a son due to family and societal pressure.

There were frequent disputes relating to landholdings, adultery and brideprice payment among the Garasia groups, which continued for several generations. Violence is a way of life and is linked to the difficult economic conditions in which Garasias live. So, they desire more sons to protect their family and resources from encroachment by others.

Badi, a 23-year-old Garasia woman, explained the importance of high fertility and the need for a minimum of three sons. During disputes relating to landholdings, adultery and brideprice payment among the Garasias, they stand united against any outsider. An outsider generally thinks twice before attacking or harming any member of a large family. For people going to work in the fields, the company and security provided by family members is essential.

Dhapi, another 35-year-old Garasia woman, who had four daughters, said her husband wanted at least three sons. He threatened to marry another woman for their old age and for economic support to the family. Their traditional lifestyle acted as a binding force to prevent them from using birth control methods.

Haski, 36, was aware of family planning methods. She came to know about it from Kamla Benji (ANM). She had five children – three daughters and two sons. She considered it a sin to use such methods. She believed that all the children are born due to the grace of God. So, after the birth of every child, she offered something to Baosi as a token of gratitude for blessing her with a child. Religion in this case acts as a deterrent against the use of family planning methods.

Health results from interaction between an individual's hereditary contribution with his natural and cultural environment. Health and disease are measures of effectiveness with which we have adapted to our environment.[46] Every culture has its own beliefs and practices regarding diseases. The system of medicine within a cultural group attempts to treat diseases in their own peculiar fashion. The significance of women's reproductive and nurturing roles for overall health and development is undeniable. Biological and social realities of their maternal role are closely associated with their health status and are major factors in the problems they face in health, employment, education and other areas.

It is imperative to face the hard facts. Women's marginal access to resources, particularly health care, is well established. While disparities in life expectancy may be narrowing, unequal sex relations, higher female and child mortality rates in large parts of our country are glaring indicators of the overall devaluation of women. It is pertinent to note that women are involved intricately in the process of food production, management and distribution. They are also chief caretakers of family nutrition, including their own. It is ironic that though they perform these activities, their control over resources is determined by certain social and cultural norms that are not always favourable to them.

In a nutshell, the concept of safe motherhood cannot be practised unless the broader issues regarding women's health are recognized and addressed with full sincerity and intensity. This is a reality but are we willing to accept it?

Notes

1. *World Health Organization Report*, 1984.
2. Lewis, Gilbert, 1976. 'A View of Sickness in New Guinea', in J.B. Loudan (ed.), ASA, *Social Anthropology and Medicine*, p. 94.
3. Ibid., pp. 49–50.
4. Ibid., p. 54.
5. Charcot in Chaudhary, Buddhadeb, 1974. *Tribal Health: Socio-Cultural Dimensions*, New Delhi: Inter-India Publications, p. 211.
6. Lewis, op. cit., p. 95.
7. Murray, Last, 1976. 'The Presentation of Sickness in a Community of Non-Muslim Hausa', in J.B. Loudan (ed.), ASA 13, *Social Anthropology and Medicine*, p. 115.
8. NSS, 1992. 'Morbidity and Utilization of Medical Services', *NSS* 42nd Round (1986–87), *Sarvekshna*, Vol. XV, No. 4, Government of India, April–June.
9. Baroda Citizens' Council et al. *Prevalence of Clinically Detectable Gynae-cological Morbality in India: Results From Four Community Based Studies* (unpublished).
10. Basu, S.K., 1992. *Health and Culture among the Underprivileged Groups in India in State of India's Health*, Edited by Alok Mukhopadhyay, Voluntary Health Association of India, pp. 175–186.
11. Field, D., 1984. 'The Social Definition of Illness', in David Tuckett (ed.), *Introduction to Medical Sociology*, London: Tavistock Publications, p. 334.
12. Ibid., p. 335.
13. Mechanic, D., 1967. *Medical Sociology*, New York: The Free Press, pp. 115–157.
14. Harvey, L., 1990. *Critical Social Research*, London: Unwin, Hyman.
15. Chant, S., 1992. 'Woman and Poverty in Urban Latin America, Mexican and Costa Rican Experiences', *London School of Economics and Political Science*, United Kingdom.
16. Schur, E., 1971. *Labelling Deviant Behaviour*, New York: Harper and Roue.
17. Hasan, K.A., 1967. *The Cultural Frontier of Health in Village India*, Bombay: Manaktalas.

18. Bang et al., 1989. 'High Prevalence of Gynaecological Diseases in Rural Indian Women', *Lancet*, 14 January; and Santhya, K.G., and G.L. Das Varma, 1988. 'Spousal Communication on Reproductive Illness: A Case Study of Rural Women in Southern India', *Paper presented at the IUSSP Seminar on Gender Inequalities and Reproductive Health: Changing Priorities in an Era of Social Transformation and Globalization*, Brazil, November.
19. Bang, R.A., and A.T. Bang, 1994. 'Women's Perceptions of White Vaginal Discharge: Ethnographic Data from Rural Maharashtra', in J. Gittellslobon et al. (eds), *Listening to Women Talk about Their Health: Issue and Evidence from India*, New Delhi: Har-Anand Publications, pp. 79–94.
20. Oommen, N., 1996. *Poverty and Pathology: Comparing Rural Rajasthan Women's Ethnomedical Models with Biomedical Modes of Reproductive Morbidity: Implications for Women's Health in India.* Dissertation submitted to the School of Hygiene and Public Health, Baltimore: Johns Hopkins University.
21. Khan, M.E., Irfan Khan and Nupur Mukerjee, 1997. 'Involving Men in Safe Motherhood', *Journal of Family Welfare*, 43, 2, June, pp. 18–30.
22. Barge, Sandhya, 1997. 'Gynaecological Morbidity: The Ignored Tragedy', *Journal of Family Welfare*, 43(2), June, pp. 18–30; and

    World Bank, 1996. *Improving Women's Health in India,* Washington, D.C.: The World Bank.
23. Ganatra, B.K., and S.S. Hirve, 1995. 'Unsafe Motherhood: The Determinants of Maternal Mortality', *Journal of the Indian Medical Association*, 93, 2, pp. 34–35; and Thaddeus, Sereen and Deborah, Maine, 1994. 'Too Far to Walk: Maternal Mortality in Context', *Social Science in Medicine*, 38, pp. 1091–1100.
24. Kakar, S., 1981. *The Inner-World: A Psychoanalytic Study of Childhood and Society in India*, New Delhi: Oxford University Press, p. 56.
25. Greer, G., 1984. *Sex and Desting*, London: Secker and Warburg.
26. Van Gennep, A., 1960. *The Rites of Passage*, Chicago: University of Chicago Press.
27. Bernstein, B., 1977. *Class, Codes and Control*, Vol. 3, London: Routledge and Kegan Paul.
28. Papanek, H., 1973. 'Men, Women and Work: Reflections on the Two Persons Career', in J. Huber (ed.), *Changing Women in a Changing Society*, Chicago: University of Chicago Press.
29. Dumont, L., 1970. *Homo Hierarchicus*, London: Weidenfeld and Nicolson.

30. Jejeebhoy, S.J., 1997. 'Addressing Women's Reproductive Health Needs, Priorities for the Family Welfare Programme', *Economic and Political Weekly*, XXXII (9 & 10), pp. 475–84.
31. Khan, M.E. et. al., 1983, 'Women and Health. A Case Study of Sex Discrimination', *Paper presented at Joint ICMR-Ford Foundation Workshop on Child Health, Nutrition and Family Planning,* Bangalore.
32. Visaria, L., 1988. *Levels, Trends and Determinants of Infant Mortality in India*, in Jain and Visaria, pp. 67–126.
33. Bose, A., 1988. *From Population to People*, Vol. 1, Delhi: B.R. Publishing.
34. Bhatia, J.C., 1988. 'A Study of Maternal Mortality in Anantpur District, Andhra Pradesh, India, Bangalore', *Indian Institute of Management*.
35. Mehta, A. and K. Jayant, 1981. 'Perinatal Mortality Survey in India (1977–79): Part I – Identification of Health Intervention Needs', *Journal of Obstetrics and Gynaecology,* 32(2), April, pp. 183–215.
36. International Institute of Population Sciences (IIPS), 1995. National Family Health Survey (MCH and Family Planning), India 1992–93. Mumbai, IIPS.
37. Seal, K.C., 1974. 'The Family Planning Programme in India', in A. Bose (et. al.), *Population in India's Development 1947–2000*, Delhi: Vikas Publishing House, p. 375.
38. Royston, E. and A. Armstrong, 1989. *Preventing Maternal Death*, Geneva: WHO, p. 184.
39. Sai, F.T., 1986. 'Family Planning and Maternal Care', *World Health Forum*, 7(4), pp. 315–340.
40. Kanitkar, Tara and B.N. Murthy, 1983. 'Factors Associated with Contraception in Bihar and Rajasthan: Findings from Recent Sample Surveys', in K. Srinivasan and S. Mukerji (eds), *Dynamics of Population and Family Welfare*, Mumbai: Himalaya Publishing House, pp. 165–198.
41. Patel, Tulsi, 1994. *Fertility Behaviour, Population and Society in a Rajasthan Village*, Bombay: Oxford University Press, p. 190–193.
42. Hiremath, S.L. and Shahida, 1999. 'Choice of Indian Women: A Study of Reproductive Behaviour' in R. Indira and Deepak Kumar Behera (eds), *Gender and Society in India*. Vol. I, New Delhi: Manak Publications Pvt. Ltd., pp. 205–214.
43. ICMR. 1989. '*Illegal Abortion in Rural Areas: A Task Force Study*', New Delhi: ICMR.
44. Ramanana, A. and U. Bambawale, 1980. 'The Mania for Sons: An Analysis of Social Values in South Asia', *Social Science Medicine*, 14B, 2, pp. 107–110.
45. Dube, L., 1983. 'Misadventures in Aminocentesis', *Economic and Political Weekly*, 18, pp. 279–80;

Jeffery, R., P. Jeffery and A. Lyon, 1984. 'Female Infanticide and Aminocentesis', *Social Science Medicine*, 19, 11, pp. 1207–12;

Kumar, D., 1983. 'Amniocentesis again', *Economic and Political Weekly*, 18, pp. 1075–76;

Kulkarni, S., 1986. 'Sex Determination Tests in India: A Survey Report', *Radical Journal of Health*, 1, 3, pp. 99–102; and

Lingam, L., 1991. 'Sex Determination Tests and Female Foeticide Discrimination before Birth', *Indian Journal of Social Work*, 3, 1, pp. 13–19.

46. Lieban, R.W., 1973. 'Medical Anthropology', in J.J. Honigman (ed.), *Handbook of Social and Cultural Anthropology*, Chicago: Rand McNally College Publishing Company.

4 Political Participation, Empowerment and Development

In societies characterized by severe inequalities, what is required is a change in the social order that results in a redistribution of resources and fruits of development. In this sense, development means more employment opportunities, more education, political participation, social and economic equality, new institutions and attitudinal change, social discipline, and the like. Development, as a process, necessitates changes in fundamental attitudes of life and work, in social, political and cultural institutions.[1]

Today, the focus of development has shifted from the growth-centred model to the human-centred model. It has been realized that development acquires its full meaning and potential only when it involves people right from the stages of formation to implementation. It is due to the myopic approach to development and lack of coordination among the various agencies involved that many development schemes end up being target-oriented, where the achievement becomes the main concern and the good of beneficiaries is either only a byproduct or is totally lost sight of.

In the last few decades, development literature has been enriched by a number of theoretical models. But, most of these theoretical formulations do not really take into account the vital role women play in creating and sustaining development. Till about the 1970s, women's role in the development process was generally overlooked and there was a general assumption that development efforts would affect both men and women in the same way. But, such a myth was soon shattered and the existing theories of development were found to be grossly inadequate in recognizing the women's perspective.[2] Boserup had drawn attention to the lacunae in the existing development highlighting women's contribution to development programmes. His seminal work exposed the absence of the gender perspective in integrating women's interests into development thought and practices. This is especially true of Indian rural women, who constitute the major segment of the female population and yet are left at the periphery of most development programmes.

Political participation of women is an important determinant of their modernization. It enables women to come out of the shackles of tradition and secluded life. It also leads to greater social and political awareness among them. Women in politics could effectively represent opinions of other women and also understand and deal effectively with the problems of society in general and women in particular. Political participation of women equips them with political competence, organizational abilities and belief in egalitarianism and democratic planning.

Realizing the need for the inclusion of women in the mainstream development process, it has been strongly felt that unless women are involved effectively in the development process, the goal of overall socio-economic development of the country cannot be accomplished. Accordingly, the policy of reservation of seats for women was adopted in respect of institutions of local self-government both in the rural and urban areas.

Political participation, viewed from a broader perspective, includes participation in any organized and deliberate activity that seeks to influence or alter the character/function/structure/political behaviour of any institution or power structure in any of the above spheres. In order to assess women's political participation, one thus has to look at their involvement in different types of mobilization such as movements and struggles. The question that needs to be investigated in depth is the one to ascertain women's participation in mass struggles and protest movements and not necessarily in formal political bodies ranging from panchayat to parliament.

Political participation of women has raised a major dilemma. On the one hand, it is the fundamental right of every citizen to contribute to the decision-making process. It is, in fact, the citizen's duty as well and is based on the presumption that each member has adequate means and conditions to achieve full realization of his or her personality as an entity in society. On the other hand, from a feminist perspective, an analysis of women's participation in the political process has questioned the narrow definition of political participation as accepted by the mainstream political scientists and policy-makers. The New Delhi Document on Women in Development (1985) recognized that despite the rapid growth of informal political activity by women, their role in the formal political structure had virtually remained unchanged. This recognition has resulted in a serious debate on the concepts and indicators for political participation.[3]

It is necessary to attempt a definition of political participation which is broader than the one covering women's participation only in electoral and administrative processes. It includes a gamut of voluntary activities with a bearing on the political processes, including voting, support of political groups, communication with legislators, dissemination of political views and opinions among the electorate and other related activities. Besides social relationships, there are spheres of power relationships which are generated and institutionalized by being used to encourage, control or move people's behaviour, attitudes and beliefs in specific directions. Political participation can be considered to include an involvement in any form of organized activity that affects or seeks to affect these power relationships. It refers broadly to 'activities by those not formally empowered to make decisions, these activities being mainly intended to influence the attitudes and behaviour of those who have powers for decision-making'. In fact, protests and demonstrations against those in power also form part of political participation. Women's participation has covered a range of activities, including movements, protests and support on all issues connected with labour, dowry, rape, domestic violence, price rise and deforestation, as also movements for the promotion of peace.[4]

Why Empower Women?

Discrimination against women from womb to tomb is well known. The National Perspective Plan for Women 1988–2000 A.D. (1988), which made a free, frank and objective analysis of the impact of developmental plans and programmes on Indian women with special reference to rural women, gives us the following profile of women in India: 'There is inequality and vulnerability of women in all sectors – economic, social, political, education, health care, nutrition and legal. As women are oppressed in all spheres of life, they need to be empowered in all walks of life.'

The concept of women's empowerment appears to be the outcome of several important critiques and debates generated by the women's movement throughout the world, and particularly by Third World feminists. Its source can be treated between feminism and the concepts of 'popular education' developed in Latin America in the 1970s.[5]

The conspicuous feature of the term 'empowerment' is that it contains the word 'power'. The process of challenging existing power relations and of gaining greater control over the sources of power may be termed 'empowerment'. This broad definition is defined by feminist scholars and activities within the context of their own regions.[6]

The first state of women's empowerment is women's awakening to the facts of their existence throughout the United States, in different ethnic groups, in different social classes and in the world around them.[7] Empowerment is the initial phase of women's liberation freedom, and equity, as well as a long range goal of women's political participation. It is the first step in a long journey towards formulation and realization of human rights and responsibilities that transcend gender role stereotypes and the objectification of women and the men.

Empowerment of women means many things to Kamla Bhasin:

- It means recognizing women's contribution, women's knowledge.
- Helping women fight their own fears, and feelings of inadequacy and inferiority.
- Enhancing their self-respect and self-dignity.
- Controlling their own bodies.
- Becoming economically independent and self-reliant.
- Women controlling resources like land and property.
- Reducing women's burden of work, specially within the home.
- Creating and strengthening women's groups and organizations.
- Promoting qualities of nurturing, caring and gentleness, not just in women but also in men.[8]

Power is the keyword of the term 'empowerment', which means control over material assets, intellectual resources, and ideology. The material assets over which control can be established may be of any type – physical, human, financial – such as land, water, forests, people's bodies and agencies, labour, money and access to money. Knowledge, information and ideas can be included in intellectual resources. Control over ideology signifies the ability to generate, capacity to propagate, capacity to sustain and institutionalize specific sets of beliefs, principles, values, attitudes, actions and behaviours 'virtually' determining how people perceive, think and function in a given socio-economic and political environment.[9]

Political power is based on the fact that there is a scarcity in society of social variables which are tangibles and intangibles as financial security, a nutritious diet, good health, meaningful and useful work opportunities for self-development and self-esteem.[10] Another way to define political power is who determines who gets what or influences whom. Understood this way, power then belongs only to those who make policy and set standards. Through collusive consensus, the politically powerful are able to maintain and perpetuate the status quo, which they then hold up as the only acceptable system and one which the powerless have no choice but to accept.

Power is important for community practitioners to understand, for they each play into the cyclical nature of powerlessness.

Political culture is the set of attitudes, beliefs and sentiments which give order and meaning to a political process and which provides the underlying behaviour in the political system. Political culture is the product of both the collective history of a political system and the life histories of the members of that system and, thus, it is rooted equally in public events and private experiences. Every society has its own set of attitudes, beliefs and sentiments which combine to develop its political culture. Political socialization determines the initial exposure to the basic political orientations and value patterns by which a person is included into the political culture.[11]

The most important goal in post-Independence India has been reconstruction of the centuries-old social system. With this view, numerous measures have been taken to alleviate the socio-economic and political conditions of the weaker sections. Systems for rendering justice have existed since long in various castes in rural and tribal India.

Caste Panchayats in Rajasthan

Self-styled caste panchayats in Rajasthan are emerging as a parallel judiciary to grant divorce, resolve legal issues, and impose penalties and punishments on individuals and groups of people. The panchayats existed during feudal days but today they are composed of unruly elements and the panches are normally persons, who with a view to wield power in their caste, preside over such panchayats having no legal sanctity.

The caste panchayat commits atrocities on the weaker sections of their community and women are the worst victims. They terrorize the aggrieved persons into compliance with their rulings and not to take assistance from any court of law. Fearing ostracism from their caste, most of the aggrieved persons are left with no option but to follow the dictates of these caste panchayats. The 'judges' of the caste panchayats use muscle power to get their judgments executed. The decisions of such panchayats have often resulted in dissolution of marriage, grant of divorce, separation of child from mother to father, etc.

Each caste has its own panchayat in Dangarwara village. Panchayats of Brahmins, Mahajans, Balais, Raigers, Rajputs, Meenas and of other communities in Dangarwara are very powerful organizations, which not only settle quarrels, but also punish the law-breakers and settle cases of marriage disputes, etc. Women are not included in traditional panchayats although decisions are taken about them. In the case of women, decisions on their marriage are taken either by parents, uncles or elder brothers. Divorce on the part of the husband is permitted among all castes except higher castes like Brahmin, Rajput and Bania or Mahajan on the basis of the proved bad character of the woman.

In the same manner, various castes have their own panchayats for solving internal disputes. Rulings of these panchayats are followed by all the caste members in conformity with the rules and rituals in each caste.

Traditional Tribal Panchayat

The Garasias have their own panchayat with an all-powerful headman called Patel. The decisions regarding all disputes are settled by the panchayat and the orders of the panchayat and Mukhiya are mandatory for both the parties in disputes. The Garasias did not consider it necessary to approach the law courts for settlement in inter- or intra-village disputes. They approached the panchayat for the purpose and honoured its decision. Thus, the state laws did not affect them. As the process of acculturation started, the Garasias also began to open out and came in contact of the caste Hindus and gradually began to accept the changing scenario. As a result, serious crimes began to be brought to courts of law. But, still, the hold of the panchayat remained firm and they accepted the decisions of the traditional *Panchas*.

All the villages of Pindwara Patta have a tribal panchayat as the apex body. The tribal panchayat is the highest tribunal to decide all inner-village disputes, all civil, criminal cases of appeals against village panchayats and to decide cases of social mobility and ex-communication. It interprets the customary law on the principle of natural justice.

The proceedings of the panchayat are always held in public, and any member of the tribe can tender new evidence at any stage of trial. The tribal panchayat is a mobile court of justice which moves from village to village whenever a dispute arises. The panchayat sessions are held either in the morning or evening and may continue for hours together. The sittings of the panchayat are held daily till the case is decided.

The Patel has come to acquire a position of social leadership. He is taken to be the wisest man and head of the clan and plays a significant role in Garasia society. At all social functions such as *namkaran,* engagement and marriage, the presence of the Patel is essential. In his absence, the name-giving ceremony has to be cancelled.

In the context of tribal as well as rural areas, the ushering of panchayati raj has created a new political unit for development. The panchayati raj involves the participation of villages at all three tiers, viz., Gram Panchayat, Panchayat Samiti and Zila Parishad, in the implementation of the development programmes. It is expected of the tribal and rural people to contribute their might in the success of such development schemes and also to participate in the panchayat elections. It is now reflected in the general awareness among the tribals towards the political process and their rights of participation in it.

Tribal and rural societies still have their traditional culture and yet changes are taking place in the wake of exposure of tribal and rural women to democratic polity in the country. It is, therefore, necessary to know the views and attitudes of women about elections, empowerment, panchayati raj and political institutions. Another point of enquiry is the consequences and aftermath of the participation of women in political activities. It is on these lines that an attempt has been made to gauge the nature and extent of the respondents' awareness about their participation in the political process.

Participation in Elections

Elections are complex events, involving individual and collective decisions which directly affect, and are affected by, all the political and social processes. They open up channels between the elite and the masses and also between the individual and the government. They are also major instruments of political socialization and participation. Elections have also been an agency for the recruitment of the elite belonging to middle and lower castes in politics who are less educated, less westernized, locally based.

Thus, an election provides an unrivalled opportunity to examine the organization, the personnel and the politics of the parties. In other words, an election gives an opportunity for the general political process. It not only involves the casting of votes but also offers chances for attending election meetings, pamphleteering and using various propaganda materials. This brings the voter face to face with the candidates, government officers and other agencies.

The number of people involved in the election process is normally quite large. The respondents were asked whether they had cast their vote regularly in elections. Table 4.1 shows that a large majority of respondents (69.6%) always voted, followed by another 22.9% who voted sporadically and 7.5% who never voted. It is interesting to note that an overwhelming proportion (80%) of tribal respondents always cast their vote. Probing deeper, it emerged that they treat election time as one big feast where they eat, drink and enjoy themselves. Participation in the election process diminishes in urban and rural set-ups where only 67.5% and 62.5% respondents, respectively, always cast their vote. Within the urban section, the level of involvement was much more in household and formal sectors respondents (75% and 80%, respectively, who always voted) and this proportion drops significantly to only 47.5% among their informal sector counterparts.

It can, thus, be inferred that increased education, exposure to media and independence have stimulated political interest and involvement amongst respondents of the urban formal and household sectors.

Table 4.1 *Voting Pattern in Elections*

Casting vote in elections	*Tribal N=80*	*Rural N=80*	*Urban*				*Total N=280*
			Household N=40	*Informal N=40*	*Formal N=40*	*Sub-Total N=120*	
Always	64(80.0)	50(62.5)	30(75.0)	19(47.5)	32(80.0)	81(67.5)	195(69.6)
Not always	13(16.2)	20(25.0)	10(25.0)	13(32.5)	8(20.0)	31(25.8)	64(22.9)
Never	3(3.8)	10(12.5)	—	8(20.0)	—	8(6.7)	21(7.5)
Total	80(100)	80(100)	40(100)	40(100)	40(100)	120(100)	280(100)

Figures in parentheses indicate percentages.

The 73rd and 74th constitutional amendments for ensuring one-third reservation for women in panchayat and municipal bodies were brought about in 1993. This ensured their participation in the political process at the grassroots level. As a consequence, today, women are matching their male counterparts stride by stride and proactively getting involved in the political process.

Although women do not have intricate knowledge of legal nuances, yet they are efficient in management of budget in meagre resources. They can sympathize with difficulties faced by womenfolk regarding access to fuel, drinking water, etc. They are well aware of the oppression faced by illiterate and financially-dependent women. Hence, they are determined to eradicate these problems and uplift the status of womenfolk. In the starting phase, men were more dominant but now women have overcome their inhibitions and are more vocal and expressive about raising issues and taking them to logical conclusions.

This is also removing disparities in their family and social life. This has drawn respect and opened new avenues for their growth.

Before implementing the Panchayati Raj system, there were a lot of unanswered questions and people were apprehensive if women who were unexposed for decades would be outgoing and could deliver speeches, organize people and present their problems effectively in front of bureaucrats. However, encouraged by an overwhelming response from women, many sections are advocating reservation of 33% seats in the state assemblies and parliament as well for women.

It is true that 33% reservation of seats in local bodies has provided opportunities to a large number of women to enter the political decision-making process, but many of these women have no identity of their own and act as mere mouthpieces of powerful men in politics. Also, the violent power struggles prevalent in many villages do not allow poor, unprotected women to contest these elections.

It is against this backdrop that the respondents were asked to give their opinion about the one-third reservation for women in legislatures and institutions of local self-government. Responses are presented in Table 4.2. Justification for the above issue was gravitated towards the urban set-up with 35% of urban respondents supporting overwhelmingly and 28.3% partially. The proportion of rural and tribal respondents offering overwhelming support reduced to 12.5% and 5%, respectively, and partial justification emerged from only 12.5% of the rural respondents.

Majority (61%) of the respondents were unable to comprehend the issue and could not frame any opinion for its justification. Lack of expenses and gruelling daily lifestyle were major reasons why 95% of tribal and 75% of rural women had no time and energy for such broader issues. Nearly 30% of urban respondents also did not elucidate. While awareness levels regarding political process have risen substantially in the urban set-up, women still feel their hands are full with their primary areas of concern (husband, children and home) and become obliviant to other issues. This reflects primarily amongst urban informal (55%), followed by household (22.5%) and formal sector respondents (10%).

Table 4.2 *Justification for One-third Reservation for Women in Parliament, Assembly and Panchayats*

Response	*Tribal N=80*	*Rural N=80*	*Urban*				*Total N=280*
			Household N=40	*Informal N=40*	*Formal N=40*	*Sub-Total N=120*	
To large extent	4(5.0)	10(12.5)	16(40.0)	7(17.5)	19(47.5)	42(35.0)	56 (20.0)
To some extent	—	10(12.5)	13(32.5)	11(27.5)	10(25.0)	34(28.3)	44(15.8)
To a lesser or some extent	—	—	1(2.5)	—	3(7.5)	4(3.3)	4(1.4)
Not justified	—	—	1(2.5)	—	4(10.0)	5(4.1)	5(1.8)
Can't say	76(95.0)	60(75.0)	9(22.5)	22(55.0)	4(10.0)	35(29.1)	171(61.0)
Total	80(100)	80(100)	40(100)	40(100)	40(100)	120(100)	280(100)

Figures in parentheses indicate percentages.

Thus, it can be concluded that educated urban respondents were more exposed to the election process and hence strongly favoured reservation for women in politics. Nearly half of the urban informal sector, rural and tribal respondents were not well-educated and neither aware nor concerned about the election process. Hence, they were non-committal regarding benefits due to reservation for women in politics. They are besieged by their own day-to-day problems and do not have much foresight to think on broader issues such as government set-up, elections, etc.

Majority of the urban formal sector respondents expressed unequivocal support for the idea because they felt that politics was a male-dominated field and unless women were given reservation, they would never get an opportunity to be at par with men.

Reserving one-third of seats in rural political bodies has several important implications for the empowerment of women. It has created a silent revolution in the country. But mere reservation in itself is not sufficient. A conducive social environment has to be created for empowering these women to face the challenges that the newly-acquired power brings.[12]

To a question regarding their active involvement in political parties or other organizations, in tribal context, a singular isolated instance came to light where a woman got elected as a member of the Panchayat Samiti from a seat reserved for ST women. She was a member of BJP. Besides political parties, women were not involved in any other organization and association.

In the rural context, we came across a woman owing allegiance to the Congress party. We also came across a Sathin attached to a Women Development Association. In the urban household sector, there was an isolated case of a woman respondent being part of a cooperative organization (Kardhani). There was no participation of the urban informal sector women in any organizational activity. This activity was most pronounced in the urban formal sector, where at least 10 respondents were part of an employee organization, two were actively involved with a women's association, three with a social organization and five (lady doctors) with different doctors' organizations.

It, thus, clearly emerges that tribal and rural women are underexposed, hesitant and unable to find time and freedom to associate themselves with any collective process. Contrary to this, urban formal sector women are educated, exposed, broad-minded and vocal and hence, eager to devote themselves actively for collective cause.

Women's Role in Development

Women do not have a significant place in the process of socio-economic development due to gender-biased attitudes and practices. The goal of development cannot be realized if women are not involved meaningfully in the development process. Not only does the failure to include them in the development process run counter to the objectives of development, it also invariably hinders the process itself. Considering the fact, the constitutional provisions in the form of 73rd and 74th amendments have been introduced to reserve seats for women in PRIs and urban local bodies (ULBs). Thus, at least in a theoretical sense, rural women are empowered to participate in the development process on an equal plane with men. Their effective participation in the development process depends, inter alia, on the nature of their outlook, values and orientation towards changing social, economic, educational and political situations.

Table 4.3a *Should Women be Active in Politics?*

Should women be active in politics?	*Tribal N=80*	*Rural N=80*	*Urban*				*Total N=280*
			Househol d N=40	*Informal N=40*	*Formal N=40*	*Sub-Total N=120*	
Yes	37(46.2)	48(60.0)	16(40.0)	21(52.5)	25(62.5)	62(51.6)	147(52.5)
No	43(53.8)	32(40.0)	24(60.0)	19(47.5)	15(37.5)	58(48.4)	133(47.5)
Total	80(100)	80(100)	40(100)	40(100)	40(100)	120(100)	280(100)

Figures in parentheses indicate percentages.

We tried to gauge the attitude of the respondents towards women becoming active in politics (see Table 4.3a). More than half were totally against women entering politics. Within this segment, the proportion of respondents varied from a high of 60% in rural to 51.6% in urban and 46.2% amongst tribal respondents. Further analysis reveals that significantly higher proportions of urban formal sector and urban informal sector (62.5% and 52.5%, respectively) were positively disposed towards women becoming active in politics in contrast to only 40% of urban household sector respondents who endorsed this point of view.

On further prodding the respondents who favoured women entering politics, Table 4.3b shows that a significant proportion (41.5%) looked upon women entering politics to solve their hardships and problems. This viewpoint had no representation from urban formal sector respondents and emerged strongly from 62.1% of tribal respondents, followed by 41.6% of rural and 56.2% and 43.2% of urban household and informal sector respondents, respectively. Another one-fifth of the total respondents opined that women entering politics would increase the prestige of women. One-third of urban formal sector and rural respondents endorsed this viewpoint and 19% of urban informal sector respondents agreed with them. It is pertinent to note that none of the urban household sector and tribal respondents agreed with this angle.

Table 4.3b *Reasons for Women Being Active in Politics*

Reasons	*Tribal N=37*	*Rural N=48*	*Urban*				*Total N=147*
			Household N=16	*Informal N=21*	*Formal N=25*	*Sub-Total N=62*	
Solve problem of women's rights	23 (62.1)	20 (41.6)	9 (56.2)	9(43.2)	—	18 (29.0)	61 (41.5)
Can work with honesty and open new avenues for job	4 (10.8)	2 (4.2)	3 (18.8)	2 (9.5)	—	5 (8.0)	11 (7.5)
Would make administration sensitive and effective	—	—	—	—	5 (20.0)	5 (8.0)	5 (3.4)
Would increase prestige of women	—	16 (33.3)	—	4 (19.0)	8 (32.0)	12 (19.6)	28 (19.0)

Cont'd...

...Cont'd

Women are active in all fields and they would excel in politics	—	—	—	—	9 (36.0)	9 (14.5)	9 (6.1)
NR/DK	10 (27.0)	10 (20.8)	4 (25.0)	6 (28.6)	3 (12.0)	13 (28.9)	33 (22.5)
Total	37 (100)	48 (100)	16 (100)	21 (100)	25 (100)	62 (100)	147 (100)

Figures in parentheses indicate percentages.

A significant portion (18.8%) of household sector women of the urban community felt that women politicians would work honestly and open avenues for new jobs. In totality, 7.5% of respondents expressed similar sentiments. About 36% of formal sector urban women (6.1% of total) felt that since women are successful in all fields, they would excel in politics. Likewise, 20% (3.4% of total) felt women entering politics would make the administration sensitive and effective. In totality, 22.5% of the respondents did not elucidate on this topic as they were either ignorant or unclear. Proportion of such respondents varied from 27% in tribal to 21% in rural and 29% in urban segment.

The above data is reflective of the background, status and living conditions of respondents. While a significant proportion of tribal, rural and informal sector urban women were illiterate, economically deprived and faced hardships with access to basic necessities, they yearned for women entering politics and solving their problems. On the other hand, most of the formal sector urban respondents were well-educated, economically self-sufficient and at a plateau where most of their basic needs are sufficed. They were confident of solving their problems on their own and hence for them the presence of women in politics would lead to an increase in prestige at best.

To expand the horizon, we discussed in detail with those respondents who were not in favour of women entering politics. A summary of their viewpoints is given in Table 4.3c. Nearly one-third could not provide any logic for their gut feeling that women should not enter politics. This lack of clarity was spread amongst 44.2% of tribal, 21.9% of rural and 27.6% of urban sector respondents. Lack of self-confidence that women can work independently emerged from 15.4% of total respondents and was concentrated amongst 31.2% of rural, 17.2% of urban respondents and within them 26.3% of urban informal sector respondents and 20.8% of urban household respondents. Apprehension that illiterate women entering politics are susceptible to exploitation was expressed by 12.8% of total respondents. However, this viewpoint was confined to tribal, rural and urban informal sectors and had no representation from urban household and formal sector respondents. Corruption in politics was cited as a major factor deterring women's entry into politics by 11.3% of total respondents and this view found endorsement in all sectors, except for tribals.

Table 4.3c *Reasons for Women Not Being Active in Politics*

Reason	*Tribal N=43*	*Rural N=32*	*Urban*				*Total N=133*
			Household N=24	*Informal N=19*	*Formal N=15*	*Sub-Total N=58*	
Cannot work independently	—	10 (31.2)	5 (20.8)	5 (26.3)	—	10 (17.2)	20 (15.4)
Domestic work would suffer	8 (18.6)	5 (15.7)	—	—	—	—	13 (9.2)
Illiterate women can be exploited	7 (16.3)	6 (18.8)	—	4 (21.1)	—	4 (6.1)	17 (12.8)
Due to patrilineal society system	9 (20.1)	—	—	—	—	—	9 (6.7)
Corruption in politics	—	4 (12.5)	4 (16.7)	5 (26.3)	2 (13.3)	11 (18.9)	15 (11.3)
Physical insecurity in politics	—	—	4 (16.6)	—	—	4 (6.8)	4 (3.0)
Family life would suffer	—	—	3 (12.5)	2 (10.5)	8 (53.3)	13 (22.4)	13 (9.1)
NR/D/K	19 (44.2)	7 (21.9)	8 (33.3)	3 (15.8)	5 (33.4)	16 (27.6)	42 (31.6)
Total	43 (100)	32 (100)	24 (100)	19 (100)	15 (100)	58 (100)	133 (100)

Figures in parentheses indicate percentages.

Women's entry into politics would lead to compromises in family life, felt 9% of the respondents. This viewpoint emerged from the urban segment and had no takers amongst rural and tribal counterparts. Similar proportion of total respondents felt that domestic work would suffer if women entered politics. However, this view remained confirmed to tribal and rural communities. Some typical responses were also observed in various categories, i.e. 20% of tribal respondents were predetermined that women cannot succeed in politics due to patrilineal society system wherein values manifested by male assertion prevail. Physical exploitation of women entering politics was feared by 16.7% of urban household sector respondents. Again, this view was singular and had no reflection in other segments.

Therefore, it can be said that apprehensions were reflective of their education level, mindset and perception of their current role and existing responsibilities.

Indian rural women are by far the most hardworking and the least rewarded. ICSSR study reports state that 'when development introduces or increases inequalities within rural society, women, at least the poor ones, become doubly unprivileged, first as members of the rural poor and then as women'.[13] Most studies on rural women who are also referred to as the 'less visible women' are of the view that prevailing models of development have not only been detrimental as 'producers' but also contributing to their marginalization due to their unequal access to employment, credit technology, education and training. It is not just with reference to economic opportunities that development has bypassed women's interest. In the matter of opportunities for education and health care – the two most important indices of development – women have lagged far behind men.

Implications of Women Entering Politics

The respondents were asked whether women's entry into politics would improve their status. Table 4.4a makes it clear that majority (52.1%) felt that women entering politics would improve their position. This feeling of optimism was highest amongst tribal respondents (56.2%) and declined to 48.8% amongst rural and 52% amongst urban respondents. It is pertinent to note that within the urban community, this feeling gravitated towards urban household sector respondents (62.5%), while majority of urban formal sector and informal sector (55% and 52.2%, respectively) respondents assumed that women entering politics would have no effect on their status.

Table 4.4a *Entry in Politics Would Improve Women's Position*

Entry in politics would improve women's position	*Tribal N=80*	*Rural N=80*	*Urban*				*Total N=280*
			Household N=40	*Informal N=40*	*Formal N=40*	*Sub-Total N=120*	
Yes	45(56.2)	39(48.8)	25(62.5)	19(47.5)	18(45.0)	62(52.0)	146(52.1)
No	35(43.8)	41(51.2)	15(37.5)	21(52.2)	22(55.0)	58(48.0)	134(47.9)
Total	80(100)	80(100)	40(100)	40(100)	40(100)	40(100)	280(100)

Figures in parentheses indicate percentages.

The respondents who replied in the affirmative were further asked as to how women politicians would improve their position. Table 4.4b reveals that nearly one-third (32.9%) felt that women politicians would inspire other women to move forward. Proportionately, this reflected more amongst rural respondents (41%) as compared to urban and tribal counterparts (33.8% and 22.2%, respectively). Amongst the urban community, this feeling was pronounced amongst formal segment respondents, followed by informal and household sector counterparts.

Women politicians would work for welfare of other women was the confidence expressed by 30% of the total respondents. This confidence was highest amongst tribal respondents and diminished as we moved to rural and urban respondents. Expectation that women politicians would fight for women's rights was felt by 12.3% of the respondents, which included 15.4% of rural and 19.3% of urban respondents. Amongst urban respondents, this drew more support from the household sector respondents (32%) as compared to 10.5% of informal and 11.1% of formal sector respondents.

Table 4.4b *Reasons for Entry in Politics*

Reasons	*Tribal N=45*	*Rural N=39*	*Urban*				*Total N=146*
			Household N=25	*Informal N=19*	*Formal N=18*	*Sub-Total N=62*	
Inspiration to move forward	10(22.2)	7(41.0)	6(24.0)	7(36.8)	8(44.4)	21(33.8)	48(32.9)
Work for welfare of women	20(44.4)	11(28.2)	5(20.0)	6(31.5)	2(11.1)	13(21.0)	44(30.1)
Would fight for women's rights	—	6(15.4)	8(32.0)	2(10.5)	2(11.1)	12(19.3)	18(12.3)
Social status would be better	—	—	2(8.0)	1(5.3)	2(11.1)	5(8.0)	5(3.4)
Assist in progress of other women	—	—	—	1(5.3)	2(11.1)	3(4.8)	3(2.0)
DK/NR	15(33.3)	5(12.8)	4(16.0)	2(10.5)	2(11.1)	8(12.9)	28(19.2)
Total	45(100)	39(100)	25(100)	19(100)	18(100)	62(100)	146(100)

Figures in parentheses indicate percentages

Thus, aspirations and expectations of respondents from women politicians are reflective of their status, mindset, and day-to-day problems they face. The formal sector urban women, in spite of being financially independent and well-educated, lack recognition and respect that they rightfully deserve, hence they strongly feel that the entry of women in areas dominated by male counterparts would be an eye-opener for society and open more such avenues in other fields, besides adding to social prestige. In the urban informal sector, respondents expect women politicians to work for their welfare and also fight for their rights. Majority of the urban informal sector women reside in slums and face an acute shortage of basic necessities and look forward for betterment in their day-to-day life. Most of the urban household sector women are financially better-off as compared to informal sector counterparts but their role in decision-making is ignored in the orthodox set-up. Hence, the majority craves for women politicians to fight for their rights. Likewise, in rural and tribal societies, the concerns are for their welfare and providing inspiration to move forward.

Almost all respondents felt that it was very important for women to participate in politics because political participation helps women come out of age-old barriers, equips them to face the world with confidence and help other women who need support.

The results why some respondents are pessimistic about women entering politics are shown in Table 4.4c.

Table 4.4c *Entry in Politics Would Not Improve Women's Position*

Reasons	*Tribal N=35*	*Rural N=41*	*Urban*				*Total N=134*
			Household N=15	*Informal N=21*	*Formal N=22*	*Sub-Total N=58*	
Cannot work without consent of husband	25 (71.4)	15 (36.6)	4 (26.6)	5 (23.8)	—	9 (15.5)	49 (36.5)
Male-centred society	—	—	5 (33.3)	4 (19.0)	5 (22.7)	14 (24.1)	14 (10.4)
Women will do their own good	—	10 (24.4)	2 (13.3)	3 (14.3)	3 (13.6)	8 (13.8)	18 (13.4)
Politics is corrupt, no further development	—	—	2 (13.3)	—	6 (27.2)	8 (13.8)	8 (5.9)
DK/NR	10 (28.6)	16 (39.0)	2 (13.3)	9 (42.9)	8 (36.7)	19 (32.8)	45 (33.6)
Total	35 (100)	41 (100)	15 (100)	21 (100)	22 (100)	58 (100)	134 (100)

Figures in parentheses indicate percentages.

Women cannot work independently and seek consent from their husbands on all issues. This opinion was expressed by 36.5% of the total respondents and proportionately such respondents were concentrated in the tribal set-up (71.4%) and reduced as we moved to rural (36.6%) and urban segments (15.5%). This view is reflective of the insecurity predominant in the above sections and found no takers in the formal sector respondents who are educated, financially independent and forward-looking.

Another significant portion (13.4%) considered women as selfish and self-centred and hence felt they would not be concerned for any greater cause. Surprisingly, none of the tribal respondents agreed to this while a significant number of urban (13.6% of household, 14.3% of informal and 13.6% of formal) as well as rural (24.4%), women echoed similar views. While 10.4% of respondents blamed male-centred society, this view was confined to the urban section and had no takers in the tribal and rural societies. Besides, within the urban setting, 27.2% of formal and 13.3% of household sector women blamed corruption in politics for their apprehension regarding non-success of women politicians. Again, this opinion did not echo in other sections of respondents.

On the consequences on the personal/domestic front due to women entering politics, an overwhelming majority (88.2%) of respondents felt the entry of women in politics will have harmful consequences on their personal life. Similar sentiments were echoed by 81.2% tribal, 94% rural and 89.2% urban women. In the urban community, 100% of households, 87.5% of informal and 80% of formal women subscribed to this view. However, 20% urban formal sector and 18.8% tribal women strongly felt that women's entry into politics would not damage their personal/domestic life.

Respondents who agreed that entry into politics for women will have harmful consequences in personal life were asked for reasons for such thinking. Results are summarized in Table 4.5.

Women's entry into politics would imbalance their domestic life, felt 27.5%, who were apprehensive that they would find less time for domestic and outside chores. This thought process was much more prevalent in tribal and rural sections (46.6% and 26.7%, respectively) as compared to 15% of urban household, 11.4% of urban informal and 25% of urban formal sector respondents.

Social and physical insecurity for women entering politics was the major apprehension expressed by 16.2% of the total respondents. While this view had no takers in formal urban section, it found support from 15.4% of tribal, 20% of rural, 17.5% of urban households and 22.9% of urban informal sector respondents. In the opinion of 15.4%

Table 4.5 *Consequences of Women Entering Politics*

Reasons	*Tribal N=65*	*Rural N=75*	*Urban*				*Total N=247*
			Household N=40	*Informal N=35*	*Formal N=32*	*Sub-Total N=107*	
Imbalance in domestic life	30 (46.6)	20 (26.7)	6 (15.0)	4 (11.4)	8 (25.0)	18 (16.8)	68 (27.5)
They can become part of conspiracy	—	—	8 (20.0)	2 (5.7)	6 (18.7)	16 (14.9)	16 (6.5)
Social and physical insecurity	10 (15.4)	15 (20.0)	7 (17.5)	8 (22.9)	—	15 (14.0)	40 (16.2)
No time for family	10 (15.3)	—	10 (25.0)	8 (22.8)	10 (31.2)	28 (26.1)	38 (15.4)
Politics is very dirty for women to be involved	—	5 (6.7)	5 (12.5)	—	8 (25.0)	13 (12.1)	18 (7.3)
Cannot work according to their wishes	—	—	—	4 (11.4)	—	4 (3.7)	4 (1.6)
Harmful for illiterate women	—	10 (13.3)	2 (5.0)	4 (11.4)	—	6 (5.6)	16 (6.4)
DK/NR	15 (23.1)	25 (33.3)	2 (5.0)	5 (14.3)	—	7 (6.6)	47 (19.0)
Total	65 (100)	75 (100)	40 (100)	35 (100)	32 (100)	107 (100)	247 (100)

Figures in parentheses indicate percentages.

of total respondents, if women entered politics, they would find less time for family life. While this viewpoint emerged from 15.3% of tribal and 25% of urban households, 22.8% of urban informal and 31.2% of urban formal sector women, it found no takers amongst rural respondents. Politics was perceived as too complicated and dirty for women to get involved by 7.3% of the respondents. This perception was confined to 6.6% of rural, 12.5% of urban household and 25% of urban formal sector respondents. On a similar wavelength, 6.5% considered women as susceptible to conspiracy on entering politics. This viewpoint emerged from 20% of household, 5.7% of informal and 18.7% of urban formal sector respondents.

Nearly similar proportion (6.4%) of total respondents was also apprehensive that politics is harmful for illiterate, ignorant and poorly informed women. Over 13% of rural, 5% of household and 11.3% of urban informal sector respondents felt as above. Nearly one-fifth (19%) of total respondents could not elucidate on the reasons for their feeling.

Women and Empowerment

That the 73rd and 74th constitutional amendments offer a legal arrangement for women to participate in PRIs is not contested by any group. But, what is contested is the consequential empowerment of women. The formal membership by reservation through election in legally-created institutions does not ensure the substantive exercise of power by women. The real empowerment works only in ambience of equal distribution of assets between males and females in all spheres of private and public life. Secondly, it is also thought that genuine empowerment of women is realized through 'politics of struggle' and not 'politics of reservation'. Empowerment by reservation buttressed with the help of NGOs and state may act as a soporific against women's struggles against the state and society and typify the project of gender discrimination and inequality. This in the long run may strengthen the status quo rather than transform it.[14]

On being asked about the need to empower women, all the respondents across all sections euphorically responded in the affirmative. They were asked to list the factors critical towards empowerment of women. Table 4.6 depicts the data obtained.

Table 4.6 *Critical Factors for Empowering Women*

Reasons	*Tribal N=80*	*Rural N=80*	*Urban*				*Total N=280*
			Household N=40	*Informal N=40*	*Formal N=40*	*Sub-Total N=120*	
Education	20 (25.0)	32 (40.0)	11 (27.5)	5 (12.5)	5 (12.5)	21 (17.5)	73 (26.0)
Through husband	25 (31.2)	12 (15.0)	8 (20.0)	10 (25.0)	4 (10.0)	22 (18.3)	59 (21.0)
Through parents	—	—	9 (22.5)	2 (5.0)	4 (10.0)	15 (12.5)	15 (5.4)
Providing basic rights	—	—	4 (10.0)	—	6 (15.0)	10 (10.0)	10 (3.6)
By reservation	—	—	2 (5.0)	—	2 (5.0)	4 (3.3)	4 (1.4)
Providing equal status	—	—	2 (5.00)	10 (25.0)	8 (20.0)	20 (16.7)	20 (7.4)
Freedom to work and in decision-making	—	8 (10.0)	4 (10.0)	10 (25.0)	8 (20.0)	22 (18.3)	30 (10.7)
DK/NR	35 (43.8)	28 (35.0)	—	3 (7.5)	3 (7.5)	6 (5.0)	69 (24.6)
Total	80 (100)	80 (100)	40 (100)	40 (100)	40 (100)	120 (100)	280 (100)

Figures in parentheses indicate percentages.

Criticality of education for empowerment was outlined by 26% of the total respondents. Surprisingly, only 17.5% of urban women agreed with it, while 40% of rural and 25% of tribal women endorsed the need of education for empowerment. Tribal and rural respondents viewed education as a necessary ingredient of women's progress and considered it to be important to increase the perception of women about local or regional problems. Education is also necessary for development of a progressive outlook. Tribal respondents were of the view that educated women can participate in any activity more meaningfully. These feelings of respondents clearly indicate that education is essential for women to perform effectively in all spheres of life.

Role of husband was emphasized for empowering women by 21% of the total respondents. While only 18.3% of urban women agreed with it, a significant proportion of tribal (31.2%) and rural women (15.1%) felt that empowerment can come best through the husband. In tribal context, women are dependent upon husbands for every small need. In the urban community, only 10% of formal sector respondents agreed with it while this proportion increased to 20% in household and 25% in informal sector women. Empowerment of women and their equal status are more easily talked about than put into practice. This is more so in a society ridden with orthodox and conservative ideals and ideologies for which religious sanction and support are not lacking. In such societies, any improvement in the status of women is almost impossible without the cooperation and change of hearts on the part of men.[15]

Freedom in work and decision-making was outlined as critical for empowerment by 11% of the respondents. While none of the tribal respondents agreed with this viewpoint, it was endorsed by 10% of rural and 18.3% of urban respondents. All this shows that the tribal women lack exposure and are myopic in their thinking.

Like husband, parents can also play a major role in empowerment since they bring up their child during their critical formative age. This was the viewpoint of 5.4% of the total respondents. Another 7.4% emphasized providing equal status for empowering women. One-fourth (24.6%) could not specify any critical factor for empowerment. Parents in the Indian family perceive the male child as a good investment. They are future assets and source of successor and care. In contrast, female children are treated as consumer goods and source of pleasure and gratification. If the women in future have to be treated at par with men, the basic attitude towards girls in the family has to change.

Women's participation in PRIs or any other association is only a minor measurement of their empowerment. Education, economy, culture and ideology are some other fields where women can enter only through comprehensive and protracted struggles. Secondly, 'empowerment' is not merely a legal or political concept. It is multilateral and multidimensional too. It also embraces social, economic and cultural dimensions.

Women's powerlessness or lack of empowerment is directly related to their unequal status within the structure of rural as well as tribal society. Women face multiple inequalities, discrimination and deprivations, which are economic, social and cultural with their root in history. To fight the war of inequality, many battles have to be waged and won.[16]

To a query regarding fields where women can be more successful, Table 4.7 represents the relevant information.

Table 4.7 *Perfection in Various Fields as Compared to Men*

Fields	Tribal N=80	Rural N=80	Urban				Total N=280
			Household N=40	Informal N=40	Formal N=40	Sub-Total N=120	
Home management	20(25.0)	39(48.7)	2(5.0)	3(7.5)	—	5(4.1)	64(22.8)
Education	12(15.0)	7(8.8)	10(25.0)	9(22.5)	3(7.5)	22(18.3)	41(14.6)
Medical	5(6.2)	8(10.0)	4(10.0)	4(10.0)	5(12.5)	13(10.8)	26(9.8)
Judiciary	—	1(1.2)	4(10.0)	—	5(12.5)	9(7.5)	10(3.5)
Welfare	—	4(5.0)	6(15.0)	—	13(32.5)	19(15.8)	23(8.0)
Administration	—	—	2(5.0)	3(7.5)	2(5.0)	7(5.6)	7(2.5)
Finance	—	—	3(7.5)	2(5.0)	10(25.0)	15(12.5)	15(5.3)
Art	—	—	—	6(15.0)	—	6(5.0)	6(2.1)
Each and every field	—	7(8.7)	6(15.0)	4(10.0)	2(5.0)	12(10.0)	19(6.8)
DK/NR	43(53.8)	21(26.3)	3(7.5)	9(22.5)	—	12(10.0)	76(27.1)
Total	80(100)	80(100)	40(100)	40(100)	40(100)	120(100)	280(100)

Figures in parentheses indicate percentages.

Nearly one-fourth (22.8%) of the total respondents indicated home management. This view was endorsed by nearly half (48.7%) of the rural and one-fourth (25%) of tribal women. In urban context, however, only 5% of the household sector and 7.5% of the informal sector women agreed. Surprisingly, not a single formal urban sector woman supported this stance. Tribal and rural women were bogged down by their own schedules and were unable to perceive any other role for women.

Women would perform better as educationists was a view endorsed by 14.6% of the total respondents. In all, 18.3% of the urban, 8.8% of the rural and 15.3 of the tribal women felt this. Women consider themselves to be more patient, tolerant and persevering as compared to male counterparts. Their natural liking for children also makes them ideally suited for the teaching profession. In the tribal context, families would prefer young girls being educated by women since they are suspicious and orthodox in nature.

Another 9.8% of total respondents felt that women might excel in medical field due to their sensitive nature and caring attitude. Similarly, 8% considered welfare as the chosen field where women can perform better than men.

Women would perform better than men in each and every field. Such confidence radiated from 6.8% of the total respondents. There were 12.5% of urban women who felt that women can excel in the field of finance too since they manage the home budget and allocate scarce resources effectively. Finally, in totality, 3.5%, 2.5% and 2.1% of total respondents indicated judiciary, administration and art as their chosen fields, respectively, where women can perform better than men.

During the course of fieldwork in Dangarwara village, the case of Kamla Meena, a 32-year-old barely literate woman, stood out. She was only able to sign. It was astonishing that she was elected as Sarpanch on the seat reserved for an ST woman, owing to her allegiance to the Congress party. On enquiry regarding the family background, it was found that her husband was only middle-pass and managed the fields. his two brothers were educated and taught in a senior secondary school. It was a collective feeling within their family that if Kamla became Sarpanch, this would provide enhanced prestige and status to her husband. Due to her illiteracy, she was drawn into a conspiracy wherein her assistant made her sign a voucher for a smaller amount and siphoned off ₹ 1,000. Due to this instance and trauma of repeated trials and explanation, she was hesitant to attend any meeting on her own and became dependent upon her husband to accompany her. On being asked if she would like to get elected again as Sarpanch, she replied in the affirmative since she felt that exposure to problems had hardened her to deal more effectively.

Then there was Pavni, a 27-year-old illiterate Garasia woman who was a member of the village Panchayat due to her loyalty to the Bharatiya Janata Party. She felt that an educated woman can participate more actively in panchayat meetings as compared to an illiterate woman like her. Although household work suffers when she goes to attend monthly meetings and the allowances are also meagre, a Sarpanch enjoys many rights and privileges, and she yearned to reach that position.

Importance of training and continuous exposure to the realities of a fast-changing world cannot be undermined in the process of empowering women. Illiteracy, ignorance and economic deprivation have long prevented them from taking an active part in the decision-making process. A training programme held sporadically cannot bring the kind of empowerment women require to run the panchayat system effectively. Until they reach a stage when they can effectively count the hurdles to emancipation, there should be repeated exposure to empowerment exercises. In fact, with increasing exposure and empowerment, women have done well.

To sum up, the importance of political participation for women can hardly be overemphasized, yet this alone is not the panacea of all the ills and wrongs plaguing the women's community. Proper primary education, increased higher education and economic independence through creating more job avenues would go a long way in preparing the base and springboard for educated and conscious women to leapfrog in the political arena.

Notes

1. Klein, P., 1979. 'An Institutional View of Development Economics', *Journal of Economic Issues*, XI (4).
2. Krishnaraj, M., 1988. *Role of Rural Women in Development*, Bombay: S.N.D.T. University.
3. *National Perspective Plan For Women, 1988*. '1988–2000 A.D. Report of the Core Group Set Up by the Department of Women and Child Development', Ministry of Human Resource Development, Government of India, p. 153.
4. Ibid., 153.
5. Walters, S., 1991. *Her Words on His Lips: Gender and Popular Education in South Africa*, ASPBAC Counter 52, p. 17.
6. Batliwala, Srilata, 1995. 'The Meaning of Women's Empowerment', *Women's World*, pp. 23–24.
7. Charlton, S.E.M., J. Everett, K. Staudt, (eds), 1989. *Women, the State, and Development*, Albany: State University of New York Press.
8. Bhasin, Kamla, 1992. 'Education for Women's Empowerment: Some Reflections', *Adult Educational Development*, March, Number 38.
9. Apte, J.S., 1995. 'Education and Women's Empowerment', *Indian Journal of Adult Education*, Vol. 56, No. 3, July–September.

10. Parenti, M., 1978. *Power and the Powerless*, New York: St. Martin's Press.
11. Verba, Sydney, 1972. 'Comparative Political Culture', in L.W. Pye, and S. Verba (eds), *Political Culture and Political Development*, Princeton, pp. 516–524;

    Pye, L.W., 1968. *International Encyclopedia of Social Science*, 12, The Free Press, p. 218;

    Johnson, H.M., 1963. *Sociology*, New Delhi, p. 110;

    Greentien, Fred, I., 1968. 'Political Socialization', *International Encyclopedia of the Social Sciences*, 14, New York, pp. 551–555;

    Raz, S.M., 1976. *The Process of Socialization*, New Delhi: Chetna Publications, p. 3;

    Dean, Jaros, 1973. *Socialization to Politics*, Nelson, p. 23; and

    Almond and Colonan (eds), 1960. *The Politics of the Developing Nations*, Princeton University Press, pp. 27–28. Also see Richard Dawson and Kenneth Prewitt, 1960. *Political Socialization*, Boston: Little Brown & Co., p. 6.
12. Mohanty, S. and N. Mohanty, 1999. 'Empowering Elected Woman Representatives of Village Panchayats: An Urgent Need', in R. Indira and Deepak Kumar Behera (eds), *Gender and Society in India*, New Delhi: Manak Publications Pvt. Ltd., pp. 128–132.
13. Majumdar, V., 1978. *Role of Rural Women in Development*, Bombay: Allied Publishers Pvt. Ltd.
14. Raghavendra Rao, J.V., 1999. 'Panchayati Raj, Women and the Problematic of Empowerment', in R. Indira and Deepak Kumar Behera (eds), *Gender and Society in India*, New Delhi: Manak Publications, p. 99.
15. Ibid., 101.
16. Lucy, T.V., 1995. 'Empowerment of Women for Sustainable Development', *Social Action*, Vol. 45, April–June.

5 Women, Economy and the Household

In all societies, economic activities constitute the main source of survival and sustenance. The nature of economic activity is determined by a number of factors, the most important being the occupation pursued by majority of its members. Every society ensures that a systematic arrangement exists for the supply and distribution of goods and services. The allocation of resources and economic roles, perhaps, determines every other form of human activity and also decides the position an individual occupies in the social hierarchy. In every society, different ways of earning livelihood have fundamental influences on the type of lives people lead.

Work, according to the Concise Oxford Dictionary, refers to the 'application of effort or exertion to a purpose'.[1] Scott's[2] definition of work consists of two connotations: (1) Disciplined and persistent activity devoted to achieving a goal, with the actual activity only instrumental to the accomplishment of the final goal of the activity. This definition contrasts work to leisure or play; (2) Work that is related to economic activity.

Both the definitions provide a wonderful meaning to the concept of work. But, in popular usage, work is restricted to mean 'gainful economic activity' to the neglect of its wider meaning.[3] William[4] has argued that the notion of work has become specialized over the last century or so, so that it refers primarily to paid employment, as opposed to other types of labour or effort. In fact, the work for economic necessity is closely related to work in other institutional spheres of life and the problems relating to the understanding of work by men and women are an outcome of the neglect of their functional interdependence. Therefore, the proper meaning of work should include work both inside and outside the home.

The phenomenon of working wives is not new to India. Women have always been working outside their homes in the fields. With the advent of industrialization, women from poorer sections started working in factories and mills as unskilled and semi-skilled labourers or as manual labour. A sizeable section of those who constitute the rural and urban poor have formed an inalienable part of the workforce in villages and cities. In sharp contrast, women from the middle and upper classes were mostly confined to homes. Indeed, it was considered demeaning for a girl, and even more so a married woman, of these classes to come out of home to take up gainful employment outside.

A number of forces of social change were unleashed which were destined to affect the lives of women, especially the middle class educated women, in significant ways. Of all these factors, the economic factor was the most powerful. The rising aspirations of the middle classes transformed the women to defy tradition and come out of the confines of their home and hearth. What is more significant is that the middle class tended to evolve its own logic to justify this action of their women going against the established traditions. Commenting on this development, Kapur[5] observes:

'The phenomenon of the increasing number of educated wives has emerged from the growing economic necessity for the wives to contribute their earnings to the family income. Since marriage is not a spiritual commission in a vacuum, but a union of two human beings who need clothes, food and a place to live in, material foundations are indispensable and a wife's participation in procuring the required family finances becomes essential in times of economic hardship. The attitude of society towards married women taking up jobs has also changed.'

In the beginning, women were supposed to take up only those jobs or occupations which were considered respectable by society like those of a teacher or doctor. But things started changing fast. Very soon, middle class women stepped out and started serving in offices as clerks, officers and in various other capacities. The emergence of urban married women as a workforce has been rightly viewed by sociologists as heralding a profound change in all vital aspects of Indian society.

Whether out of sheer economic necessity or due to increasing opportunities arising from the spread and utilization of opportunities, women are entering into the public and private, formal and informal sectors of the Indian economy in increasing numbers today.

Working women come face-to-face with a paradoxical situation with the alternatives being adherence to customary patterns or the adoption of innovative models. The dilemma is not easy to resolve for working women in a traditional society. The strategic patterns of adjustment with the two roles differ across differential social strata and also from individual to individual, which makes generalization quite difficult.

The number of working women has risen sharply and vital changes in the social, cultural and structural spheres of the Indian society have also contributed significantly. Traditionally, women's role was confined to look after the household and her employment outside was alien to the traditional norms. Her role of a mother and housewife widened after the spread of education of girls and constitutional measures providing equality to women in matters of opportunities. The increase in female employment brought to fore the problem of compatibility of family and work life. The adjustment to social changes is generally associated with a high balance between satisfaction and tensions. Hence, the need for good adjustment.[6]

In the above context, the observation of Anderson[7] is very apt. He says, 'Good adjustment cannot be defined once and for all in any simple or complete fashion. It must be defined in terms of meeting the problems appropriately to the level of development. What is good adjustment at one age level may be poor adjustment at another.' However, the traditional bias against working women, though in a lesser degree, has made good adjustment between the two roles of working women more challenging. The working of wife/mother outside the home necessitated re-arrangement of familial roles and tasks. To pursue double roles, the working homemaker has to adhere to a stricter time schedule and arrange things more systematically. This entails greater mental and physical alertness. Thus, changed ways of thinking and behaviour emerge in the household. These may lead to changes in work division, marital relationship, relations with in-laws, authority pattern within family, etc.

When a housewife takes on a working role, she not only finds a change in her status within the family and outside it, but also takes upon herself increasing pressures to reconcile the dual burden of the two roles located in different sectors of the society in house and workplace, and thereby arises the need for proper adjustment between the two.

Working women have to make an adjustment between dual roles of a family member and a working woman. She has to fulfil her commitments towards her family and job. This situation becomes more piquant if she fails to make a proper adjustment. On one hand, she has to meet the demands of her family as a mother or wife and on the other she has to discharge duties connected with her job. Good adjustment is achieved primarily through a balance between the two roles. However, when she attaches more importance to one particular role, it leads to role conflict.

The present study is more focussed on attitudes, problems, and work environment for working women in various strata of society. As a corollary would be an attempt to gauge the fine balance of their dual roles, adjustment made for household responsibilities and the level of control regarding allocation of earning mode.

At the outset, we probed into the daily schedule, lifestyle and working conditions of the Garasia tribal community. As the study progressed, the importance of tribal women as significant contributors to tribal economy was well realized. Their roles stretched beyond the confines of home to the forest for collecting fuel, fodder, forest produce, etc. They actively participated in all agricultural activities except ploughing. To substantiate family income, they walked long distances to work as manual/unskilled labourers at mines, factories, etc. All this was in addition to fulfilling their basic responsibilities of home management.

Garasias' Economy

Garasias are dependent on agriculture as their mainstay. Their entire energy is directed towards obtaining the maximum yield from land. Due to the topography of this area, *valro* (shifting system of cultivation) was adhered to by the Garasias. Women played an important role in *valro* and were considered equal partners with men. Today, Garasias have taken to settled agriculture. Most of Garasias working on their small plots of land have adopted plough cultivation. Wherever ploughing is done, it is considered the master operation and other operations are accorded secondary importance. Men are generally the steers or ploughs.

Makka (maize) is the major crop for the Garasias and most other farmers in Sirohi district. It is sown once a year before the monsoon rains start in July and harvested between the end of October and beginning of November. Besides maize, some Garasias grow wheat in the winter season. Sharing the field with wheat could be *jawar* (millet), *jou* (barley), *channa* (gram) or *rayda* (rapeseed). They also grow some vegetables around wells, and on the thorn fences directly outside their huts during rainy seasons. Agricultural crops are susceptible to climatic vagaries, insects and pests, floods, etc. The tribals naturally attribute these misfortunes to the displeasure of Gods of climate, field and land. They develop practices to appease the various Gods connected with agriculture by offering sacrifices. At the time of ploughing and harvesting, Bhomiya and Khetrapal are worshipped and blessings are sought for good and bumper crops.

Cooperation is the central feature of economic activities among the Garasias. The cooperative behaviour and the system of cooperative farming is a part of their historical tradition which has been handed down from generations. The lack of material resources is compensated by the human cooperative spirit. The major agricultural operations such as *bhavli* (sharing of water), *halmo* (friendship) and *helaru* (cooperative association of a large number of persons) are carried out jointly, singing while working.

Bhavli

In a Garasia village, where irrigation facilities do not exist, possession of a source of irrigation (i.e. a well) is a big asset. Wells play an important role in agriculture. A Garasia owning a well would permit another Garasia to operate it in lieu of some reward or joint cultivation. They work and behave as if all the holdings are jointly owned and perform all the agricultural operations jointly. In this system, resources and produce are both shared and individually owned and consumed according to certain rules and well-defined norms.

Halmo

This is a traditional system of cooperation by exchanging labour on a small scale, on the basis of need. *Halmo* is evoked when enough members of a family are not available to perform the work and they have to seek cooperation from others. In *halmo*, no wages or share of crop is given; instead, meals on working days are provided.

Helaru

Helaru is a form of cooperative association of a large number of persons, thus different from than *halmo*. *Helaru* is resorted to bring grass, collection of wood for construction of houses, weeding, harvesting where greater number of labourers are required to finish the work. It may also be used for public utility works like tanks, constructing *devara* (temple), etc.

Generally, *haga* (true brothers) form a share group in a well and also irrigate a common section of land around it. The *haga* are all required to bring their *hals* (ploughs) and oxen and are later accompanied by their wives who sow the seed. Each house has one or two ploughs and usually, a pair of oxen. The ploughing is done by all the brothers together in their shared plot in the fertile area.

Garasias and Forests

The economy of the Garasia revolves around the ecological setting of the homeland. The forests provide them raw material for their shelter, various household articles, agricultural implements and indigenous medicines. These are also an abundant source of fuelwood. Garasias also depend upon the forests for eking out a measured living by making basket, rope, plate and by lac cultivation. The Garasias gather wild cereals (*mal, kura, kodara, rang*), vegetables (*turiya, jhalra, pankoda, jumka, koli, phong, ahor, seel, kohra*) and fruit (mango, papaya, *ber, tibirna, dongla, chibra, mahua*, wild dates) from forests. The leaves of *tendu, khajoor* and *khakhara* are used in *bidi* and basket-making, respectively. Liquor is extracted from the flowers and bark of *mahuva, ber* and *babool* trees. Oil is also extracted from the seed of Gawar, *malkangni, chirmi, karanj, ratanjot* and *mahuva* seeds. The stalks of *bhindi, ambadi*, wild date (*khajoor*) and *munj* when split yield a fibre which is used in making ropes. The stalks of *munj (Aristida hystrix)* are used in making arrows, thatching the roofs, preparing litter around the altar with its leaves and making girdles with its fibre extracted from the upper leaf.

The economic activities of the Garasia women are also centred around the forests. Women, young and old, go to the forests for collecting firewood, roots, tubers, etc. as they have to depend on such forest products for subsistence. The economic activities in relation to the forests are performed mainly by Garasia women. Many edible roots, tubers, fruits, leaves, flowers of different trees are available in the forests round the year and these are collected by girls/women of all ages for subsistence. Adolescent boys and girls take their cattle to the grazing ground which happens to be in the forest region. These adolescent girls also collect twigs from the forests which are used as firewood. Garasias are also expert in *dhamino* (fishing). They catch fish from the *nadi* (pond), *valoo* (rivers) and tanks and they are very fond of eating fish. *Maid* (honey) selling is one of the subsidiary economic activities of the Garasias. They are expert beekeepers and specialize in the art of not only collecting honey but also of controlling bee behaviour.

The livestock has been one of the most valuable assets for the Garasias. Every house takes special care of them. The animals are reared to provide power, transportation, manure and fuel. Bullocks, cows, sheep, goats and dogs are the main varieties of livestock kept by the Garasias. Cows, goats and bullocks are also reciprocated on important societal functions and marriage ceremonies. The bullocks are the main draft animal being harnessed to covets, plough and employed for the purposes. While cows, buffaloes, sheep and goats supply milk, meat, wool and skin, goats are used for sacrifices to the Gods and Baosis, and dogs provide safety at night.

Scarcity of cultivable land, lack of irrigation resources and dependence on monsoons offer low yields which are hardly sufficient for subsistence of tribal farmers. Lack of modern means of farming, irrigation facilities, and non-availability of high-yielding seeds add to their woes and they are unable to undertake farming as a full-scale commercial activity to raise their standard of living. This has been explored in detail by Maya Unnithan Kumar,[8] who says that these factors, coupled with rising contingency costs related to health care, essential items of clothing, rising brideprice and other expenses for ritual occasions, make their economic condition even more miserable. Attempts are made by Garasias to supplement agricultural production by working as manual labourers and collecting forest produce such as fruits, vegetables, bee honey and selling them in market areas. They travel great distances in search of work at factories or mines. Garasia women's problems are accentuated by the new forest policies which are not very friendly towards them. Their economic roles are closely related to forests and increasing deforestation and lack of access to forest produce have intensified their state of economic dependence. Their traditional occupations, such as basket weaving, coal making, leaves, etc. have suffered under the impact of the new forest legislation.

Working Hours for Women

Workers in the organized sector of economy have fixed hours of work and are entitled to many benefits. But, the informal sector is characterized by irregular work schedules and absence of incentives. The respondents were asked about their daily work schedule (Table 5.1):

Table 5.1 *Working Hours of Working Women*

Working women	*Tribal N=30*	*Rural N=30*	*Urban*			*Total N=140*
			Informal N=40	*Formal N=40*	*Sub-Total N=80*	
Up to 4 hours	—	—	3(7.5)	—	3 (3.7)	2 (2.2)
5–6 hours	—	7(23.3)	12(30.0)	7(17.5)	19(23.8)	26(18.6)
7–8 hours	—	15(50.0)	19(47.5)	15(37.5)	34(42.5)	49(35.0)
9–10 hours	30(100.0)	6(20.0)	6(15.0)	18(45.0)	24(30.0)	60(42.8)
11–12 hours	—	2(6.7)	—	—	—	2(1.4)
Total	30(100)	30(100)	40(100)	40(100)	80(100)	140(100)

Figures in parentheses indicate percentages.

Respondents working for 9–10 hours every day were 43% in number. They included all working women in the tribal community and the proportion of such respondents reduced to 30% and 20% in urban and rural sectors, respectively. This was mainly due to the basic difference in the nature of work. While tribal and rural women were involved in manual labour-based activities, urban formal sector respondents were office-going professionals and urban informal sector women were engaged in productive work in the confines of their homes.

Income Levels of Respondents

'More work and less reward' seems to be the typical feature of most informal sector jobs. There is no periodic pay rise, nor do salaries keep in tune with the cost of living index. We tried to plot the earnings of respondents on a continuum from less than ₹ 500 at one end and between ₹ 1,000–14,999 at the other end. Results are tabulated in Table 5.2.

It is evident from the table that 38.5% of the total respondents have to make ends meet with monthly earnings between ₹ 500–999. They included 42.5% of urban informal sector, 70% of rural and 53.3% of tribal women. More than one-fourth (26.4%) of the respondents were earning even less than ₹ 500 per month. The maximum proportion of such respondents was in the tribal category (46.6%), followed by 26.6% of rural and 18.8% of urban respondents. All these respondents were involved in non-specialized labour-intensive and low-paid jobs. However, none of the urban formal sector respondents fell in this category. Another 6.4% of the total respondents who acknowledged earning between ₹ 1,000–1,999 included 10% of urban sector and 3.3% of rural women. Such respondents were engaged in handicraft and providing value-added products and services to increase their earnings.

Extent of Control over Self-earnings of Women

Very often, the contribution that a woman makes to the household determines her status in the household. On the other hand, it may also be argued that the status of a woman in the household may decide as to what extent she can have some control over her own earnings. Often, women are not recognized for what they are in terms of their likes, hobbies, interests or aspirations. There is no or limited concept of women's autonomy; the resources that belong to the woman – her earnings, whatever property or assets she may own, her time, her abilities – are considered to be rightfully at the disposal of the household. How those resources are to be distributed or allocated is also the prerogative of the household.

Women generally have limited powers to take decisions relating to their earnings. Almost always a woman's earning is considered the family's earnings and it is true that most women spend the entire earnings on the family. Working respondents were asked about the extent of self-earnings they could retain. Table 5.2a presents the data:

Table 5.2a *Extent of Self-earning Retained*

Portion	*Tribal N=30*	*Rural N=30*	*Urban*			*Total N=140*
			Informal N=40	*Formal N=40*	*Sub-Total N=80*	
No portion	15(50.0)	13(43.3)	18(45.0)	11(27.5)	29(36.2)	57(40.7)
10%	4(13.3)	2(6.7)	3(7.5)	1(2.5)	4(5.0)	10(7.1)
1/4 portion	2(6.7)	3(10.0)	2(5.0)	—	2(2.5)	7(5.0)
1/2 portion	—	—	4(10.0)	1(2.5)	5(6.2)	5(3.5)
3/4 portion	—	—	1(2.5)	3(7.5)	4(5.0)	4(2.8)
Full	9(30.0)	12(40.0)	12(30.0)	24(60.0)	36(45.0)	57(40.7)
Total	30(100)	30(100)	40(100)	40(100)	80(100)	140(100)

Figures in parentheses indicate percentages.

Respondents who retained a portion of the earnings were 40.7% in total. A total of 60% of urban formal, 30% of urban informal, 40% of rural and 30% of tribal women formed this group of respondents. In sharp contrast, nearly one-fourth (24.3%) of the respondents acknowledged that they did not retain any portion of their earnings. Maximum proportion of such respondents belonged to tribal sector (50%), followed by rural and urban respondents. Within urban sector, the proportion of informal sector respondents was much higher as compared to formal sector counterparts.

A small proportion (7%) said they retained one-fourth of their earnings. This section comprised 5% informal urban sector, 10% rural and 6.6% tribal women. Half of the earnings were retained by only 3.5% of the total respondents. Nearly 3% of the total respondents said they retained three-fourth of their earning. All these respondents again belonged to the urban sector and the proportion of urban formal sector respondents was three times their informal sector counterparts.

In tribal and rural contexts, the wants and desires of the respondents are very limited and their concept of self-indulgence is hardly found. Hence, in majority of the cases, women do not retain any portion of their earnings and handed over the entire amount to their husbands or in-laws. In the urban informal sector, the household economic needs remain unfulfilled even after contribution of working respondents. Hence, women cannot afford to spend much for their own use. Majority of the urban formal sector respondents retained their self-earnings and allocated judiciously for self and family requirements.

Table 5.2b *Money for Personal Requirement is Sought From*

From whom retained money	*Tribal N=15*	*Rural N=13*	*Urban*			*Total N=57*
			Informal N=18	*Formal N=11*	*Sub-Total N=29*	
Husband	12(37.5)(80.0)	8(25.0) (61.5)	12 (37.5) (66.6)	—	12 (37.5) (41.3)	32(100) (56.1)
Mother-in-law	3(33.3) (20.0)	3(33.3) (23.1)	3(33.3) (16.7)	—	3(33.3) (10.34)	9(100) (15.8)
Father-in-law	—	2(33.3) (15.4)	3(50.0) (16.7)	1(16.7) (9.1)	4(66.7) (13.8)	6(100) (10.5)
Common fund of husband and wife	—	—	—	10(100) (90.9)	10(100) (34.4)	10(100) (17.6)
Total	15(100)	13(100)	18(100)	11(100)	29(100)	57(100)

Figures in parentheses indicate percentages.

The respondents who did not retain any portion of self-earning were asked as to how they fulfilled their personal requirements.

Results, in Table 5.2b, reveal that the respondents depending upon their husbands for fulfilling their personal requirements were 56% in total. The proportion of such respondents was at peak in the tribal category (80%), followed by rural (61.5%) and urban categories (41.3%). Another 18% of total respondents drew money from the common fund of husband and wife for fulfilling personal requirements. All these respondents belonged to the urban formal sector. Nearly 16% of the total respondents asked for money from their mother-in-law and this included the highest proportion of rural respondents (23%), followed by 20% of tribal and 10% of urban respondents. All these urban respondents belonged to the informal sector.

Respondents who acknowledged asking their father-in-law for monetary requirements were 10.5% in aggregate. Proportion of such respondents was 15.4% in rural set-up and reduced marginally to 13.8% in the urban set-up.

Thus, majority of the tribal and rural women depended upon their husbands for fulfilling their personal requirements. Two-third of the urban informal sector women were also in the same category, while one-third sought money from in-laws. Even earning respondents in above sections did not have any control over their earnings. In contrast, majority (10 out of 11) of urban formal sector respondents were not dependent on their husband/in-laws for fulfilling the requirements.

As already observed, the rural, tribal and poor females had little control over the family income to which they were a major contributor. Even in regard to their personal needs, these women had to depend, by and large, on the consent of some or the other male or female in the family. Elsewhere, women only had a right to maintenance but no right to land and income, though they had a larger participation in economic activities and a more decisive role in family management than their counterparts elsewhere. We, therefore, asked our respondents regarding their freedom in access to their earnings and the results are tabulated in Table 5.3.

Nearly one-fourth (22.8%) felt it was unthinkable to spend out of their own earnings. In all, 37.5% of the urban informal sector and 56.6% of rural women constituted this category. However, none of the urban formal sector and tribal respondents fell in this category. Another section of respondents, who could spend according to their requirements, comprised 22.1% of the total and included 27.5% of urban formal, 17.5% of urban informal, 10% of rural and 33.3% of tribal respondents.

Table 5.3 *Freedom in Access to Earnings*

Earning	*Tribal N=30*	*Rural N=30*	*Urban*			*Total N=140*
			Informal N=40	*Formal N=40*	*Sub-Total N=80*	
According to requirements	10(33.3)	3(10.0)	7(17.5)	11(27.5)	18(22.5)	31(22.1)
According to planning	—	4(13.3)	8(20.0)	8(20.0)	16(20.0)	20(14.3)
According to any limit	—	—	—	15(37.5)	15(37.5)	15(10.7)
According to wishes	—	—	—	4(10.0)	4(10.0)	4(2.8)
According to some limit	15(50.0)	1(3.3)	10(25.0)	2(5.0)	12(30.0)	28(20.0)
Absolutely not	—	17(56.7)	15(37.5)	—	15(37.5)	32(22.8)
NR/DK	5(16.7)	5(16.7)	—	—	—	10(7.1)
Total	30(100)	30(100)	40(100)	40(100)	80(100)	140(100)

Figures in parentheses indicate percentages.

Thus, it can be concluded that the freedom to spend one's earnings is more pronounced in the tribal and urban formal society. Even informal sector urban and rural women could not spend according to their wishes and were dependent on male members for their basic requirements too. It is indeed ironic that they have little control over their own hard-earned incomes.

Dimensions of Indulgence for Women

The respondents were asked regarding their indulgence if given the freedom to spend their earnings. Data is tabulated in Table 5.4.

As expected, the circle of aspirations is different in tribal, rural and urban contexts. The urban formal sector women were inclined to spend on personal requirements, needs of the family and children, besides leisure activities. They did not have much fancy for jewellery and clothes. In contrast, their tribal and rural counterparts counted to accumulate jewellery, aspired to build a house and spend on the needs of the children and family. Urban informal sector was unique in the sense that it had a rub-off effect of both the rural background and urban exposure. Hence, their desires were divided proportionately, i.e. accumulating jewellery, savings, building a house, spending on clothes and more modern ones like spending on leisure activities, needs of the family and children and personal requirements.

Table 5.4 *Freedom to Spend Self-earnings*

Ways of spending	*Tribal N=30*	*Rural N=30*	*Urban*			*Total N=140*
			Informal N=40	*Formal N=40*	*Sub-Total N=80*	
Accumulate money for jewellery	9(30.0)	8(26.7)	5(12.5)	—	5(6.2)	19(13.6)
Accumulate money for house	6(20.0)	4(13.3)	5(12.5)	—	5(6.2)	15(10.7)
Saving for depositing	3(10.0)	6(20.0)	4(10.0)	4(10.0)	8(10.0)	17(12.1)
Spend on clothes	—	4(13.3)	6(15.0)	—	6(7.5)	10(7.1)
Leisure activity	—	—	4(10.0)	6(15.0)	10(12.5)	10(7.1)
Needs of the family	6(20.0)	—	7(17.5)	5(12.5)	12(15.0)	18(12.8)
Spend on children	4(13.3)	6(20.0)	6(15.0)	8(20.0)	14(17.5)	24(17.1)
Personal requirements	—	2(6.7)	2(5.0)	14(35.0)	16(20.0)	18(12.8)
DK/NR	2(6.7)	—	1(2.5)	3(7.5)	4(5.0)	6(4.3)
Total	30(100)	30(100)	40(100)	40(100)	80(100)	140(100)

Figures in parentheses indicate percentages.

It is a common belief that mothers are more affectionate, accommodating and splurge money on children as compared to fathers. The respondents were asked whether they conformed to it.

Majority (60%) of total respondents agreed with the query and this included 52.5% of urban (37.5% formal; 67.5% informal), 60% of rural and 76.7% of tribal respondents. It is interesting to note that only in the urban formal sector the majority (57.5%) opined that their husbands tend to spend more on the needs of their children.

Myers and Indriso[9] have summarized the findings of a number of recent studies showing that men and women have separate obligations and priorities for meeting family needs. Although there are variations by cultural context, yet results suggest that women generally show greater and steadier allocational inputs than men for children's nutrition and health needs. A study among agricultural workers in South India indicates that though the amount contributed to household maintenance by men is sometimes greater than the women's contribution in absolute terms, the proportion of men's contribution to men's earnings is always much lower than that of women's.[10] The mother's income seems to be a better predictor of a child's nutritional status than the father's income, where men's and women's responsibilities for family food supply are separate.[11]

To another query, on 'which specific needs of children did expenses take place', the responses are outlined in Table 5.5. Majority (59%) of the total respondents said they spend on daily requirements of children, i.e. food, fruits, sweets, etc. This comprised 10.2% respondents of urban formal and 18.4% of urban informal sector. The proportion rose to 30.6% in rural and 40.8% in the tribal context. Another 14.5% said they spend on entertainment needs of children such as games, comics, movies, video games, chocolates in urban segment and toys (*romakiya*), balloons, handmade things, etc. in rural and tribal segments. An overwhelming majority (80%) of such respondents were clustered in urban formal (30%) and urban informal (40%) segments. This proportion dropped to 10% in rural, but increased to 30% in the tribal context. Similarly, 12% of the total respondents preferred to spend on educational needs of children. It is interesting to note that 50% of such respondents belonged to the urban informal sector and the remaining 30% and 20% were from the urban formal sector and rural background, respectively.

Table 5.5 *Specific Needs of Children*

Needs of children	*Tribal N=23*	*Rural N=18*	*Urban*			*Total N=83*
			Informal N=27	*Formal N=15*	*Sub-Total N=42*	
Daily requirement	20(40.8)(87.0)	15(30.6) (83.3)	9(18.3) (33.3)	5(10.2) (33.3)	14(28.5) (33.3)	49(100) (59.0)
New clothes	—	—	4(100) (14.8)	—	4(100) (9.5)	4(100) (4.8)
Education	—	2(20.0) (11.1)	5(50.0) (18.5)	3(30.0) (20.0)	8(80.0) (19.0)	10(100) (12.0)
Entertainment	3(40.0) (13.0)	1(10.0) (5.6)	3(40.0) (11.1)	5(30.0) (33.3)	8(80.0) (19.5)	12(100) (14.5)
Any wishes	—	—	4(100) (14.8)	—	4(100) (9.5)	4(100) (4.8)
NR	—	—	2(50.0) (7.4)	2(50.0) (13.4)	4(100) (9.5)	4(100) (4.8)
Total	23(100)	18(100)	27(100)	15(100)	42(100)	83(100)

Figures in parentheses indicate percentages.

Desire to spend on education was much exhausted in urban informal sector respondents. And, only about 5% of the total respondents said they preferred to spend on new clothes for children. All these respondents belonged to urban informal segment. Similar percentage of urban informal sector respondents were spending according to whims and fancies of their children.

Sharing Household Responsibilities of Working Respondents

One of the major sources of domestic conflict in families where both the spouses work outside is the issue of sharing domestic responsibilities. Gender stereotypes firmly embedded in the social psyche have forced women to accept sole responsibility for tasks such as child rearing, household chores, etc. However, there is a gradual change in the attitude of some men to the issue of sharing domestic responsibilities and in such homes where both spouses share domestic work, there is lesser degree of tension. A family does not necessarily mean only the husband, wife and their children. At times, it also includes parents of spouses, siblings and other relatives. Given the fact that most families in India are formed on the lines of a patrilocal type of residence, it is the woman who is expected to shift to her husband's house. The saying that in India a woman is married not to an individual but a family typically reflects the state in which most married women are placed. The attitudes of other members of the family towards their work go a long way in determining the type of work and family life of married women. The respondents were asked as to who looked after their household responsibilities while they were away at work.

Majority of rural respondents (36.7%) were able to elicit support from in-laws as compared to rural and urban counterparts (16.7% and 15%, respectively). Even in the urban sector, this trend gravitated towards formai sector respondents. One-fifth (20%) of working respondents found support from in-laws in managing household affairs. Nearly one-tenth (9.3%) of the respondents depended upon their near relatives (sister-in-law) for overseeing household work while they were away at work. Thus, it can be inferred that the disintegration of the joint family system in tribal and urban societies has led to such problems and burden of household responsibilities has shifted to children, husbands and neighbours/close relatives. However, urban formal sector respondents are able to afford to employ full/part-time servants to get relief. It is interesting to note that 12.5% of the urban formal sector respondents said their husbands shared household responsibilities since they were working. However, there were no such instances in the urban informal sector, rural or tribal sections.

Alternatives of Child Care for Working Mother

Contemporary literature on gender abounds with references to 'dual parenting'. Yet, in reality, its practice is extremely limited. A lot of tension between spouses and between working mothers and other relatives emanates from lack of proper arrangements for child care. Whether or not women work outside their homes, they are made to feel that they are primarily responsible for child care. In fact, a woman is made to develop a guilty feeling if she gives priority to her career over her 'mothering' responsibilities. It is also true that in many families children are showered not only with undue attention but are also overprotected. With most men hardly participating in child care functions, women are left with little choice but to accept that responsibility. We asked our respondents who took care of children while they were away from home. Table 5.6 contains the details.

Table 5.6 *Alternatives of Child Care for Working Mother*

Alternatives of child care	*Tribal N=30*	*Rural N=30*	*Urban*			*Total N=140*
			Informal N=40	*Formal N=40*	*Sub-Total N=80*	
In-laws	12(40.0)	4(13.3)	2(5.0)	11(27.5)	13(16.3)	29(20.7)
Parents	—	—	1(2.5)	4(10.0)	5(6.3)	5(3.5)
Husband	—	—	1(2.5)	3(7.5)	4(5.0)	4(2.9)
Servant/maid	—	—	—	7(17.5)	7(8.7)	7(5.0)
Leaves child in creche	—	—	—	3(7.5)	3(3.7)	3(2.1)
Elder children	12(40.0)	14(46.7)	6(15.0)	6(15.0)	12(15.0)	38(27.1)
Other	—	2(6.7)	—	—	—	2(1.4)
NA	6(20.0)	10(33.3)	30(75.0)	6(15.0)	36(45.0)	52(37.2)
Total	30(100)	30(100)	40(100)	40(100)	80(100)	140(100)

Figures in parentheses indicate percentages.

More than one-fourth (27%) depended upon their elder children to take care of younger siblings. This trend was strongly reflected among rural respondents (46.7%) and mitigated as we moved to tribal (40%) and urban set-ups. (15%). In the tribal context, women with singular children do not work far from their home but once they have two or more offsprings and feel the older one can take care of younger sibling, they start working at more distant places. In-laws looked after children in 20.7% cases. Maximum (40%) of such cases were in tribal set-up, followed by urban and rural set-ups. It is interesting to note that although majority lived in nuclear families in tribal areas, still the in-laws took care of the younger lot. Since urban formal sector respondents had more spending power, 17.5% of such respondents could afford to employ a servant/maid, whereas 7.5% left their children in a creche. Such instances were unheard of in urban informal, rural and tribal segments.

Facets of Discrimination for Working Respondents

Wage levels of women are much less than what is due to them as per the law and also than their male colleagues. The respondents were asked about specific problems they face at their workplace. Responses are shown in Table 5.7.

Table 5.7 *Problems Experienced at Workplace*

Problems experienced	*Tribal N=30*	*Rural N=30*	*Urban*			*Total N=140*
			Informal N=40	*Formal N=40*	*Sub-Total N=80*	
Long working hours and less pay	15(50.0)	8(26.7)	6(15.0)	—	6(7.5)	29(24.2)
No facility to keep kids at work	—	2(6.7)	2(5.0)	—	2(2.5)	4(3.3)
No facility for toilets, drinking water, etc.	—	4(13.3)	2(5.0)	—	2(2.5)	6(5.0)
Behaviour of male colleagues and male domination	—	3(10.0)	2(5.0)	4(10.0)	6(7.5)	9(7.5)
Excess work	—	—	—	8(20.0)	8(10.0)	8(6.7)
No facility for first aid	—	3(10.0)	2(5.0)	—	2(2.5)	5(4.1)
No specific problem	10(33.3)	4(13.3)	—	24(60.0)	24(30.0)	38(3.2)
Verbal harassment by masters	—	3(10.0)	—	—	—	3(2.5)
NR/DK	5(16.6)	3(10.0)	26(65.0)	4(10.0)	4(7.4)	12(10.0)
Total	30(100)	30(100)	40(100)	40(100)	80(100)	140(100)

Figures in parentheses indicate percentages.

The data reveals that within the urban formal sector, majority (60%) of the respondents denied facing any specific problem. However, 10% outlined domination of male colleagues, while 20% complained about excess work. Moving over to urban informal sector, 43% respondents said they were asked to put in long work hours with meagre salary. Another 14.4% complained regarding lack of basic amenities like drinking water, toilets, etc. Similar proportion of women was of the view that there was no facility to keep children at workplaces. Another 14.3% complained of male domination while a similar number of women indicated no facility for first aid.

More than one-fourth (26.7%) of rural respondents complained of long working hours and meagre salary. Women workers in village were also discriminated against in a number of ways. The big farmers and upper-caste Jagirdars still hold sway on the poor, illiterate, low-caste women and landless labourers. Due to illiteracy and ignorance, these women are undergoing regular exploitation.

Dilating on the problem of economic exploitation vis-à-vis the relationship between work and wages, it was pointed out that the statutory provision regarding payment of minimum wages, i.e. ₹ 32 per day was not being followed in most cases; the norm of equal wage for equal work was not being adhered to either. Another 13.3% complained of lack of facilities. One-tenth were perturbed by male domination and another one-tenth by verbal harassment. However, 13.3% of rural respondents denied facing any of the above specific problems. In tribal context, while 17% of respondents could not elaborate, one-third denied facing any specific problem. Thus, for majority (50%) of respondents, long working hours and low remuneration remained the main problems.

Dimensions of Sexual Harassment at Workplace

Women workers also face another type of gender-specific discrimination and oppression at their place of work. A severe problem is of sexual harassment, which is perpetuated not just by the employer but also by workmates. Majority of respondents suffer this silent humiliation and are unable to draw enough courage to denounce it. The respondents were asked regarding various manifestations of this harassment. The results are shown in Table 5.8.

As expected, 46.4% of the total respondents had not experienced any sexual harassment. Most of them, however, said they had heard of other women having experienced it. These included 74.5% of urban formal sector, 2% of urban informal sector and 23.5% of rural respondents. One-tenth (10%) said they were perturbed by lewd comments of superiors, colleagues and customers. Such respondents included 18.2% of urban formal sector, 45.5% of urban informal sector and 36.4% of rural women. According to 8% of total respondents, they faced humiliation in spite of their sincerity towards work. In all, 44.4% of urban informal sector and 55.6% of rural respondents were included in this category. Then, physical molestation emerged as a means of harassment among one-tenth (10%) of urban informal sector respondents and this was unheard of in any other section. And finally, 13.3% of rural women complained of visual harassment, that is obscene pictures and writing on walls, workplaces, making suggestive gestures, etc.

Table 5.8 *Harassment Experienced by Working Women*

Kind of Harassment	*Tribal N=30*	*Rural N=30*	*Urban*			*Total N=140*
			Informal N=40	*Formal N=40*	*Sub-Total N=80*	
Passing lewd comments	—	4(36.4) (13.3)	5(45.5) (12.5)	2(18.2) (5.0)	7(66.6) (8.8)	11(100) (10.0)
Physical molestation	—	—	4(100.0) (10.0)	—	4(100.0) (5.0)	4(100) (3.6)
Visual harassment	—	4(100) (13.3)	—	—	—	4(100) (3.6)
Humiliation	—	5(55.6) (16.7)	4(44.4) (10.0)	—	4(44.4) (5.0)	9(100) (8.1)
NA	—	5(16.1) (16.7)	26(83.4) (65.0)	—	26(83.8) (32.5)	31(100) (28.2)
DK/NR	—	12(23.5) (40.0)	1(2.0) (2.5)	38(74.5) (95.0)	39(76.5) (48.7)	51(100) (46.4)
Total	—	30(100)	40(100)	40(100)	80(100)	110(100)

Figures in parentheses indicate percentages.

It is pertinent to note that none of the tribal respondents complained of any harassment. This is precisely because disrespect for any married Garasia woman becomes an issue of prestige for the entire Garasia community to take revenge. Hence, they derive fearful respect at workplace from their non-tribal colleagues and superiors. Such exploitation and harassment are also confined to rural and urban informal sector women who suffer silently due to insecurity of losing their jobs.

Dilemmas and Afterthoughts of Working Women

Once the wife/mother starts working, it requires realignment of familial roles and responsibilities. Sandwiched between demands of dual roles, a working homemaker has to work within a stricter time schedule. It requires greater mental and physical alertness and a change in thinking and behaviour in the household. This may also lead to change in marital relationship and relationship with in-laws and the authority pattern within the family.

A woman is drawn in a dilemma of somewhat contradictory role perceptions. The loyalties, interests and aims differ between home and the workplace and demand different individuals. Working respondents were asked regarding such problems and the responses are tabulated in Table 5.9.

Most of the urban formal sector women bore a guilt of neglecting their basic household responsibilities. In spite of keeping a servant or depending upon other household members, the finer points of household management suffered due to lack of supervision. She tried to compensate by involving herself on holidays and after working hours to make up for her lack of presence. Condition of most urban informal sector working women was even more miserable since they were living in crowded slums that lack basic amenities like clean and regular drinking water, which makes management of household responsibilities even more difficult. The menfolk did not share their worries to the same extent. As household members and labourers, women increasingly had to face the hard and oppressive realities of life. Rural and tribal working women have to walk long distances for going to place of work. They leave early and return late and due to their absence, basic household activities such as collecting fuel, fodder, drinking water, preparing meals suffer. Under the circumstances, they can cook only after their return from work and wash clothes only on weekends. Nearly 18% of total respondents regretted that they had little time for leisure activities due to their dual roles. Amongst these were 12.5% of urban (both formal and informal) and 50% of tribal women. The concept of leisure varied across different strata. For both urban formal and informal sector urban women, it meant going to movies, eating out, going for outings, while for rural and tribal women, it included finding time for self-indulgence – that is bathing, gossip with neighbours, relatives, going to fairs, visiting relatives in neighbouring villages.

Table 5.9 *Household or Other Problems Experienced by Working Women*

Problems	*Tribal N=30*	*Rural N=30*	*Urban*			*Total N=140*
			Informal N=40	*Formal N=40*	*Sub-Total N=80*	
No leisure activity	15(50.0)	—	5(12.5)	5(12.5)	10(12.5)	25(17.9)
Household work suffers	8(26.7)	10(33.3)	10(25.0)	17(42.5)	27(33.8)	45(32.1)
Does not take proper care of children	2(6.6)	8(26.7)	4(10.0)	4(10.0)	8(10.0)	18(12.8)4.
Tension in family	5(16.7)	4(13.3)	6(15.0)	4(10.0)	10(12.5)	19(13.6)
No time for self	—	2(6.7)	6(15.0)	2(5.0)	8(10.0)	10(7.1)
Less time for interaction with relatives	—	4(13.3)	2(5.0)	5(12.5)	7(8.7)	11(7.9)
No problem	—	—	—	2(5.0)	2(2.5)	2(1.4)
NR/DK	—	2(6.6)	7(17.5)	1(2.5)	8(10.0)	10(7.1)
Total	30(100)	30(100)	40(100)	40(100)	80(100)	140(100)

Figures in parentheses indicate percentages.

For some respondents (13%), tensions of office overflowed and affected their family life. Such women comprised 10% of urban formal sector, 15% of urban informal sector, 13.3% of rural and 16.7% of tribal respondents. Handling increased workload might lead to a delay in returning home from work and leads to flaring up of tension with in-laws, husband, etc. This factor was experienced by all women in varying degrees since their relatives and husbands were unable to appreciate the pressure and demands of workplace. Lack of time and energy to take care of children pinched nearly 13% of the respondents. Interaction with relatives suffered due to paucity of time in case of 8% of total respondents. Another 7% had little time to spend on their own due to pressing demands both at workplace and home.

Quantifying Economic Value of Household Women

In all traditional societies, women are involved in varying degrees in food production, management and distribution. Women are also chief caretakers of family nutrition, including their own. Despite the fact that these activities are performed by women, their control over resources is determined by certain social and cultural norms which are not always favourable to them.

The value of women's work in creating and maintaining the household stock of human capital through cooking, cleaning, nursing and raising children is often valued rhetorically, but less often valued in national data, where housewives are often listed among dependent or non-working members of society. Neo-classical, new household economists, and Marxists as well as many feminists are documenting the productive nature of such work, its contribution to national welfare, and the necessity of including its value in national accounts.[12]

Amartya Sen has suggested that the balance of power in the household is based on perceptions of economic contributions, which in turn supports notions of the legitimacy to claims to infra-household distribution and allocation. Women's perception of their lesser claim is further disadvantaged by their perception of self-interest being conflicted with family well-being.[13] Women are seen as actors, but acting not in their self-interests but persuading goals related to family welfare.

The household is a fundamental production unit in every type of economy. The ultimate purpose of production activities carried out at the household level is to meet the basic needs of household members. The world around, it is primarily women who manage and perform household production. Women's ability to manage resources in such a way to produce goods and services for consumption in the household and to produce products that can generate some cash income greatly influences the level of living achieved by households in developing countries.

The innumerable production activities, carried out mainly by women within the household sector, are of critical importance for society's survival, growth and development. Household production is essential for providing the calories that produce energy with which to work in any sector of the economy. The level of any individual's health is largely determined by the household's ability to produce basic shelter and food. Furthermore, the household is society's primary institution for the replacement and development of human capital for the process of reproduction, socialization and nurturance. The household sector thus fulfils a vital role in contributing to the welfare of the society.[14]

The nature of household production was formally recognized and conceptualized by Reid.[15] She defined household production as those unpaid activities which are carried on by and for the members (of the household), and might be replaced by market goods or paid services if circumstances such as income, market conditions and personal inclinations permit the services being delegated to someone outside the household group.

A variety of classification schemes have been used to categorize activities that constitute household production. Several of these have been developed for studies of time allocation in United States.

The following list from a study in the 1970s conducted by NE 113 Regional Research Committee[16] includes:

- Food preparation and after-meal clean-up
- Shopping
- Care of clothing and household lines
- Care of family members
- Management, including account-keeping

These categories of household production are too limited for developing countries.

Acharya and Bennett[17] distinguish three types of production activities: conventional economic activities, extended economic activities and domestic activities. Conventional economic activities are those activities generally included in official economic activity reports (e.g. manufacturing, agriculture, animal husbandry and market activities). Extended or facilitating economic activities include food processing, fuel and water collection, and manufacturing for home use. In fuel-scarce areas, the production of fuel may involve gathering cow-dung and processing it into fuel *patties* or walking miles in search of twigs and wood. A realistic assessment of women's household production in developing countries must include these extended economic activities. Domestic activities include cooking, cleaning, child care, and all other works conventionally termed 'services'.

In this section, we dissect the day-to-day life of household women in tribal, rural and urban communities and analyse their feelings, desires and aspirations.

Self-perception of Housewives

'Women are seen as financial dependents, with no capital and no income' has been a prevailing paradigm. Their roles are defined as wife, mother and consumer. It is assumed that their work, which they perform for non-economic reasons, is house work and child care. The farm, worked by men, is economically productive, while the household consumes production. Their work in agriculture farm is long, hard and unpaid. The male head of the household makes all decisions, presumably in a more or less altruistic way. Women are seen as legal minors whose interests are taken care of by the men in the household. The policy recommendations address only their roles as wives and mothers, and do not consider economic incentives.

We, therefore, tried to gauge from the respondents the economic perceptions of their household work. As per the data presented in Table

5.10a, it can be seen that a significant number of our of respondents (62% of the total) said yes to the economic value of their work.

Table 5.10a *Economic Value of Household Work*

Household work has any economic value	*Tribal N=50*	*Rural N=50*	*Urban (Household) N=40*	*Total N=140*
Yes	20(40.0)	30(60.0)	37(92.5)	87(62.2)
No	—	10(20.0)	—	10(7.1)
NR/DK	30(60.0)	10(20.0)	3(7.5)	43(30.7)
Total	50(100)	50(100)	40(100)	140(100)

Figures in parentheses indicate percentages.

This feeling was strongest amongst the urban household women as 92.5% of them replied in the affirmative, whereas only 40% of tribal and 60% of rural women were of the same view. However, 20% of rural respondents (7.1% of total) did not attach any economic value to household work. We asked our respondents to explain the reasons for their thinking so, which are summarized in Table 5.10b.

It was observed that more than one-third (34%) of the respondents felt household work led to savings. These included 37.5% of urban household, 46% of rural and 20% of tribal women. Another 17.8% considered their natural instinct and ability in doing household chores. This viewpoint was concentrated amongst 40% of tribal and 10% of rural respondents. The perception of an ideal tribal wife is one who can carry out domestic chores efficiently and is attentive towards the needs of husbands on return from work. Any laxity regarding non-preparation of food or non-availability of water is looked down upon and such irritants are the starting points for quarrels and domestic violence. One-tenth of rural women (3.6% of total) believed it to be their duty to perform such roles. Overall environment and upbringing of the girl child in tribal and rural areas is gravitated towards making her realize her required roles as wife and mother. This myopic attitude is unable to broaden her horizons and mental set-up to perceive any role beyond the confines of the household. In contrast, in the urban household sector, women perform their household chores due to choice and not because of any duty. Another 14% of the total respondents believe that their primary responsibility is to take care of the husband, children and elders. In all, 17.5% of urban household sector, 6% rural and 20% tribal respondents conform to above.

Besides, 25% of (urban) household women (7.1% of total) felt that household work is labourious, consumes a lot of time and involves adequate planning.

Table 5.10b *Reasons for Viewpoint*

Reasons	*Tribal N=50*	*Rural N=50*	*Urban (Household) N=40*	*Total N=140*
Household work leads to savings	10(20.0)	23(46.0)	15(37.5)	48(34.3)
Proper utilization and no wastage	—	4(8.0)	5(12.5)	9(6.4)
This work involves hard work, planning and time	—	—	10(25.0)	10(7.1)
Proper care of husband and children	10(20.0)	3(6.0)	7(17.5)	20(14.3)
This is one's duty and good service	—	5(10.0)	—	5(3.5)
Only women can do this work/ability to household work	20(40.0)	5(10.0)	—	25(17.8)
NR/DK	10(20.0)	10(20.0)	3(7.5)	23(16.4)
Total	50(100)	50(100)	40(100)	140(100.0)

Figures in parentheses indicate percentages.

Another 6.5% of the total respondents were of the opinion that this leads to proper utilization and prevents wastage of resources. A total of 12.5% of urban household and 8% of rural respondents held this thinking. The proportion of total respondents who were convinced that household work can be efficiently carried out by women but with a thinking that it leads to saving, proper utilization of resources and requires lots of planning to take care of their husband and children stood at 17.8%.

Career Aspirations of Non-working Respondents

We asked our non-working respondents that given a chance, what would be their favourite vocation. Relevant data can be seen in Table 5.11.

Since urban household sector women were relatively more educated, exposed and lived in an environment where means and opportunities were plenty, more than one-third (37.5%) said they would take up a job in any segment from various existing opportunities. Nearly one-fourth (22.5%) craved to take up teaching professions while 15% were inclined to conduct hobby classes at home. Of the remaining, while

5% each wanted to set up a designing institute and a business of their own, 15% were unsure and did not elaborate immediately.

Table 5.11 *Respondents' favourite work*

Work Preference	*Tribal N=50*	*Rural N=50*	*Urban (Household) N=40*	*Total N=140*
Labour	30(60.0)	14(28.0)	—	44(31.4)
Teaching	—	4(8.0)	9(22.5)	13(9.3)
Job	—	—	15(37.5)	15(10.8)
Business	—	2(4.0)	2(5.0)	4(2.8)
Designing institute	—	—	2(5.0)	2(1.4)
Hobby classes	—	10(20.0)	6(15.0)	16(11.4)
NR/DK	20(40.0)	20(40.0)	6(15.0)	46(32.8)
Total	50(100)	50(100)	40(100)	140(100)

Figures in parentheses indicate percentages.

In rural context, while most (28%) of the respondents, who were mainly illiterate, said that they would do labour-oriented jobs, 20% were imaginative and wanted to take hobby classes like painting, stitching at home, 8% had the self-confidence to take up teaching, and 4% were inclined to establish some business.

Similarly, in the tribal context, majority of respondents (60%) wanted to do labour-oriented jobs and the remaining could not elucidate as opportunities to work are scarce.

We also asked our respondents whether they had faced a situation where in spite of talent and desire, they were not permitted to work. Responses, which are displayed in Table 5.12a, reveal that majority (63%) replied in the affirmative and proportion of such respondents was highest amongst rural (76%) and reduced to 60% amongst tribal and 50% amongst urban household sector respondents.

Table 5.12a *Capable but not allowed to work*

Capability of doing work but not allowed	*Tribal N=50*	*Rural N=50*	*Urban (Household) N=40*	*Total N=140*
Yes	30(60.0)	38(76.0)	20(50.0)	88(63.0)
No	14(28.0)	11(22.0)	19(47.5)	44(31.4)
NR/DK	6(12.0)	1(2.0)	1(2.5)	8(5.7)
Total	50(100)	50(100)	40(100)	140(100)

Figures in parentheses indicate percentages.

Roadblocks in Working Outside

On specific hindrances, as shown in Table 5.12b, while majority (50%) of urban household sector women cited non-cooperation from family as the main hindrance in working outside, 30% pointed out small children and 15% said they were overloaded with household work. Moving over to the rural context, while non-cooperation from family remained the dominant factor (26.3%), 13.2% said they did not have the freedom to move outside and work due to the orthodox set-up in the upper-caste rural system. Likewise, while 21% women were overloaded with household work, in 16% cases, their health did not permit to move outside for work. Another 13% were preoccupied with taking care of small children, whereas 8% were made to realize that prestige of household would come to an end if they ventured out for work. This factor emerged strongly in upper-caste rural Rajput families, where families may suffer from poverty but do not send their wives/daughters-in-law for work outside the confines of home.

Table 5.12b *Nature of Hindrance*

Roadblocks in Working Outside	*Tribal N=30*	*Rural N=38*	*Urban (Household) N=20*	*Total N=88*
Non-cooperation from family	—	10(26.3)	10(50.0)	20(22.7)
No freedom to go outside for work	16(53.3)	5(13.2)	—	21(23.9)
Small children	12(40.0)	5(13.2)	6(30.0)	23(26.1)
Due to health problem	—	6(15.8)	—	6(6.8)
Overloaded household work	—	8(21.0)	3(15.0)	11(12.5)
Prestige of household	2(6.7)	3(7.9)	—	5(5.7)
NR/DK	—	1(2.6)	1(5.0)	2(2.3)
Total	30(100)	38(100)	20(100)	88(100)

Figures in parentheses indicate percentages.

In the tribal set-up, more than half (53.3%) of the respondents acknowledged that they did not have the freedom to go outside for work due to suspicious nature of their husbands and prevalence of extra-marital affairs in tribal society. Moreover, 40% of respondents had small children while 6.7% considered going out for work as adverse to the prestige of the family. These women mainly belonged to the families of the elite within the tribal society.

Dispensable Income

Non-working respondents were asked if they regularly got pocket money and their level of satisfaction with the same.

Table 5.13a *Regularly Get Pocket Money*

Get Pocket Money Regularly	*Tribal N=50*	*Rural N=50*	*Urban (Household) N=40*	*Total N=140*
Yes	40(80.0)	20(64.0)	35(87.5)	107(76.4)
No	10(20.0)	16(32.0)	5(12.5)	31(22.2)
NA	—	2(4.0)	—	2(1.4)
Total	50(100)	50(100)	40(100)	140(100)

Figures in parentheses indicate percentages.

More than three-fourths (76.4%) confirmed receiving pocket money. These included 87.5% of urban household, 64% of rural, and 80% of tribal respondents. Levels of satisfaction were graded on a scale from absolutely satisfied to not-at-all satisfied, and the results are deputed in Table 5.13a.

Table 5.13b *Level of Satisfaction with Pocket Money*

Response	*Tribal N=40*	*Rural N=32*	*Urban (Household) N=35*	*Total N=107*
Absolutely satisfied	4(10.0)	—	10(28.5)	14(13.0)
Satisfied	25(62.5)	18(56.2)	20(57.1)	63(58.9)
Not satisfied	11(27.5)	8(25.0)	5(14.3)	24(22.4)
Not-at-all satisfied	—	6(18.7)	—	6(5.6)
Total	40(100)	32(100)	35(100)	107(100)

Figures in parentheses indicate percentages.

While 28.5% of household sector respondents were absolutely satisfied, 57% were satisfied while 14.3% were not satisfied with the pocket money required. In rural community, none of the respondents was absolutely satisfied, though, 56% were satisfied, 25% were not satisfied and 18.7% not at all satisfied. A sharp contrast emerges between urban household sector and rural respondents, pointing to the male-dominated orthodox and self-centred rural set-up where women have little access to economic resources. In the tribal society, 10% of respondents were absolutely satisfied, 62.5% satisfied and 27.5% not satisfied with the pocket money. The high level of satisfaction with regard to pocket money amongst tribal respondents can be attributed to lack of exposure and a simplistic, hardworking lifestyle.

Feeling of Helplessness due to Financial Dependency

Feeling of helplessness was acknowledged by 45% and the proportion of such respondents was maximum in rural sector (68%) and reduced to 37.5% and 28% amongst urban household and tribal set-ups, respectively. More than half of the respondents (51.5%) denied facing helplessness or financial insecurity. This mindset was strongest amongst tribal respondents (68%) and reduced to 57.5% in urban household sector and diminished to 30% amongst rural respondents.

Table 5.14a *Feeling of Helplessness Due to Financial Dependency*

Response	*Tribal N=50*	*Rural N=50*	*Urban (Household) N=40*	*Total N=180*
Yes	14(28.0)	34(68.0)	15(37.5)	63(45.0)
No	34(68.0)	15(30.0)	23(57.5)	72(51.4)
NR/DK	2(4.0)	1(2.0)	2(5.0)	5(3.5)
Total	50(100)	50(100)	40(100)	140(100)

Figures in parentheses indicate percentages.

For the respondents who expressed this feeling of helplessness, the reasons were analysed. Results are shown in Table 5.14b.

Table 5.14b *Specific Reasons for Feeling Helpless*

Response	*Tribal N=14*	*Rural N=34*	*Urban (Household) N=15*	*Total N=63*
Less earning, more requirements	4(28.6)	12(35.3)	4(26.7)	20(31.8)
Husband does not give enough money	—	6(17.6)	—	6(9.5)
To be self-dependent	—	4(11.8)	6(40.0)	10(15.9)
Can take good care of children	—	8(23.5)	2(13.3)	10(15.9)
Husband is drunkard	—	4(11.8)	1(6.7)	5(7.9)
Lack of outside exposure	10(71.4)	—	2(13.3)	12(19.0)
Total	14(100)	34(100)	15(100)	63(100)

Figures in parentheses indicate percentages.

In totality, 63 out of 140 respondents expressed a feeling of helplessness. These included 15 respondents from urban household, 34 from rural and 14 from tribal backgrounds. Urban household sector respondents who wanted to be independent were 40% while 26.7% were depressed due to less earnings and more requirements of urban life. Another 13.3% felt guilty that they lacked outside exposure and a similar proportion wanted to take good care of children. In a singular instance, the husband was a drunkard, resulting in misery for the respondent.

Feeling of helplessness was much more pronounced in the rural set-up, where 35% of respondents were perturbed by less earnings and more household requirements. Nearly one-fourth (23%) wanted to take good care of children while 17.6% were anguished since their husbands did not give enough money. Another 12% wanted to be independent while a similar proportion were depressed since their husband was an alcoholic. Amongst tribal respondents, majority, i.e. 71%, said they lacked outside exposure while for 29%, less earnings and more requirements were the major cause of concern.

Table 5.15a *Benefits in Going to Work Away from Home*

Benefits in going to work away from home	*Tribal N=50*	*Rural N=50*	*Urban (Household) N=40*	*Total N=140*
Yes	10(20.0)	19(38.0)	23(57.5)	52(37.1)
No	40(80.0)	31(62.0)	17(42.5)	88(62.9)
Total	50(100)	50(100)	40(100)	140(100)

Figures in parentheses indicate percentages.

To our query whether they desired any benefits while going away from home for work (Table 5.15a), an overwhelming majority (63%) of respondents who replied in the negative were 42.5% from urban household, 62% from rural and 80% from tribal sectors and from the respondents who replied in the affirmative, we asked regarding the range of benefits they desired from working outside home. Results are given in Table 5.15b.

Table 5.15b *Reasons for Benefits Derived in Working Away From Home*

Benefits	*Tribal N=10*	*Rural N=19*	*Urban (Household) N=23*	*Total N=52*
Economic independence	8(33.3) (80.0)	12(50.0) (63.2)	4(16.7) (17.4)	24(100) (46.2)
Opportunity for outside exposure	—	5(50.0) (26.3)	5(50.0) (21.7)	10(100) (19.2)
Personality development	—	—	9(100.0) (39.1)	9(100) (17.3)
Improvement in condition of household	—	2(40.0) (10.5)	3(60.0) (13.0)	5(100) (9.6)
DK/NR	2(50.0) (20.0)	—	2(50.0) (8.7)	4(100) (7.7)
Total	10(100)	19(100)	23(100)	52(100)

Figures in parentheses indicate percentages.

Respondents who outlined economic independence as the major benefit of this process constituted 46% and included 16.7% of urban household sector, 50% of rural and 33.3% of tribal women. Nearly 19.2% of the total respondents stated opportunity of outside exposure as the main charm. Also, outside work will give them an opportunity to meet other women. They can share their feelings with them. So, work is also an outlet for social amity and camaraderie, for sharing their ideas. They can remain away from daily routine of their household for at least some hours. These included similar percentage (i.e. 50) of women in rural and urban household sectors. Another 39% of urban household sector women (17.3% of total) felt that this had led to personality development and they were able to overcome inhibitions and their attitude had become more flexible and accommodating. However, this view was not shared by their rural and tribal counterparts.

Feeling that outside work and extra earning improves the overall condition of the household emerged from 10% of the total respondents; 13.7% of urban household sector and more than 10% of rural respondents agreed.

On the other hand, for those respondents who were non-working, we tried to analyse any benefits they gained while working within the household and results are shown in Table 5.15c.

Table 5.15c *Benefits in Working Within Household*

Benefits	*Tribal N=40*	*Rural N=31*	*Urban (Household) N=17*	*Total N=88*
Family life moves peacefully	25(71.4) (62.5)	7(20.0) (22.6)	3(8.6) (17.6)	35(100) (39.8)
House remains organized	—	4(50.0) (12.9)	4(50.0) (23.5)	8(100) (9.0)
Proper upbringing of children	—	5(55.6) (16.1)	4(44.4) (23.5)	9(100) (10.2)
Total care and control of family	—	—	3(100) (17.7)	3(100) (3.4)
No sarcastic remarks by others	—	7(100) (22.6)	—	7(100) (7.9)
Besides household, can take care of cattle and crops	15(71.4) (37.5)	6(28.6) (19.3)	—	21(100) (23.9)
DK/NR	—	2(40.0) (6.6)	3(60.0) (17.7)	5(100) (5.7)
Total	40(100)	31(100)	17(100)	88(100)

Figures in parentheses indicate percentages.

Family life moves smoothly and peacefully as 40% of the total respondents were able to devote their entire time and energy for household responsibilities. Day-to-day life was devoid of tensions, misunderstanding between husband and wife and they were able to take complete care of family. This group of respondents included 8.6% of urban household sector, 20% of rural and 71.4% of tribal respondents. Nearly one-fourth (23.7%) of the total respondents felt they can take care of cattle and crops, besides household responsibilities by staying at home. This view was confined to rural and tribal set-ups and included 28.6% of rural and 71.4% of tribal respondents.

The view that a non-working housewife can ensure proper upbringing of children was expressed by 10.2% of the respondents. Entire burden of domestic chores is upon the housewife and this relieves children to attend school and study at home. Proper nutritious diet leads to their good physical and mental development. In all, 44.4% of urban household sector and 55.6% of rural respondents agreed with the viewpoint. House remains organized as they are non-working. This was the opinion of 9% of the total respondents and included 50% of urban household sector and 50% of rural respondents.

Adequate care and total control in family matters were the major benefits of staying at home, as described by 17.7% of urban household sector women. According to more than one-fifth (22.6%) of rural respondents, staying at home spared them of sarcastic remarks generally passed on working women. However, this view had no significant respondents among urban household and tribal societies.

Upper, middle and lower caste rural women perform back-breaking tasks for their households, just like their tribal counterparts. In order to get social and emotional acceptance in the conjugal family, the women work hard in as well as outside the house. Household work and managing cattleshed is primarily women's responsibility among all castes in rural areas. This is besides their other major responsibilities such as upbringing of children, organizing the household, caring for elderly members, and cooking. They milch and feed cattle, clean the shed, make cow-dung and also smear the house with dung and mud paste at regular intervals. Entire food processing, such as chaffing, pounding, grinding and fetching water and fuel collection, is the sole responsibility of women. They process and store certain food items for the whole year. The young daughter-in-law takes up strenuous chores, while the mother-in-law does the lighter ones. Except for Rajput women, all other women join their men in agricultural and non-agricultural works. Peasant artisans and lower middle caste and lower caste women usually work on their family farms or on leased lands. The upper caste women also work hard. They perform all the household duties, besides wage labour.

Notes

1. Sykes, J.B. (ed.), 1993. *The Concise Oxford Dictionary of Current English,* p. 1241.
2. Scott, W.P., 1988. *Dictionary of Sociology,* Delhi: Goyal Saab Publishers and Distributors, p. 446.
3. Delamont, S., 1980. *The Sociology of Women,* George Allen and Unwin.
4. William, K., 1976. *Key Words,* London: Fontana Croom Helm.
5. Kapur, Promilla, 1974. *Marriage and the Working Women in India,* New Delhi: Vikas Publishing House.
6. Nair, K.S., 1970. 'Women's Two Roles', *Social Welfare,* December.
7. Anderson, J.E., 1949. *The Psychology of Development and Personal Adjustment,* New York: Molt, p. 429.
8. Unnithan, Kumar, Maya, 1997. *Identity, Gender and Poverty,* Oxford: Berghanhn, p. 30.
9. Myres, Robert and Cynthia, Indriso, 1987. 'Women's Work and Child Care: Supporting the Integration of Women's Productive and Reproductive Roles in Resource-Poor Households in Developing Countries', *Paper prepared for the Rockefeller Foundation/IDRC Workshop on Gender, Technology and Development,* February, 26–27.
10. Mencher, John P., 1988. 'Women's Work and Poverty: Women's Contributions to Household Maintenance in South India', in Daisy Dwyer and Judith Bruce (ed.), *A Home Divided: Women and Income in the Third World,* Stanford CA: Stanford University Press.
11. Engle, Patricia L., 1983. 'The Effect of Maternal Employment on Children's Welfare in Rural Guatemala', *Child Development and International Development: Research Policy Interfaces, New Directions for Child Development,* Vol. 20, San Francisco: CA.,

    Kumar, Shubh K., 1978. 'Role of Household Economy in Child Nutrition at Low Incomes: A Case Study of Kerala', *Occasional Paper No. 95,* Cornell University and US/AID Tad-c-1327; and

    Popkin, Barry M., 1983. 'Rural Women, Work and Child Welfare in Philippines', in M. Buvinic, M.A. Lycette and W.P. Mc Greevey, (ed.), *Women and Poverty in the Third World,* Baltimore, M.O.: The Johns Hopkins University Press.

12. Acharya, Meena and Lynn, Benett, 1983. 'Women and the Subsistence Sector: Economic Participation and Household Decision-making in Nepal', *Working Paper No. 526,* Washington, D.C.: The World Bank;

    Goldschmidt-Clermont, Luisella, 1987. *Economics Evaluations of Unpaid House Work: Africa, Asia, Latin America and Oceania,* Geneva: International Labour Office; and

    World Bank, 1981–1991, 'Living Standards Measurement Projects', Various titles, Washington, D.C.: World Bank.
13. Sen, Amartya K., 1990. 'Gender and Cooperative Conflict', in Irene Tinker (ed.), *Persistent Inequalities,* New York and London: Oxford University Press.
14. Nickols, Sharon Y. and Kamala, Srinivasan, 1994. 'Women and Household Production', in Romy Borooah (et al.), *Capturing Complexity,* New Delhi: Sage Publications India Pvt. Ltd, pp. 102–122.
15. Reid, Margaret G., 1934. *Economics of Household Production,* New York: Wiley and Sons.
16. NE 113 Regional Research Committee, 1981. 'Family Time Use: An Eleven-State Urban/Rural Comparison', *Bulletin VPI-2,* Blackburg, VA: Virginia Agricultural Experiment Station.
17. Acharya, Meena, 1982. 'Time Use Data and the Living Standards Measurement Study', *LSMS Working Paper No. 18,*. Washington, D.C.: The World Bank.

6 The Modernizing Context

Gender, Body and Sexuality

Cultural concepts of feminine and masculine, and the ideology of gender, have meant that throughout the world, women continue to occupy a disadvantageous position in production and are assumed to be primarily responsible for reproduction (biologically, but also in terms of socialization). Not only do men and women allocate labour and receive differently, they also consume, utilize and receive resources, goods and services quite distinctly.[1]

Gender asymmetry is a universal fact of life. In many societies around the world, women are discriminated against by law and by custom, rendering them among the vulnerable and disadvantageous social group. As Papanek[2] puts it: '... Gender differences, based on the social construction of biological sex distinctions, are one of the great 'fault lines' of societies – those marks of differences among categories of persons that govern the allocation of power, authority and resources.' What then is gender? Gender is a cultural construct of sex roles, a definition of 'masculine' and 'feminine' and of the prerogatives of male and female. While culturally and historically bound, gender commonly is a function of power relations and the social organization of inequality.

Feminist scholars defined gender as the social organization of sexual difference, or a system of unequal relationships between the sexes. DeLauretis[3] has elaborated on the concept and the social fact of gender in the following way:

Cultural conceptions regard male and female as two complementary yet mutually exclusive categories into which all human beings are placed and constitute within each culture a gender system, that correlates sex to cultural contents according to social values and hierarchies. Although the meaning may vary with each concept, a sex gender system is always intimately interconnected with political and economic factors in each society. In this light, the cultural construction of sex into gender and the asymmetry that characterizes all gender systems cross-culturally (though each in its particular ways) are understood as systematically linked to the organization of social inequality.

Gender relations, on the one hand, are socially constructed as a result of the behaviour of women themselves. It is important to realize that gender relations are historical, changeable and subject to change through daily events and periodic moments of crisis and transformation.

In fact, men and women reflect biological similarities to a greater degree than biological differences. Society and culture have suppressed the natural similarities between the sexes and exacerbated the differences. They are governed by rules and practices through which society ensures that male and female are channelled into being men and women. Biological arguments about women's suitability for certain types of work operate under such premises.

Therefore, one's gender determines the life experiences one will be exposed to, i.e. access to education, work, resources, health, freedom of movement, relationship, sexuality, ability to make decisions and act autonomously. In different cultures, gender and gender relations constitute power relations with wider implications for access and control over resources (economic or political), including decision-making. In such a situation, women receive the smallest share. It is important to remember that the interests and needs of women and men in any family structure may be quite different because they are mainly based on their social roles, power and differences of status vested in these roles.

Men and women have performed different roles in life from time immemorial. In most societies, women are identified as being mothers, housekeepers and/or homemakers, whereas men are identified as breadwinners. On the whole, it is possible to list out the roles ascribed to men and women by the four institutions which shape human life, namely, the household, community, market and state. The roles identified in each of these sectors are basically common or similar in most societies. In actuality, the rules, resources, people, activities and power relations in these four institutions determine the roles that ought to be played by women and men.[4]

Discrimination against a girl begins from the moment she is born. Many controls and curbs are imposed on her. She is discriminated against in allocation of food and other resources. When she reaches the age of puberty, her free movement is severely curtailed. It is unfortunate that the improvement in the socio-economic status of a household only works in containing a girl's movement in the name of tradition or prestige rather than allowing her freedom of movement. Poverty may, however, force her to work for wages. Girls are made to understand that they must work at home and help their mothers in the performance of domestic chores. Parents feel that they are training their daughters to be effective homemakers and it is considered that the normally accepted gender stereotype for a girl is to take upon domestic responsibilities. Besides, she is compelled to keep mum and grows up amidst constraining situations. She is always made to feel that she has got a body to be afraid of. There is a conscious mystification of one's sexuality. Thus, girls have the constant feeling of inferiority and fear. At the same time, boys are pampered and trained to be domineering and rule their female family members.

Gender inequality is defined as the 'departure from parity in the representation of women and men in key dimensions of social life'.[5] Krishna Raj[6] says that inequalities and gaps are seen in the following major areas of life: employment, education, health, leisure, participation in public life and in opportunities for enrichment of personality.

Discrimination occurs due to several factors; sometimes it is self-imposed, sometimes it has religious sanctions and sometimes it is due to other cultural norms and at other times, it is externally imposed; the external agent normally being the employer. All these have a cumulative effect on women and thus they become vulnerable to exploitation.

Theories of gender inequalities look at women's status in most situations as different and less privileged than men. Liberal feminism explains gender inequality by using the concept of sexism – an ideology similar to racism, which consists partly of prejudice and discriminatory practices against women. According to these theorists, because of sexism, females are socialized from childhood onwards that they can move into their adult roles as dependent, mindless, subconsciously depressed beings, created by the constraints and requirements of their gender specific roles.[7]

The female body and female sexuality are tied to the reproductive process within the confines of marriage, in which the male normally dominates. Women are told to accept societal practices and that not doing so would be unnatural. The gynaecological practices of the nineteenth and twentieth centuries, *sati* in India, foot-binding in China, genital mutilation in Africa and witch-hunting in Europe are examples of women being drawn into compliance.

Differences between various societies are highlighted in distinctive dressing pattern, typical jewellery and attitudes and behavioural norms of women in public places. Attitudes and sexuality of women are further reflected in institutions of marriage, family, etc. within each community.

This chapter is an attempt to study constraints faced by women in the tribal, rural and urban communities of Rajasthan.

Women as Weaker Sex

The principle of protection is the basic consideration regarding female sexuality. The responsibility for protection of an unmarried girl lies with her natal or patrilineal male kin, particularly fathers and brothers. This responsibility for protection gives males the right to exercise power over the females in their charge and often dictates every facet of their behaviour. A proper demeanour is essential for remaining safe and above reproach. Downcast eyes and shrinking body, almost creating a private, sacrosanct space for oneself within a public space such as a road, constitute a part of this demeanour. Girls prefer to move in groups rather than alone.

The protection continues, to a greater or lesser degree, until a woman reaches menopause. Both seclusion and segregation are part of it. The perennial fear of misbehaviour and the fear of assault are expressed in the imposition of control over women's physical movement and their association with males. Linked to this is the notion that a woman's purity is fragile: the pollution she incurs through sexual intercourse is internal, whereas that incurred by man is only external.[8]

Women are considered as a weaker sex. They are given a subordinate status in the society. She is protected by the father in her childhood, by the husband in her adulthood and by the son in her old age. The male-dominated paternal system allows her to survive as a secondary member of the family and lower citizen of society.

The respondents were asked about these perceived notions that they are the weaker sex. Table 6.1 portrays the answers.

The respondents wholeheartedly endorsing the prevalent notion that women are the weaker sex were 58% in total. The proportion of such respondents was high amongst rural respondents (75%) as compared to their urban and tribal counterparts (51.6% and 50%, respectively).

Table 6.1 *Women as Weaker Sex*

Response	*Tribal N=80*	*Rural N=80*	*Urban*				*Total N=280*
			Household N=40	*Informal N=40*	*Formal N=40*	*Sub-Total N=120*	
To a large extent	40 (50.0)	60 (75.0)	30 (75.0)	32 (80.0)	—	62 (51.6)	162 (57.9)
To some extent	30 (37.5)	12 (15.0)	4 (10.0)	2 (5.0)	—	6 (5.0)	48 (17.1)
To a little extent	—	3 (3.8)	4 (10.0)	3 (7.5)-	15 (37.5)	22 (18.3)	25 (8.9)
Not at all	—	—	2 (5.0)	1 (2.5)	25 (62.5)	28 (23.3)	28 (10.0)
NR/DK	10 (12.5)	5 (6.2)	—	2 (5.0)	—	2 (1.7)	17 (6.1)
Total	80 (100)	80 (100)	40 (100)	40 (100)	40 (100)	120 (100)	280 (100)

Figures in parentheses indicate percentages.

Even amongst urban respondents, this viewpoint drew support mainly from informal and household sector women and not a single formal sector woman agreed with them. As against this, 17% of the total respondents acknowledged that women are a weaker sex to some extent. This feeling was high amongst tribal respondents (37.1%) and declined as we moved towards rural and urban segments (15% and 5%, respectively). One-tenth of the total respondents were more self-confident and felt they were not weaker than their male counterparts. However, this view was restricted to urban respondents (23.3%) and within them found concurrence primarily with formal sector respondents (62.5%). Nearly 9% of total respondents felt that they were marginally weaker and this view was confined to 18.3% of urban and nearly 4% of rural respondents.

Thus, a comparative examination brings to light the fact that a cleavage between the mindset of urban formal sector and other respondents is glaring and obvious. This section is well-educated, born and brought up in a modern, less restrictive environment and hence radiates the confidence of being lesser than none. Such feelings are lacking not only in tribal and rural communities but also in the majority of their counterparts in household and informal sections of the urban community.

Women in Patriarchal Society

Patriarchy is a structure underlying the subordination of women. While Lesigner defines patriarchy as the complex of ideology and institutions that maintain male privilege, according to Chen, it is a set of social relations with a material base which enables men to dominate women.[9]

The concept of patriarchy is difficult to grapple with, though women face it in various spheres of everyday life. This concept is widely debated and various explanations and definitions have been forwarded. At one level, patriarchy is understood as an ideology which arises out of men's power to exchange women between kinship groups; as a symbolic male principle; to express male control over women's sexuality and fertility; and to describe the institutional structure of male domination.[10] At another level, the concept of patriarchy characterizes the structures and social arrangement within which women's oppression is organized and maintained. Patriarchy is viewed as an institutionalized social practice diffused through all spheres of social life. Thus, patriarchy not only extends to the family but also to the control of the economy, polity, religion, medical science and many other institutions. This spread of patriarchal practice can be understood as 'extended patriarchy'.[11]

Since time immemorial, women have been subjugated and relegated to the background of our social fabric. Social order confined their activities within the four walls of the house and they are perceived to reproduce life and take care of household affairs. These activities are considered insignificant as compared to those that their male counterparts perform, i.e. producing material goods. Males defined the social order and established norms of morality for women's behaviour. Thus emerged a patriarchal social order where males are in a commanding and dominating position.

It was found that the respondents across all communities unanimously blamed the patriarchal society as the cause of all the ills and wrongs which are plaguing women. We probed further to examine their agony and determined the reasons for feeling so.

From the data presented in Table 6.2, it is clear that 31.4% of the respondents felt that the patriarchal society imposes constraints in social life and entails rigidity. The proportion of rural respondents holding this opinion was slightly higher (35%) as compared to their tribal and urban counterparts (31% and 27.5%, respectively). Within urban society, this viewpoint emerged from 25% each of the formal and household sector respondents and increased to 37.5% in the informal sector.

Table 6.2 *Demeaning of Women in Patriarchal Society*

Response	*Tribal N=80*	*Rural N=80*	*Urban*				*Total N=280*
			Household N=40	*Informal N=40*	*Formal N=40*	*Sub-Total N=120*	
Rigidity and constraints in social life	25 (31.3)	28 (35.0)	10 (25.0)	15 (37.5)	10 (25.0)	35 (29.1)	88 (31.4)
Physical insecurity	20 (25.0)	25 (31.3)	10 (25.0)	10 (25.0)	5 (12.5)	25 (20.8)	70 (25.0)
Denial of right in ancestral property	—	2 (2.5)	8 (20.0)	—	20 (50.0)	28 (23.3)	30 (10.7)
Economic dependency	5 (6.2)	20 (25.0)	12 (30.0)	15 (37.5)	4 (10.0)	31 (25.8)	56 (20.0)
Denial of religious rights	20 (25.0)	—	—	—	—	—	20 (7.1)
DK/NR	10 (12.5)	5 (6.2)	—	—	1 (2.5)	1 (0.8)	16 (5.7)
Total	80 (100)	80 (100)	40 (100)	40 (100)	40 (100)	120 (100)	280 (100)

Figures in parentheses indicate percentages.

Constraints imposed by society and their ramifications on the day-to-day life of women vary across strata. The concept of seclusion and observance of *purdah* is not uniform and class acts as an important variable in this respect. In rural areas, lower-caste working women do not generally observe *purdah* and this practice is confined to women from well-to-do families only where they were secluded and confined to their houses. This practice also varies among regions, communities and according to the level of education.

In the tribal community, girls are free from all restrictions till the time they get married. Married Garasia women also observed *purdah* and were confined to their husband's home. Shame and honour were associated with their conduct with in-laws and village elders in their affinal village. Although they were restricted from socializing in their in-laws' village, they could freely meet people from their natal village. She has no right to land or property or even her own children. In any eventuality of divorce or death of the husband, she may move away and remarry but her children remain with her husband's family. In case of remarriage, her new husband is required to pay compensation to her previous husband or brideprice to her parents. Such issues are settled through the Caste Panchayat where tribal women have neither representation nor any right to express themselves. They remain mute spectators and have no control on their sexuality.

Even in the rural context, women have little say in day-to-day decisions regarding religious functions, marriages, family affairs, etc. The magnitude of rigidity is slightly reduced in the urban household and informal sectors due to more exposure to urban lifestyles. It is only in the urban formal sector that women have become economically independent and have broken the shackles of rigidity and constraints faced by others. However, even working/professional formal sector women experienced unique constrains and had to strike a fine balance between their household and professional responsibilities.

One-fourth (25%) of the total respondents were of the opinion that the patriarchal society inculcated among them a feeling of physical insecurity. A total of 21% of the urban respondents held the above perception, which increased to 25% in the tribal and 31% in the rural community. Even within the urban section, this feeling was witnessed in household and informal sectors (25% each) as compared to only 12.5% in the formal sector. Only 11% of the total respondents felt the pinch that they were denied the right to ancestral property. These feelings had no relevance for tribal respondents and found favour with only 2.5% of rural respondents. Such feelings mainly emerged from 50% of urban formal sector and 20% of urban household sector respondents.

The data clearly points to the fact that right from birth, a girl child is considered and made to realize that she is *paraya dhan* (other's property) and has no right over her father's property. It is ironic that even in her husband's home, her status is no better. A married woman foregoes the claim from her ancestral property in favour of her brother as she feels she can depend upon him for protection through her entire life.

Seen from the total perspective, 20% of respondents said that control over resources remained with male members, which made them economically vulnerable. Surprisingly, this insecurity was predominant in urban (26%) and rural (25%) respondents only. Only 6.2% of tribal respondents shared this viewpoint. Amongst urban respondents, 37.5% of informal, 30% of household and only 10% of formal sector women expressed this. In the rural as well as urban informal sector, even working women have to give their earnings to male members of the household. In contrast, only 10% of the formal sector respondents were economically insecure. Self-reliance of formal sector respondents was reflective of their higher education, exposure and self-confidence.

Respondents who said that societal norms denied them religious rights constituted 7% of the total set. These feelings were confined to tribal respondents. It is ironic that even after marriage, a Garasia wife is considered an outsider in her husband's clan. She is not entitled to cook, distribute and eat in religious feasts. This remains a prerogative of the Garasia menfolk.

Put briefly, tribal women have no significance during religious rituals at the family or community level and remain passive observers. This is in total contrast to the norms of rural and urban societies where a wife is regarded as *ardhangini* (better half) and no religious activity can culminate in her absence.

Since patriarchal society is responsible for the lower status of women, the respondents were asked whether they think that a matriarchal society can benefit women? Results are tabulated in Table 6.3.

Table 6.3 *Views of Respondents on Matriarchal Society*

Matriarchal Society can benefit women?	*Tribal N=80*	*Rural N=80*	*Urban*				*Total N=280*
			Household N=40	*Informal N=40*	*Formal N=40*	*Sub-Total N=120*	
Agree	10(12.5)	25(31.3)	30(75.0)	25(62.5)	35(87.5)	90(75.0)	125(44.6)
Undecided	—	20(25.0)	5(12.5)	10(25.0)	—	15(12.5)	35(12.5)
Disagree	—	15(18.7)	5(12.5)	5(12.5)	5(12.5)	15(12.5)	30(10.7)
DK/NR	70(87.5)	20(25.0)	—	—	—	—	90(32.2)
Total	80(100)	80(100)	40(100)	40(100)	40(100)	120(100)	280(100)

Figures in parentheses indicate percentages.

Respondents agreeing with the standpoint were 44.6% and included 75% urban, 31% rural and 12.5% tribal respondents. Within the urban society, the lion's share, i.e. 87.5% was bagged by the formal sector respondents, followed by 62.5% of informal sector and 75% of household sector respondents. As against this, respondents who were sceptical that such an arrangement would lead to any improvement in the status of women were 12.5% in total. In all, 12.5% of the urban respondents of all sectors and 19% of the rural respondents subscribed to this opinion. The data highlighted that while a little more than one-tenth (10.7%) of the total respondents were undecided on this issue, nearly one-third (32%) were unable to comprehend and hence did not reply. The tribal respondents outnumbered the rural ones in this category. Thus, it can be said that majority of urban and rural respondents favoured a matriarchal society. However, most of the tribal respondents were unable to understand and reply on this issue.

Female Body and Social Control

'... to control women's bodies is to control their personalities and represent an act of authority over the body in the interests of public order organized around male values of what is rational.'[12] Male and female bodies were seen to be different in structure and function. Men and women are different because the active male was said to have bigger brains, more intelligence, whereas females were said to be passive and sluggish.[13]

Whenever a woman succumbs to temptation or becomes a victim of social violence, she cannot easily remain within the folds of respectability. A woman who has been raped is not easily accepted even by her own family. Women routinely suffer whenever there is caste or communal violence or a struggle between landowners and tenants or labourers. It is well accepted that poor or low-caste women in rural areas as well as urban slums are available for sexual abuse by those possessing economic, political or merely physical power.

Changes in Dressing Pattern

The traditional attire of Rajasthani women is losing out to modern urban influences. Dressing is considered an expression and extension of one's personality. Even tribals are very conscious of their personal grooming and make-up even when going out for work. In response to a question whether they approved of wearing modern western dresses, such as jeans, skirts, midis, minis, etc. the answers were varied. These can be seen in Table 6.4.

Disapproval of such influences in dressing patterns emerged from 37% of the total respondents and included nearly 50% of urban and 56% of rural respondents. Within the urban setting, the informal sector women (67.5%) predominated their counterparts in household sector (50%) and formal sector (30%). In contrast, nearly 14% of the total respondents opined that women should be free to wear as per their liking. This found favour amongst 45% of urban formal sector women while only 10% women in informal sector and 30% in household sector followed them. Besides, 6.3% of the rural respondents also agreed with above.

Table 6.4 *Approval of Modern Attire by Respondents*

Response categories	*Tribal N=80*	*Rural N=80*	*Urban*				*Total N=280*
			Household N=40	*Informal N=40*	*Formal N=40*	*Sub-Total N=120*	
Agree	—	5(6.3)	12(30.0)	4(10.0)	18(45.0)	34(28.3)	39(13.9)
Undecided	5(6.3)	10(12.5)	5(12.5)	8(20.0)	10(25.0)	23(19.2)	38(13.6)
Disagree	—	45(56.2)	20(50.0)	27(67.5)	12(30.0)	59(49.2)	104(37.1)
DK/NR	75(93.7)	20(25.0)	3(7.5)	1(2.5)	—	4(3.3)	99(35.4)
Total	80(100)	80(100)	40(100)	40(100)	40(100)	120(100)	280(100)

Figures in parentheses indicate percentages.

Of the remainder, a total of 13.6% respondents were undecided on this issue, while about 35% were not exposed enough to understand and addressed this issue in the right perspective. Thus, in brief, the approval of choosing western dress emerges strongly from only the urban sector respondents.

Free Movement of Women

Traditionally, women are considered to require protection and guidance, hence they seldom ventured out alone and were confined to and involved in household chores. With passage of time, women have become more outgoing. The respondents also expressed their views on this (Table 6.5).

Nearly 23% were in favour of freer movement of women. This view was confined to 52% of urban respondents and found favour amongst only 2.5% of rural respondents. None of the tribal respondents shared this viewpoint. Around 52% of the respondents did not approve of women moving alone. This insecurity was more predominant in tribal (77.5%) respondents, followed by their rural counterparts (69%). Within urban community, this disapproval emerged from 40% of informal sector, 25% household sector and only 5% of formal sector women. The data is clearly illustrative of the fact that the needs and requirements of urban lifestyle, coupled with education and exposure, have led to acceptability of more outgoing roles for women.

Table 6.5 *Free Movement of Women*

Response categories	*Tribal N=80*	*Rural N=80*	*Urban*				*Total N=280*
			Household N=40	*Informal N=40*	*Formal N=40*	*Sub-Total N=120*	
Agree	—	2(2.5)	20(50.0)	12(30.0)	30(75.0)	62(51.7)	64(22.9)
Undecided	10(12.5)	12(15.0)	10(25.0)	12(30.0)	8(20.0)	30(25.0)	52(18.6)
Disagree	62(77.5)	55(68.8)	10(25.0)	16(40.0)	2(5.0)	28(23.3)	145(51.7)
DK/NR	8(10.0)	11(13.6)	—	—	—	—	19(6.8)
Total	80(100)	80(100)	40(100)	40(100)	40(100)	120(100)	280(100)

Figures in parentheses indicate percentages.

Women's Control over Fertility

The most important fact in a woman's life is to experience motherhood. However, it is ironic that even this decision is not within her control. She is looked upon to meet the needs of the household and also satisfy the sexual urge of her husband. Caught in this conflict, she becomes a mute spectator and loses control even over her own body. There is hardly any gap between marriage and childbirth and she is torn in the cycle of frequent childbirths. This is more so in rural and tribal areas where their husbands are insecure and want to burden their young wives with family responsibilities at the earliest. Family planning loses its relevance due to overbearing societal and family pressures for an ideal family with many children. The respondents were asked as to how they empathized with this situation (Table 6.6).

Table 6.6 *Women's Control over Fertility*

Response categories	*Tribal N=80*	*Rural N=80*	*Urban*				*Total N=280*
			Household N=40	*Informal N=40*	*Formal N=40*	*Sub-Total N=120*	
Agree	15(18.8)	40(50.0)	20(50.0)	27(67.5)	30(75.0)	77(64.2)	132(47.1)
Disagree	20(25.0)	20(25.0)	16(40.0)	5(12.5)	10(25.0)	31(25.8)	71(25.4)
Undecided	45(56.2)	20(25.0)	4(10.0)	8(20.0)	—	12(10.0)	77(27.5)
Total	80(100)	80(100)	40(100)	40(100)	40(100)	120(100)	280(100)

Figures in parentheses indicate percentages.

Respondents who wholly or partly endorsed the view that a woman should have the right to decide when to have children constituted nearly half (47%) of the total. Such respondents included 64% urban, 50% rural and nearly 19% tribal women.

As against this, respondents who disagreed with this were nearly one-fourth (25.4%) of the total and comprised 25% each of tribal and rural women.

Thus, it can be inferred that in the tribal society, children are considered to belong to father's lineage and Garasias strongly believe that women merely provide the space for development and structure of the child in the womb. Genetic content for the child is believed to be provided by *admi ka pani* (semen). With such conditioning, majority of tribal women were either undecided or disagreed that women should have any right regarding childbirth.

Such traditional and faulty myths are broken by changing viewpoint of rural respondents. Hence, half of the respondents vocally supported the right of women and deciding when to have children.

Urban household sector is nearly equally divided amongst those approving and disapproving of such empowerment of women. It is interesting to note that two-thirds of the informal sector women supported empowering women in this context. This may be because this section bears the maximum brunt due to lack of resources, no education and difficulty in coping with household and other responsibility.

Adding another dimension, the respondents were asked to think hypothetically if the status of women would be better if they were devoid of the process of maternity. Table 6.7a indicates that nearly half (48.2%) the respondents agreed that the status of women would be better in this respect. In all, 62.5% of urban, 50% of rural and 25% of tribal women were of this opinion. Disagreement with the hypothesis emerged from 22.2% of the total respondents. Tribal women give utmost importance to their fertility and consider early and numerous childbirths as a means of securing their stronghold in the husband's family. Divorce is common if she is unable to give birth to children. In rural and urban societies, the psychological importance of motherhood is well realized and hence one-fourth (25%) of the respondents find absence of this aspect unimaginable. Nearly 20% were undecided on this issue.

The respondents who said that absence of maternity would improve the status of women were asked to elucidate the reasons: Table 6.7b.

Table 6.7a *Views of Women on Maternity*

Response categories	*Tribal N=80*	*Rural N=80*	*Urban*				*Total N=280*
			Household N=40	*Informal N=40*	*Formal N=40*	*Sub-Total N=120*	
Agree	20(25.0)	40(50.0)	30(75.0)	15(37.5)	30(75.0)	75(62.5)	135(48.2)
Disagree	40(50.0)	20(25.0)	10(25.0)	10(25.0)	10(25.0)	30(25.0)	90(32.2)
Undecided	20(25.0)	25(20.0)	—	15(37.5)	—	15(12.5)	55(19.6)
Total	80(100)	80(100)	40(100)	40(100)	40(100)	120(100)	280(100)

Figures in parentheses indicate percentages.

More than one-fourth (26.7%) said that women would be better off without maternity as this would significantly reduce their level of responsibility. Besides rural society, such feelings were also more pronounced in the formal and informal sectors of the urban society. Since the household sector women are geared towards handling household responsibilities, very few agreed with these feelings.

Table 6.7b *Benefits from Lack of Maternity*

Benefits	*Tribal N=20*	*Rural N=40*	*Urban*				*Total N=135*
			Household N=30	*Informal N=15*	*Formal N=30*	*Sub-Total N=75*	
Stronger body	5(25.0) [18.5]	10(25.0) [37.0]	8(26.7) [29.6]	4(26.6) [14.8]	—	12(16.0)[44.4]	27(20.0)[100.0]
Physical/mental toughness	—	—	14(46.6) [51.8]	3(20.0) [11.1]	10(33.3) [37.0]	27(36.0) [100.0]	27(20.0)[100.0]
Less emotional	—	8(20.0) [44.4]	5(16.6) [27.7]	—	5(16.6) [27.7]	10(13.3)[55.5]	18(13.3)[100.0]
No responsibility	5(25.0) [13.8]	10(25.0) [27.8]	1(3.3) [2.7]	5(33.4) [13.8]	15(50.0) [41.6]	21(28.0)[58.3]	36(26.7)[100.0]
No death during pregnancy	10(50.0)[37.0]	12(30.0) [44.4]	2(6.6) [7.4]	3(20.0) [11.1]	—	5(6.7) [18.5]	27(20.0)[100.0]
Total	20(100)	40(100)	30(100)	15(100)	30(100)	75(100)	135(100)

Figures in parentheses indicate percentages.

Belief that lack of maternity would not result in any death during pregnancy emerged from 20% of the respondents. Such women comprised 18.5% of the urban sector and this number increased to 37% in tribal and 44.4% in rural areas, respectively. Within urban society, this view was confined to 11.1% in informal sector and 7.4% in household sector. The data is reflective of the level of health care facilities available to pregnant women across all sections. Pregnancy-related deaths were negligible amongst urban formal sector respondents, hence none of the respondents expressed this viewpoint.

Again, one-fifth of the total respondents opined that women would be devoid of physical weakness ones they were spared from this cycle of motherhood. This view came from 44.4% urban, 37% rural and 18.5% tribal respondents. It was also observed that numerous and frequent pregnancies with little spacing placed immense strain on the malnourished and weak body structure of respondents in all communities. Due to their socio-economic conditions, they were unable to voice their opinion as to when to have children. They succumbed to family pressure and went all out to please their husband. It is pertinent to note that none of urban formal sector respondents belonged to this category as they were mostly self-reliant and assertive about their feelings.

Similar proportion (20%) of the total respondents felt that women would be physically and mentally tougher like men if they did not undergo the process of motherhood. All these respondents belonged to urban society and included 37% in formal sector, 11.1% in informal sector and 51.8% in household sector. And, finally, nearly 13% were of the view that women would be less emotional in such a situation. These feelings were confined to 55.5% of urban and 44.4% of rural women.

Significance of Menstrual Process in Woman's Life

In medicine, menstruation is considered a disorder, as impure and having an adverse impact on women's life. It is described in negative terms, as failed production because egg implementation does not take place.

These metaphors come alive when a menstruating woman is confined to a room and her movement curtailed. The initiation rituals for females emphasize infertility, unlike the ones for males. The woman is acknowledged as a 'concrete sexual being' for the rest of her life. Thus, the orientation of the body is based on the concept of purity and protection of females. The woman has to maintain laws regarding pollution and purity for life. When women go to lead a sexually active life, they feel their bodies are submitted and used and are a continuous source of pollution. The 'Hindi tests' emphasize the women's accessibility to the male, her return to purity and her obligation to increase the linkage.[14] The female body absorbs the sins of the husband and any danger to him. The maternal body is symbolic of regenerating of the maternal and social universe. The proponents of the argument believe that women produce 'perishable bodies' and men produce 'enduring symbol', therefore, men are superior to women and must control women.[15] Female sexuality is controlled to maintain the super status of men. Despite several variations, it becomes abundantly clear that there are many restrictions on menstruating women, with their bases in the beliefs of the people that this particular bodily process makes women distinctly inferior to men. The respondents were asked if they felt that their menstrual process relegated them to a status lower than men. The results in Table 6.8 show that a big majority (72%) replied in the affirmative. Proportion of such respondents was only 44% in urban community, which rose significantly to 87.5% in rural and 97.5% in tribal community. Within urban community, this feeling was more predominant amongst three-fourths of the informal sector respondents.

Table 6.8 *Inferior Status Due to Menstrual Process*

Inferior status due to menstrual process	*Tribal N=80*	*Rural N=80*	*Urban*				*Total N=280*
			Household N=40	*Informal N=40*	*Formal N=40*	*Sub-Total N=120*	
Yes	78(97.5)	70(87.5)	15(37.5)	30(75.0)	8(20.0)	53(44.2)	201(71.8)
No	2(3.75)	10(12.5)	25(62.5)	10(25.0)	32(80.0)	67(55.8)	79(28.2)
Total	80(100)	80(100)	40(100)	40(100)	40(100)	120(100)	280(100)

Figures in parentheses indicate percentages.

The prohibition on religious activity during menstruation was universal in all the three communities: tribal, rural and urban. However, the extent of restrictions, taboos and prohibitions regarding daily lifestyle were more stringent in tribal and rural set-ups. Tribal women referred to the menstrual process as *gaaba aave*. During this period, the husband cooks for the entire family and they are not allowed to touch even water vessels. They are prohibited to enter fields during sowing and threshing as this can lead to various crop diseases and also reduce the yield. They have to be very careful in disposing of their menstrual pads as these can be misused by *Devala* as menstrual blood is believed to attract evil spirits, ghosts and even some Hindu deities.

In the rural set-up, restrictions remain broadly the same; however, their level varies amongst castes. Women of upper castes are expected to follow stricter rules of behaviour during menstruation and keep themselves aloof from ordinary circulation and household activities. In contrast, women of middle and lower castes feel that bathing and washing of their hair suffices to make them fit for cooking and most other household jobs.

In urban context, these restrictions are diluted and many urban educated families, even among upper castes, have done away with restrictions on routine activity during menstruation. However, menstruating women of all castes across all societies still keep themselves away from taking part in rituals and worship. Majority consider this as a natural biological process and feel that this in no way demeans the status of women in society.

Women's Image in Mass Media

Media of mass communication plays a crucial role in social change. As Kamla Bhasin puts it: 'More frightening than the direct reach of media, however, is its indirect influence. By gradually shaping public opinion, personal beliefs and even people's self-perception, media influences the process of socialization and shapes ideology and thinking.'[16]

Media is often said to lead people's thoughts and mould public opinion. Press, radio, television and films have a very important role to change the standard of women mass of India.

By offering information or entertainment, media reflects images of society consciously or unconsciously. But, when it comes to projecting the image of women, every mass media portrays a regulative image. Media images of women are, by and large, confined to the traditional archetypes – treating women in their domestic roles and sexual appeal – ignoring their significant contribution to society. Women's struggles for economic independence, political and legal rights, for a meaningful identity within marriage and for relevant education fail to get adequate coverage even in the government-controlled electronic media.

According to Kirti Kumar, the portrayal of women in advertisements reinforces and creates the impression of women being used as a mere sex symbol. Advertisements use beautiful women to sell the products to both male and female consumers by virtue of the two-dimensional role as housewife, mother and daughter and her function as a decorative sexual object. Women's entire being is reduced to her physical appearance. Advertisers exploit women's sex appeal by vulgar exposure of her body. Both in their context and presentation, such advertisements are aimed at attracting male consumers. Such a distorted portrayal of woman is not only humiliating and dehumanizing, it also reinforces male sexist attitude towards treating women as a play thing.[17]

Saroj Zaveri says such a portrayal of women conveys that the woman is only a toy and anybody can take liberty with her. This type of depiction is responsible for various offences like violence, kidnapping, abduction and rape. In the social frame as it is, women are not still bold enough either to fight this type of violence or to expose them. As such, the bad elements get the licence for playing mischief.[18]

According to Mala Gupta, there is a feeling of remorse on seeing the distorted pictures/photos, mostly with overexposed women. These appear often undesirable and vulgar. Many a time, it is not possible to watch them in the presence of one's daughter, sister or mother. The main objective of the advertisers is to attract customers with a view to earning money by sale of their products. But this they do with the least respect and regard to women and society and its effect on the younger generation. Women are being portrayed negatively to the young boys and girls with scant regard to Indian culture.[19]

Projections of rape and sex in the media have incurred the wrath of women, who have become extremely conscious of their rights and responsibilities. Scores of women's organizations have vehemently protested against this practice either in movies, advertisements or in posters, handbills and at other places. Some individuals have also written to the authorities to tighten curbs on advertisements giving too much exposure of the weaker sex.

The National Commission for Women recently called on the women members of Parliament and voiced its ire at the 'sacrilege' being committed on them. It demanded that the government should evolve a 'decent' media policy on the portrayal of women in films and other media in a 'positive manner'. The Commission also expressed its resentment against frequent depiction of gang-rapes. In buses, molestation of women is a common occurrence and this can be attributed mostly to watching of films and TV serials. Thus, women organizations strongly feel that the moral standards in society are going down. They have urged the authorities to come down heavily on anti-social elements. Social values are being forgotten, imitation of foreign culture seems to be the order of the day and this has already proved disastrous. The quality has completely vanished and today people by and large see the most ghastly scenes of violence and crimes against women.[20]

The respondents were asked about the portrayal of women as sex symbols in advertisements. Tribal and rural respondents were not exposed and were mostly unaware of the complexities of this issue. However, in some cases, they hesitantly acknowledged an increase in sex-related crimes due to percolation of such urban influences in their society.

Urban respondents were more vocal and vehemently denied any justification for these trends. According to them, exposure and depiction of women as objects of consumption had led to the overall deterioration of moral standards and resulted in an increase in instances of molestation, rapes, gang-rapes, etc. Merely enacting laws won't help, collective efforts are required by intellectuals, literates and women organizations to denounce such inferior portrayal of women. All conscious citizens have to raise their voice against the unfair projection of women in the media. Only then can this vicious cycle be broken.

Notes

1. Moghadam, Valenline M., 1990. *WIDER Research for Action – Gender, Development and Policy: Towards Equity and Empowerment,* World Institute for Development Research of the United Nations University.
2. Papanek, Hanna, 1989. *Socialization for Inequality: Entitlements, the Value of Women and Domestic Hierarchies,* Mimeo, Centre for Asian Development Studies, Boston University.
3. De Lauretis, Teresa, 1989. *Technologies of Gender,* Bloomington: University of Indian Press.
4. Rao, Sudha and M.D. Gayatri Devi Dutt, 1999. 'Gender Bias and Socialization through the Primary School Curriculum in Karnataka', in R. Indira and Deepak Kumar Behera (eds), *Gender and Society in India,* New Delhi: Manak Publications Pvt. Ltd., pp. 142–154.
5. Young, F.L. Fort and M. Danner, 1994. 'Moving from the Status of Women to Gender Inequality', *International Sociology,* 9(1): 55–77.
6. Krishna Raj, M., 1989. 'Women's Issues in India: Is the Feminist Perspective of the West Totally Irrelevant to India', *Seminar Abstract, Research Unit on Women's Studies.* UGC Project No. 38.
7. Lengermann, P.M. and J.M.N. Brantley, 1988. 'Contemporary Feminist Theory,' in George Ritzer, *Contemporary Sociological Theory,* New York: Alfred A. Knopf, pp. 296–309.
8. Dube, Leela, 1997. *Women and Kinship: Comparative Perspectives on Gender in South and South-East Asia,* New Delhi: Vistar Publications, pp. 49–59.
9. Palriwala, R., 1990. 'Introduction' in Leela Dube and Raja Palriwala (eds), *Structures and Strategies: Women, Work and Family,* New Delhi: Sage Publications, pp. 41–45.

10. Rowbotham, Shiela, 1981. *The Trouble with 'Patriarchy' in No Turning Back: Writing from the Women's Liberation Movement 1975–80.* London: The Woman's Press, pp. 72–78.
11. Fisher, Sue, 1987. 'Good Women After All: Cultural Definitions and Social Control,' in J.F. Mc Donough and R.C. Saari (eds), *The Trapped Women: Catch 22 in Deviance and Control*, Newbury: Sage.
12. Turner, Bryan S., 1984. *The Body and Society: Explorations in Social Theory,* New York: Basil Blackwell.
13. Martin, Emily, 1987. *The Woman in the Body: A Cultural Analysis of Reproduction,* Boston: Press Boston.
14. Das, Veena, 1988. 'Feminity and Orientation to the Body', in Kaurna Chanana (ed.), *Socialization, Education and Women*, New Delhi: Orient Longman, pp. 193–207.
15. Ortner, S.B., 1974. 'Is Female to Male as Nature is to Culture?', in M.A. Rosaldo and L. Lamphere (eds), *Women, Culture and Society,* Stanford: Stanford University Press, pp. 67–68.
16. Bhasin, Kamala and Bina Agarwal (eds), 1984. 'Women and Media', *Kali for Women*, Delhi.
17. Kumar, Kirti, 1993. 'Mass Media is Promoting Gender Inequality', *Kurukshetra,* December, pp. 5–7.
18. Zaveri, Saroj, 1993. 'Stop Negative Portrayal of Women in Mass-Media!', *Kurukshetra,* December, p. 23.
19. Gupta, Mala, 1993. 'Let Mass Media Help Build Positive Public Opinion about Women's Concerns', *Kurukshetra,* December, pp. 31–33.
20. Kaur, P.C., 1993. 'Curb This Obscenity Galore in Mass Media!', *Kurukshetra,* December, pp. 39–40.

7 Women, Leisure and Freedom

Women have to shoulder multifarious responsibilities. This workload keeps them busy for most of the time. In this context, it was pertinent to examine another aspect of their daily life, which is related to leisure time, or free time for enjoying with family and friends, listening to radio, watching television, going to movies, fairs, etc. The mode of utilization of leisure time also needed to be investigated as it too formed an important aspect of their life. It reflected their taste, degree of social interaction, intensity of their love for art and culture as well as their interest in different fields of activity.

Social adjustment enables a person to participate in social functions, enjoy the company of others, seek meeting with other people, etc. A socially adjusted person establishes spontaneous, easy and smooth interpersonal relationship. It promotes interaction and provides the opportunity of relaxation. The importance of leisure cannot be overemphasized as it relieves a person from tension. Work produces not only exhaustion but strain too. Leisure may be considered a compensation for hard work. 'Leisure is a source of relaxation from mental and nervous strain and fatigue caused by tensions.'[1]

Leisure is defined as a quality of human experience that has elements of choice and enjoyment associated with it. It is a personal aspect of people's lives that connects both active and passive forms of engaging activity. It is also a dimension of people's lives which occurs separate from or connected to other dimensions such as paid work, housework, religion, volunteering or family activities. It encompasses physical activities like sports as well as arts, away from home involvements and hobbies at home.[2] Leisure is commonly associated with a part of life where individuals exercise freedom of choice. As a corollary, leisure time is generally characterized by liberation from the constraints associated with employment, domestic work and other social obligations.

A number of scholars have observed that leisure affords people time and space to relax and recuperate from the stress and fatigue of daily activities. At the same time, it not only offers opportunities to express individuality and to be creative, it provides an important context for social network to be established and maintained.[3] Leisure is also seen as an avenue for the promotion of health through the psychological benefits associated with enjoyable leisure activities and sociability.[4]

Modi[5] has rightly pointed out that 'leisure is a social phenomenon that can be understood and explained only in the context of a social organization. Social structure influences the nature and form of leisure and its activities. In a given society, at a particular time, it allows, dictates or is conductive to a particular mode of leisure. It not only determines the form and nature of leisure but also determines the extent and limits of participation. The answer to questions such as *who* would participate, *in what, with, whom, when* and *where* and *up to what extent* is determined by the social structure of a society according to its nature and organization'.

Parker[6] argues that leisure activities are 'conditioned by various factors associated with the way people work'. In particular, he suggests, the amount of autonomy people have at work or, in other words, the amount of freedom to take decisions and organize their work, the degree of involvement they find in work and the level of intrinsic job satisfaction are directly related to their leisure activities. According to him, relationship between work and leisure falls into three main patterns: the extension pattern, the neutrality pattern and the opposition pattern.

In the extension pattern, work extends into leisure. There is no clear dividing line between the two. Activities in both spheres are similar, and work is a central life interest in family, rather than leisure. Time for activities, which can be defined exclusively as leisure, is short and is used mainly for the development of personality.

In the neutrality pattern, a fairly clear distinction is made between work and leisure. Activities in the two spheres differ and family life and leisure, rather than work, form the central life interest. This pattern is associated with occupations providing a medium to low degree of autonomy which require the use of only some of the individual's duties, and where satisfaction is with pay and working conditions rather than work itself. Hours of leisure are long compared to the extension pattern and are used mainly for relaxation. Leisure is often family-centred involving activities in which time is spent with family.

In the opposition pattern, work is sharply distinguished from leisure. Activities in the two are very different and leisure forms the central life interest. Hours of leisure are long and used mainly to recuperate from and compensate for work.

Leisure is a complex phenomenon. The very meaning of the term has changed continually. At times it has referred to a state of freedom, an absence of obligations, a cluster of activities; at others, it has suggested a mood of contemplation.[7]

Miller and Robinson[8] believe that leisure and recreation as cultural recreation are cultural universals, being found as common elements in the behaviour of individuals in all societies. According to Kaplan[9], the essential elements of leisure are:

- an antithesis to work as an economic function;
- a pleasant expectation and recollection;
- a minimum of involuntarily social role obligations;
- a psychological perception of freedom;
- a close affinity with cultural values;
- the inclusion of an entire range from inconsequence and insignificance to weightiness and importance; and
- often, but not necessarily, an activity characterized by the element of play.

For Kaplan, leisure is none of these by itself but all of them together within one or the other.

From the earliest days of civilization, man's leisure, recreation and play have been integrated with arts and creative expression. Not only is it true that even for the most primitive man there was leisure time, but also that the quality of leisure and level of civilization in any society were interlinked.

Culture can be viewed as the foundation of human life. It is the sum total of knowledge acquired through learning and shared experiences by members of a group. To agree with experts, culture is also an evolving heritage emanating from the life it nourishes.[10] The culture of a people encompasses all relations involving the vast majority of human activities, including those performed during free time. A greater portion of the culture of people or society finds its origin in free time.[11]

Leisure activities may be academic or intellectual, socio-religious, home-making and family-life activities or free-choice activities. Besides these preferred hobbies may include painting, gardening, writing stories, outdoor games or religious functions. Home-making activities include cooking and decorating the house, while academic leisure activities include reading and writing. Socio-religious activities include working for some welfare association or attending religious congregations. Free-choice activities may be listed as watching television or listening to radio, knitting, gardening, outdoor games, painting, gossiping, visiting friends, attending parties, going for a picnic or to movies, etc. Thus, these multiple activities may be performed by a person as a mode of utilization of his or her leisure time.

Leisure-time activities of tribal, rural and urban communities are vast and varied. A systematic study of these activities, therefore, required some broad classification in order to avoid confusion and overlapping. It was both convenient and congenial to bank upon the pattern of classification provided by Ishwar Modi in his book, *Leisure, Mass Media and Social Structure* (1985). This book contains almost all leisure time activities of social groups falling in urban, rural and tribal settings.

In this chapter, we examine the extent, dimensions and ramifications of leisure with reference to our women respondents in diverse backgrounds.

Average Leisure Time Available

At the outset, we attempted to examine the extent of leisure time at the disposal of respondents. Their responses, as tabulated in Table 7.1, reveal varied duration of leisure hours ranging from less than two hours to more than three hours per day.

Table 7.1 *Daily Leisure Time*

Leisure Time (hrs)	*Tribal N=80*	*Rural N=80*	*Urban*				*Total N=280*
			Household N=40	*Informal N=40*	*Formal N=40*	*Sub-Total N=120*	
< 2	51(63.8)	52(65.0)	6(15.0)	34(85.0)	8(20.0)	48(40.0)	151(53.9)
2–3	20(25.8)	18(22.5)	12(30.0)	6(15.0)	15(37.5)	33(27.5)	71(25.4)
> 3	9(11.2)	10(12.5)	22(55.0)	—	17(42.5)	39(32.5)	58(20.7)
Total	80(100)	80(100)	40(100)	40(100)	40(100)	120(100)	280(100)

Figures in parentheses indicate percentages.

The concept of leisure and its prevalence is more uncommon in rural and tribal set-ups, where the lifestyle demands extended working hours in the household as well as fields. A typical day for a tribal or a rural woman begins early in the morning with taking care of animals and cleaning the household and fetching drinking water. After preparing food, she goes to the fields and slogs till late afternoon. In the evening, again, she prepares food and feeds family and before sleeping, starts preparing for the next day. Hence, it is obvious that a woman gets very little time for self-indulgence. This trend can be further realized when we study distribution of women having more leisure time and invariably we find most of such respondents belonging to the urban set-up. Within urban community, 85% respondents belonged to the informal sector while 15% and 20% belonged to household and formal sectors, respectively. It is pertinent to note that urban informal sector women, crushed between dual responsibilities of household and outside work, have relatively limited leisure time at their disposal.

Respondents who enjoyed leisure activities for two to three hours daily constituted 27.5% of urban, 22.5% of rural and slightly less than 25% of tribal respondents. Amongst urban, while 37.5% were attached to the formal sector, the corresponding figures of respondents in the informal and household sectors were 15% and 30%, respectively. And, the remaining 21% of the total respondents had more than three hours of leisure time. Within the urban respondents of this category, more than half (55%) from the household sector and 42.5% from the formal sector and none from the informal sector had more than three hours of leisure time. It is interesting to note that in spite of their professional responsibilities, 42.5% of the formal sector respondents had maximum leisure time. This may be because of financial independence that they are able to afford part-time/full-time domestic help for managing routine chores. An appreciable member (55%) of household sector women also enjoy more than three hours of leisure time. This can be attributed to the fact that they are able to wind up domestic chores by late morning and enjoy privacy in leisure time before children return from school. The only exception seems to be in the case of informal sector respondents, where the majority (85%) get even less than two hours of leisure time since they are sandwiched between household and work pressure. It was observed that younger women in tribal and rural set-ups had a tight and hectic schedule with little time for leisure and relaxation. It is the middle-aged or older womenfolk who have relatively much more free time at their disposal.

Preferred Leisure and Recreational Activities

The respondents were asked to specify their preferred leisure and recreational activities (Table 7.2).

The three categories that emerged as preferred leisure activities were group-oriented, family-oriented, and economic and self-employing. Nearly one-fourth (24.6%) of the total respondents preferred to remain occupied with group-oriented activities. While in the rural and tribal contexts, the nature of such activities was confined to chatting, gossiping, meeting friends, relatives, neighbours, etc. and visiting fairs and *melas*, in case of urban respondents, such activities included social gatherings, attending and throwing parties, going to coffee houses, restaurants, shopping, etc. with friends, relatives and colleagues.

Table 7.2 *Preferred Leisure and Recreational Activities*

Activities	*Tribal N=80*	*Rural N=80*	*Urban*				*Total N=280*
			Household N=40	*Informal N=40*	*Formal N=40*	*Sub-Total N=120*	
Group-oriented	25 (31.3)	25 (31.3)	8 (20.0)	6 (15.0)	5 (12.5)	19 (15.8)	69 (24.6)
Family-oriented	21 (26.2)	10 (12.5)	9 (22.5)	8 (20.0)	9 (22.5)	26 (21.7)	57 (20.4)
Economic and self-employing	17 (21.3)	20 (25.0)	5 (12.5)	10 (25.0)	2 (5.0)	17 (14.2)	54 (19.3)
Quietistic	5 (6.3)	6 (7.5)	7 (17.5)	8 (20.0)	7 (17.5)	22 (18.3)	33 (11.8)
Artistic and cultural	4 (5.0)	—	—	—	—	—	4 (1.4)
Religious	8 (10.0)	5 (6.2)	1 (2.5)	—	—	1 (0.8)	14 (5.0)
Audio-visual	—	8 (10.0)	4 (10.0)	5 (12.5)	7 (17.5)	16 (13.3)	24 (8.5)
Intellectual	—	—	3 (7.5)	—	8 (20.0)	11 (6.7)	11 (3.9)
Hobby-oriented	—	4 (5.0)	3 (7.5)	3 (7.5)	—	6 (5.0)	10 (3.6)
Games and sports	—	—	—	—	2 (5.0)	2 (1.6)	2 (0.7)
Deviant	—	29 (2.5)	—	—	—	—	2 (0.7)
Total	80 (100)	80 (100)	40 (100)	40 (100)	40 (100)	120 (100)	120 (100)

Figures in parentheses indicate percentages.

More than one-fifth (20.4%) of the respondents relished family-oriented activities during leisure time. They devoted their attention to the needs and wants of children and elders in their family and talked about family issues. Another 19.3% were found engaged in self-employing activities during their free time. Tribal and rural women find very little time for self-indulgence. Whatever respite they get from their hectic schedule, they devote to non-routine works. In case of urban respondents. the major self-employing activities include cleaning house, washing clothes, shopping, and the like.

Other activities which provide relaxation and recreation to a total of 11.8% respondents fall under the category of quietistic activities, and include sitting idle, catching a nap, walking in the garden, taking rest, etc. Audio-visual means of entertainment are preferred by 8.5% of the total respondents. Effect of such means is already quite dominant in urban households and is percolating to rural areas too. However, tribal areas are insulated from the influence of these means. For another 5% of respondents, who enjoyed religious activities, were of the view that these also helped them in gaining mental peace and tranquillity. Nearly 4% of the respondents (limited to urban set-up) were satisfying their intellectual and sensitive quotient by reading and writing.

Viewed from the three broad groups under study, it was found that nearly one-third (31.3%) of the tribal (Garasia) respondents preferred group activities such as chatting and gossiping. This was their emotional outlet where they discussed family and societal issues. They loved to go to the marketplace with other women or visited fairs and festivals where they enjoyed without any inhibition. Indulging in family-oriented activities during leisure found favour with 26.2% of Garasia women. Keeping themselves occupied with self-employing and economic activities were preferred by more than one-fifth (21.3%) of tribal respondents. One-tenth (10%) of these respondents found solace in religious activities. Another 5% respondents in this category exhibited artistic and cultural traits, which found expression in decorating walls and floors with *mandana,* comprising motifs of floral, animals and birds, etc. Only 6.3% of respondents preferred quietistic activities such as sitting idle, day-time sleeping, etc. to relax.

In the rural context, the pattern of preferred leisure activities was quite similar to tribal counterparts with majority (31.3%) of the respondents preferring group-oriented activities, followed by economic and self-employing (25%), family-oriented (12.5%), audio-visual (10%), quietistic (7.5%), religious (6.2%), hobby-oriented (5%) and deviant activities (2.5%). While the proportion of women preferring group-oriented activities remained the same as in tribal context, the proportion of rural women preferring family-oriented activities reduced to 12.5% as compared to 26.2% of their tribal counterparts. It is interesting to see the influence of audio-visual aids as the preferred means of entertainment for 10% of rural respondents. Rural respondents found time to listen/watch their favourite programmes on radio/TV and also occasionally went to see films. In contrast, tribal respondents are relatively less exposed to these modern means of entertainment. In all, 5% of rural respondents utilized their free time for pursuing hobbies.

Amongst urban household sector respondents, three major recreational activities fall under the category of 'family-oriented', followed by 'group-oriented' and 'quietistic' activities. Nearly one-fourth (22.5%) of household sector women utilized their spare time in family-oriented jobs, while one-fifth (20%) gossiped with friends, relatives and neighbours or went out with them for shopping, or for watching movies. This class of respondents was more well-off financially and they attended and threw parties to enjoy in the company of friends. Lazing around and idly passing their leisure time, literally doing nothing, was preferred by 17.5% of respondents. This provides an insight into the lack of pressure in the lifestyle of urban household sector respondents. The proportion of women in the urban household category productively using their free time for activities like cleaning, reorganizing household things, cooking snacks, etc. stood at 12.5%. One-tenth (10%) of them relaxed by watching their favourite soap operas or family serials and watching films and film-based programmes. This section of women was educated, exposed and sensitive to issues, hence 7.5% of them preferred leisure activities such as reading and writing, exhibiting their intellectual bent of mind. Similar proportion (7.5%) of respondents pursued hobbies such as gardening, embroidery, painting, cooking special dishes, etc.

Urban informal sector respondents were found sandwiched between the dual pressure of household and outside responsibilities and belonged mainly to the lower economic class of society, which was struggling for basic necessities. While a total of 25% of these women engaged themselves in self-employing and economic activities, 20% of them were tied up in family-oriented works and a similar proportion (20%) recouped their energy levels and relaxed by quietistic activities.

This was followed by 15% of respondents who preferred group-oriented activities and 12.5% who spent their leisure by watching TV and listening to radio. Pursuing their hobbies like embroidery, needle work, etc. in their free time was preferred by only 7.5% of the respondents.

In the urban formal sector, a little less than one-fourth (22.5%) women indulged in family-oriented activities, followed by one-fifth (20%) who were inclined towards intellectual activities. This radiates their sensitive and creative quotient and intensity and urge to satisfy the same. Another 17.5% respondents preferred to watch TV serials, listen to radio, music, etc. or enjoyed movies in cinema halls. Quietistic activities such as sitting idle, sleeping during daytime to pass away idle time, were preferred by another 17.5% of respondents. Similarly, 12.5% of women indulged and enjoyed group-oriented activities as chatting, socializing, shopping, eating out, going to parties, etc. A small percentage (5%) kept themselves occupied with activities like household rearrangement, visiting beauty parlour, etc. in the free time. Another 5% played or viewed indoor and outdoor games.

Exposure to Television

Advent and spread of television has been rapid and it has entrenched itself as the most popular means of mass media. With more than 80% of the population covered by TV networks, its influence can hardly be overemphasized. Emergence of private Indian and foreign networks and the content of programmes being fed have left the urban and rural audiences gaping with open mouths. This forceful impact has raised moral and ethical questions as the content of programmes at times is not in tune with our lifestyle.

The respondents were asked regarding the exposure to television and Table 7.3a shows the statistics:

Table 7.3a *Watching TV Regularly*

Watching TV regularly	*Tribal N=80*	*Rural N=80*	*Urban*				*Total N=280*
			Household N=40	*Informal N=40*	*Formal N=40*	*Sub-Total N=120*	
Yes	—	30(37.5)	39(97.5)	29(72.5)	40(100.0)	108(90.0)	138(49.3)
No	80(100.0)	50(62.5)	1(2.5)	11(27.5)	—	12(10.0)	142(50.7)
Total	80(100)	80(100)	40(100)	40(100)	40(100)	120(100)	280(100)

Figures in parentheses indicate percentages.

While tribal respondents did not have access to even basic amenities of modern life, i.e. electricity, the question of their exposure to television does not arise. Even in rural areas, 62.5% respondents did not watch television, maybe due to non-availability of sufficient number of TV sets in the village. Moreover, women cannot watch TV in the presence of male members of the household due to *purdah* system. In sharp contrast, merely one-tenth (10%) of urban respondents were not exposed to television and this comprised 27.5% of informal sector and 2.5% of household sector respondents. All the urban formal sector respondents enjoyed watching television.

For those respondents who watched television, the time spent was also recorded and Table 7.3b shows that majority (59.4%) of the respondents spent 30–60 minutes on watching television everyday.

Table 7.3b *Time Spent on Watching TV Everyday*

Time in minutes	*Rural N=30*	*Urban*				*Total N=138*
		Household N=39	*Informal N=29*	*Formal N=40*	*Sub-Total N=108*	
Below 30	2(33.3) [6.7]	—	4(66.7) [13.8]	—	4(66.7) [3.7]	6(100.0) [4.3]
30–60	14(17.1) [46.7]	20(24.4) [51.3]	18(21.9) [62.1]	30(36.6) [75.0]	68(82.9) [62.9]	82(100.0) [59.4]
60–120	4(17.4) [13.3]	9(39.1) [23.1]	2(8.7) [6.9]	8(34.8) [20.0]	19(82.6) [17.6]	23(100.0) [16.7]
Above 120	2(16.7) [6.7	8(66.7) [20.6]	—	2(16.7) [5.0]	10(83.3) [9.3]	12(100.0) [8.7]
Do not watch regularly	8(53.3) [26.6]	2(13.3) [5.1]	5(33.3) [17.2]	—	7(46.7) [6.5]	15(100.0) [10.9]
Total	30 [100]	39 [100]	29 [100]	40 [100]	108 [100]	138 [100]

Figures in parentheses indicate percentages.

Majority of urban formal sector respondents being tied down with their official and household responsibilities were able to spend only 30–60 minutes on watching television. Similar is the trend for the informal sector respondents. However, the household sector women had much more spare time at their disposal. An appreciable percentage (26.6) of the rural respondents watched television sporadically.

Table 7.3c *Favourite TV Programmes*

Programme	*Rural N=30*	*Urban*				*Total N=138*
		Household N=39	*Informal N=29*	*Formal N=40*	*Sub-Total N=108*	
TV serials	26(86.6)	15(38.5)	22(75.9)	10(25.0)	47(43.5)	73(52.9)
Films	2(6.7)	8(20.5)	3(10.3)	—	11(10.2)	13(9.4)
Programmes based on film songs	2(6.7)	8(20.5)	3(10.3)	13(32.5)	24(22.2)	26(18.8)
News and debates on current affairs	—	8(20.5)	1(3.4)	17(42.5)	26(24.1)	26(18.8)
Total	30(100)	39(100)	29(100)	40(100)	108(100)	138(100)

Figures in parentheses indicate percentages.

Respondents were asked about their favourite programmes and their responses (Table 7.3c) revealed that while majority (53%) watched serials, nearly one-fifth (19%) were interested in film song-based programmes and a similar proportion watched news and programmes related to current affairs regularly. A little less than one-tenth (9.4%) had shown in interest in watching films only. This broad data, when dissected, revealed the following trends in rural and urban societies: while majority (87%) of the rural respondents were keen on watching TV serials based on religious and social themes, only 6.7% were interested in watching films since cinema halls are not present in the near vicinity. Another 6.7% watched film-based song programmes and these were of the younger age group.

Within the urban informal sector, trends were similar to that of the rural respondents wherein 76% respondents preferred watching serials while a little more than one-tenth (10.3%) each films and film song-based programmes. It is interesting to note that 3.4% of such women also expressed interest in news and current affairs programmes. Within the urban household sector, the spread amongst various categories was more with 38.5% preferring to watch serials while 20.5% were interested in films as they had more spare time in their daily schedule. Slightly more than one-fifth (20.5%) respondents each watched song-based programmes and news and current affairs, respectively. So far as the urban formal sector respondents are concerned, 42.5% were interested in watching news and current affairs programmes while 32.5% watched programmes based on film songs and another 25% serials. The preference for programmes illustrates the educational level, lifestyle, aspirations and mindset of the respondents.

Listening to Radio

Since it is within the reach of the less privileged sections and is also independent of the compulsions of electricity, its popularity was presumed in rural and tribal areas. However, the responses were contrary to expectations as is evident from Table 7.4a.

Table 7.4a *Listening to Radio*

Listening to radio	*Tribal N=80*	*Rural N=80*	*Urban*				*Total N=280*
			Household N=40	*Informal N=40*	*Formal N=40*	*Sub-Total N=120*	
Yes	20(25.0)	10(12.5)	26(65.0)	19(47.5)	23(57.5)	68(56.7)	98(35.0)
No	60(75.0)	70(87.5)	14(35.0)	21(52.5)	17(42.5)	52(43.3)	182(65.0)
Total	80(100)	80(100)	40(100)	40(100)	40(100)	120(100)	280(100)

Figures in parentheses indicate percentages.

Regularity in listening to radio was exhibited by only 35% of the total respondents and this constituted majority (57%) of the urban, 12.5% of the rural and (25%) of the tribal respondents. Urban sample comprised 57.5% of the formal sector, 47.5% of the informal sector and 65% of the household sector respondents. Shortage of time, low literacy level and lack of relevant and interesting programmes could be the main reasons why this low-cost medium has not attained popularity in tribal and rural areas. Within the urban community, however, this medium of entertainment is more popular among household sector women who enjoy this simultaneously with their household work.

The respondents were asked about the time spent on listening to radio. Responses were grouped in four categories in Table 7.4b.

Table 7.4b *Time Spent on Listening Radio*

Time in minutes	*Tribal N=20*	*Rural N=10*	*Urban*				*Total N=98*
			Household N=26	*Informal N=19*	*Formal N=23*	*Sub-Total N=68*	
Below 15	4(20.0)	—	—	4(21.1)	—	4(5.9)	8(8.2)
15–30	—	—	—	6(31.5)	—	6(8.8)	6(7.1)
Above 30	—	—	15(57.7)	—	10(43.5)	25(36.8)	25(25.5)
While doing other jobs	16(80.0)	10(100.0)	11(42.3)	9(47.4)	13(56.5)	33(48.5)	59(60.2)
Total	20(100)	10(100)	26(100)	19(100)	23(100)	68(100)	98(100)

Figures in parentheses indicate percentages.

Majority (60.2%) of the total respondents, comprising 48.5% of urban, 100% of rural and 80% of tribal respondents, said they did not have any predetermined time and listened to radio while doing other household jobs. Within the urban community, such women included 56.4% in the formal sector, 47.4% in the informal sector and 42.3% in the household sector. Thus, it is evident that radio plays an important role as a passive, non-obtrusive entertainer which can be relished while pursuing other household jobs.

More than one-fourth (25.5%) of the respondents listened to radio for more than 30 minutes. They included 43.5% formal and 57.7% household sector respondents, with no representation from any other section of the society. Listening to radio for less than 15 minutes was preferred by only 8% women in totality and half of such respondents belonged to urban informal sector and another half to tribal society. Another 6% of the total respondents spent between 15–30 minutes on this activity and all these came from the urban informal class.

Viewing Cinema

Cinema is the cheapest form of entertainment and has a deep impact on ideas, beliefs and attitudes of people. D.P. Mukerji writes: 'Indian films are, in fact, one long exercise in wish fulfilment and offer tempting avenues of escape from the drudgery of family life and disappointments in the love that might have been.'[12] Film songs are very popular throughout India. The responses regarding exposure to cinema are tabulated in Table 7.5a.

Table 7.5a *Watching Movies in Cinema Halls*

Response	*Tribal N=80*	*Rural N=80*	*Urban*				*Total N=280*
			Household N=40	*Informal N=40*	*Formal N=40*	*Sub-Total N=120*	
Yes	6(7.5)	11(13.8)	33(82.5)	19(47.5)	38(95.0)	90(75.0)	107(61.8)
No	74(92.5)	69(86.2)	7(17.5)	21(52.5)	2(5.0)	30(25.0)	173(38.2)
Total	80(100)	80(100)	40(100)	40(100)	40(100)	120(100)	280(100)

Figures in parentheses indicate percentages.

Watching movies in cinema halls was preferred by 61.8% of the total respondents. This data implies that watching films in cinema halls is preferred by only well-educated and financially well-off women of the formal and household sectors of urban community and majority of tribal and rural women were not exposed to cinema.

From the respondents who denied seeing movies in cinema halls, the reasons were asked. Respondents who could not watch movies outside due to restrictions from husbands/elders constituted 29.4% of the total set. Such restrictions, which were limited to only 11.7% of urban women, witnessed a significant increase among the rural (39.2%) and tribal (49%) women. The lifestyle in villages and tribal areas is not conducive for a woman to move alone for watching a movie without her husband. Lack of time/interest on the part of their husbands forces them to curtail their own feelings. More than one-fifth (21%) of the total respondents had never watched a movie and so did not have any inclination for seeing it. One-third of such respondents came from the rural background while two-thirds belonged to the tribal society. In total, 16.2% of the respondents were not able to do so as they had no cinema hall in vicinity. About 28.6% of such respondents were from the rural background while 71.4% belonged to the tribal set-up. Respondents who did not have spare time out of their daily hectic schedule to watch movies in cinema halls were nearly 14% of the total set. Even amongst the urban community, this view emerged from 29.2% of informal and 8.3% of the household sector respondents. Another 13% yearned to watch movies but could not spare money for doing so. They included 40.9% urban, 36.4% rural and 22.7% tribal women. All such urban respondents were from the informal sector. Lack of appeal of subject and content of movies was the primary reason why 5% of the respondents did not watch movies. These included 44.4% of urban and 55.6% rural respondents.

Further, to a query regarding preference for partners while going to cinema halls, we received the following responses (Table 7.5b):

Table 7.5b *Preferred Movie Partner*

Preference for the movie partner	*Tribal N=6*	*Rural N=11*	*Urban*				*Total N=107*
			Household N=33	*Informal N=19*	*Formal N=38*	*Sub-Total N=90*	
With spouse	5(14.3) [85.3]	2(5.7) [18.2]	12(34.3) [36.4]	8(22.9) [42.1]	8(22.9) [21.1]	28(80.0) [31.1]	35(100.0) [32.7]
With children and spouse	—	3(10.0) [27.3]	10(33.3) [30.3]	2(6.7) [10.5]	15(50.0) [39.5]	27(90.0) [30.0]	30(100.0) [28.0]

Cont'd...

...Cont'd

With children	—	—	7(46.6) [21.1]	4(26.7) [21.0]	4(26.7) [10.5]	15(100.0) [16.7]	15(100.0) [14.1]
With other family members	1(7.7) [16.7]	6(46.2) [54.5]	2(15.3) [6.1]	3(23.1) [15.7]	1(7.7) [2.6]	6(46.1) [6.7]	13(100.0 [12.1]
With colleagues and friends	—	—	2(14.3) [6.1]	2(14.3) [10.5]	10(71.4) [26.3]	14(100.0) [15.6]	14(100.0) [13.1]
Total	6 [100]	11 [100]	33 [100]	19 [100]	38 [100]	90 [100]	107 [100]

Figures in parentheses indicate percentages.

The data reveals that nearly one-third (32.7%) of the total respondents preferred to watch movies with their spouses. The proportion of such respondents was much higher in the urban society. This came down to 14.3% in case of tribal and 5.7% in case of rural women. Watching movies along with both spouse and children was preferred by 28% of the total respondents; 90% of such respondents belonged to the urban background, the concept being complete family entertainment. Another 14% respondents in total preferred to watch movies only with their children. All these respondents were from urban community. In such cases, the husband may not be able to accompany due to paucity of time and hectic schedule. Since most urban families are nuclear families, they enjoy going to movies with their children. Such phenomenon is much more pronounced in case of household sector women.

The propensity to watch movies along with friends/colleagues was exhibited by 13% of the total respondents, who were mainly hailed from the urban society. As against this, respondents preferring to watch movies with close relatives stood at 12% of the total set. Prevalence of this trend was much more enhanced in rural areas too, where 46% respondents expressed this viewpoint and 7.7% of tribal counterparts also agreed with them. This helps in concluding that rural society still endorses the values of joint family and women are more comfortable and open with their relatives.

Reading Newspapers

Reading of a newspaper is an important benchmark for gauging the literacy level and also social, political and cultural awareness and involvement of any society.

Table 7.6 *Regularly Reading Newspapers*

Regularly reading newspapers	*Tribal N=80*	*Rural N=80*	*Urban*				*Total N=280*
			Household N=40	*Informal N=40*	*Formal N=40*	*Sub-Total N=120*	
Yes	—	4(5.0)	35(87.5)	7(17.5)	40(100.0)	82(68.3)	86(30.7)
No	80(100.0)	76(95.0)	5(12.5)	33(82.5)	—	38(31.7)	194(69.3)
Total	80(100)	80(100)	40(100)	40(100)	40(100)	120(100)	280(100)

Figures in parentheses indicate percentages.

Nearly 31% of the total respondents acknowledged reading newspapers. The proportion of such respondents was much higher in formal (100%) and household (87.5%) sector of the urban society as compared to only 17.5% in informal sector and 5% in rural areas. As expected, none of the tribal respondents read newspapers as they were mostly illiterate.

Reading Magazines and Periodicals

Periodicals of general interest and specific subjects broaden our perspective and simulate social and moral issues and dilemmas to contemplate and experiment in real-life situations.

A total of 27.5% of respondents were regular in reading periodicals. As expected, they mostly included urban women (100% formal and 72.5% household). While the formal preferred to read magazines of specific interest areas such as medicine, management, finance, etc. besides magazines of general interest, the household women have much spare time and read after completing their household responsibilities, i.e. usually in the afternoon. This inclination towards reading magazines was much weaker in the urban informal sector where only 15% respondents acknowledged this and representation of rural women in this class was almost insignificant (2.5%).

Table 7.7 *Interest in Reading Magazines*

Interest in reading magazines	*Tribal N=80*	*Rural N=80*	*Urban*				*Total N=280*
			Household N=40	*Informal N=40*	*Formal N=40*	*Sub-Total N=120*	
Yes	—	2(2.5)	29(72.5)	6(15.0)	40(100.0)	75(62.5)	77(27.5)
No	80(100.0)	78(97.5)	11(27.5)	34(85.0)	—	45(37.5)	203(72.5)
Total	80(100)	80(100)	40(100)	40(100)	40(100)	120(100)	280(100)

Figures in parentheses indicate percentages.

We enquired from respondents as to how they procured these periodicals.

It can be inferred that avenues and options for quenching knowledge thirst are varied for urban household and formal sector respondents which include structured means such as subscribing on one hand and unstructured means like borrowing from friends/colleagues. In contrast, most of urban informal sector respondents do not invest in buying magazines and seek favour from their neighbours in this regard. Rural respondents are dependent mainly upon local hawkers for supplying magazines or they purchase whenever they visit any book stall.

Lifestyle and the socio-economic environment of respondents not only influences the extent to which they procure magazines, but also the choice of magazines read by them.

In totality, 40.3% of respondents preferred to read magazines related to women such as *Manorama, Grah Shobha, Sarita, Femina* and *Women's World*. Such magazines recorded the maximum readership and were first priority for all respondents across all classes and sections. Second priority was accorded to general interest magazines such as *Outlook, Week, India Today*, etc. which were favoured by about one-fourth (24.6%) of the total respondents. This was followed by magazines related to profession/career/technical issues such as *Competition Success Review, Competition Master, Business India, Business World*, etc. and were liked by nearly one-tenth (10.3%) of the total respondents. Nearly one-tenth (9.1%) of the total respondents opted for reading literary magazines such as *Kadambari, Navneet, Readers Digest*, etc. to satisfy their urge for creative and provocative literature. Health and religious magazines such as *Nigrogadham, Swasthya Patrika, Sadhu Samaj, Kalyan, Amar Sandesh*, etc. were at fifth priority, being preferred by only 6.5% each of the total respondents. And, finally, preference for light and entertaining magazines based on films and gossips such as *Madhuri, Filmfare*, etc. was exhibited by only 3% of the total respondents.

An introspection into various categories and sections of the respondents reveals their distinctiveness in preference for magazines. The only exception seems to be magazines related to women's topics which have a universal appeal and are preferred by all respondents. All women of rural grounding preferred to read only the above category of magazines.

In the urban society household sector, respondents accorded first priority (34.4%) to women's magazines, followed by magazines of general interest (27.6%), and literary magazines (10.3% each), religious and professional/career-related magazines (6.8% each) and film-based magazines (3.4%). Put briefly, the preference of varied magazines by the urban household sector women illustrates their desire to keep themselves abreast of major developments in the socio-economic, cultural and political environment.

In sharp contrast, the circle of concern for urban informal sector women is limited and besides 83.3% who prefer women magazines, the remaining 16.7% prefer to read light magazines based on films.

Formal urban sector respondents showed similar trends by giving first priority (35%) to women's magazines, followed by general interest magazines (27.5%). However, as compared to only 6.8% of household respondents, more than double (15%) of formal respondents preferred to read profession/technical/career-related magazines. This demonstrates their progressive outlook and desire to succeed in life by self-development. One-tenth (10%) of urban formal sector respondents also preferred to read literary magazines. Religious magazines were accorded more priority (7.5%) as compared to magazines related to health issues, which were preferred by only 5% of respondents.

Gossiping

Gossiping is a universal phenomenon which refers to chatting with relatives, neighbours, friends and co-workers, and is characterized by light-hearted talking which might touch any topic casually and informally. Respondents across all classes unanimously acknowledged gossiping. Family members and relatives outnumbered (36.8%) the other gossip partners. Respondents who preferred them included 18.3% from the urban sector and this proportion increased significantly to 50% and 51.3% among rural and tribal women, respectively. Even amongst urban, this comprised 12.5% of formal, 15% of household and 27.5% of informal sector respondents. Since topics of gossiping revolved around familial issues, tribal and rural respondents were most comfortable discussing them with other family members too.

Nearly one-fifth (19%) of the respondents preferred gossiping with colleagues and friends. Within the urban community, the proportion of such respondents was much higher. Another 19% of the rural and 12.5% of the tribal respondents were also comfortable in discussing issues with friends and colleagues. Such activities normally took place in mines/workplace or while working together in fields during daytime.

Preference for light conversation on varied topics with children was shown by nearly 16% of the respondents. This phenomenon was more pronounced in the urban set-up. Most of the modern urban households are nuclear families with one or two children, and here parents act as friend, philosopher and guide to their own children.

Respondents who preferred gossiping with their spouses constituted 14.6% of the total set, and contained one-fourth (25%) of the urban as against only 8.7% and 5% of rural and tribal respondents, respectively. A total of 13.9% of the respondents gossiped freely with neighbours. They included 11.7% of urban, 12.5% of rural and 18.8% of tribal respondents.

Having realized the fact that all respondents indulged in gossiping and also having analysed their gossip groups, we further enquired from them regarding topics and contents of such discussions. This open-ended question fielded numerous and varied responses which were clubbed into six categories, viz., social, economic, familial, religious, cultural and general.

Topics on which women respondents gossiped the most fell under 'familial' category (37.1%), followed by social (21.8%), religious (16.8%), economic (12.9%), cultural (6.8%) and general (4.2%). It can be clearly established that cutting across boundaries of caste, education level, economic status or rural and urban background, the circle of concern for almost all respondents remains their family and society.

In the tribal society, half of the respondents usually gossiped on familial issues and another one-fourth on religious issues. This is followed by 18.8% respondents who discussed social issues and 6.3% economic issues. The tribals have been cut off from the mainstream and development taking place in urban and rural areas does not percolate to influence their lifestyle. This makes them religious-minded, which reflects in their topics of daily conversation.

Most of the rural respondents (37.5%), like their tribal counterparts, gossiped on familial issues, followed by social (25%), religious (18.8%), economic (12.5%), cultural (2.5%) and general (2.5%) issues. There is a marked increase in the percentage of rural respondents gossiping on economic issues as compared to their tribal counterparts. For them, matters relating to land, agriculture, crops, cattle, capital and earnings are of great concern and form an inherent part of their discussions. Increased literacy levels and increasing exposure of rural women have also prompted a few of them (2.5%) to gossip on cultural issues and another 2.5% on general/recreational issues.

Moving towards the urban society, we found that the maximum number of respondents (28.3%) gossiped on social issues. This is followed by social (21.7%), economic (17.5%), culture (14.2%), religious (10%) and general (8.3%) issues. Increased proportion of household sector women gossiping on economic issues reflects growing insecurity in the urban middle class due to limited means of earning on one hand and spiralling cost of living on the other. This is accentuated by increasing aspirational levels.

Half of the informal sector respondents gossiped on familial issues and another one-fourth on economic issues. This is followed by social (20%), religious (12.5%), cultural (5%) and general/recreational (2.5%) issues in order of priority. Majority of informal sector respondents are not well-educated and work hard to make both ends meets in urban cities. This reflects in their concern for economic issues during gossips. In case of formal sector respondents, the gossip topics in the priority order were: familial (25%), social (25%), cultural (22.5%), general/recreational (15%), economic (7.5%) and religious (5%).

With growth in the status, due to increased education, economic welfare or empowerment, women's interest in cultural topics has also enhanced. Thus, the preference for cultural issues for gossiping increases from 2.5% in rural respondents to 14.2% in urban respondents. Hectic lifestyle and tendency to consider religion as a personal activity reflects in only 10% of the urban women gossiping on religious themes as compared to 25% of tribal and 18.8% of rural women.

Urban respondents, particularly those from the formal sector, are well placed in high-paying jobs. As a consequence, only 7.5% of them are bothered enough to gossip on economic issues as compared to their informal (25%), household (20%) counterparts. And, the tendency to gossip on general/recreational issues increases to 6.3% among urban women as compared to 2.5% among rural women, which demonstrates their confidence to discuss without inhibition any topic.

Pilgrimage

Visiting holy places is an important milestone in the lifespan of a spiritual person. Respondents who acknowledged going for pilgrimage stood at 36.8% and this included 52.5% of urban respondents; this proportion dropped significantly to 18.8% in rural and 31.3% among tribal respondents. Even amongst urban, majority (67.5%) of respondents who had gone on pilgrimage were from the formal sector, followed by household (50%) and informal (40%) respondents. It is obvious that such religious excursions consume time and money and since both these commodities are scarce in tribal and rural communities, only a limited number of women had gone for pilgrimage.

Our subsequent question regarding details of pilgrimage made by respondents yielded unique and numerous responses. The pilgrimage of 60% of tribals (Garasias) was confined to local temples and places of worship such as Sawaliya Mata, Tilkar Bhagwan, Asapuri Mata, Gopeshwar Mahadev, etc. Garasias have great faith in Goddess Amba and visited Ambaji situated in Gujarat, close to the border of Abu Road. Garasias go annually to Ambaji after Holi, especially if there has been a death in the family or if a specific vow has to be made. The rest of the 40% of tribal respondents had gone on a regional pilgrimage. Major places of worship are located in the close vicinity and hence none of the respondents had ever ventured out for pilgrimage to other parts of the country.

Taking into account the rural respondents, 20% of them visited local deities such as Tejaji, Hanuman Mandir and Radhaswami Temple. However, in two-third (66.7%) cases, they had gone for regional religious excursions to places such as Pushkar, Galtaji, Khatu Shyamji, etc. These places are in the range of 60–200 km from their native village. In case of 13.3% respondents, they had also made distant pilgrimages such as Mathura and Vrindavan.

Viewed in terms of the three sub-sectors within the urban society, in the household sector, while 20% respondents had visited places in regional areas such as Pushkar, Khatu Shyamji, Salasar, Bhartrihari, Narayani Mata, Pandupole, etc. situated within 100–200 km, 80% had gone to far-flung places within the country and of these, 20% had visited riversides/seashores (Haridwar, Dwarka, Prayag, Rameshwaram, Puri, Banaras, etc.), 40% to mountains (Badrinath, Kedarnath, Vaishno Devi, etc.) and the remaining 20% plains (Ayodhya, Tirupati, Mathura, Vrindavan, Shirdi, etc).

Since informal sector respondents had limited resources and could not afford to stay away from work at length, most of them satisfied their spiritual thirst/hunger by visiting local (12.5%) and regional (62.5%) places of worship.

In the formal sector, only 3.3% of respondents visited regional places of worship and 96.7% visited diverse and distant pilgrimages throughout the country.

Outing and Holidaying

Nearly half (46.8%) of the total respondents did opt for an outing: 72% of urban, 31% of rural and 25% of tribal respondents. Within the urban community, there was a tilt towards formal and household sectors (100% and 75%, respectively) as compared to informal sector (40%).

Majority of the tribal respondents (70%) went for local outing (market place, tehsil). Garasia women feel more free outside their husband's village in the marketplace where they gossip and joke while selling their produce or items gathered from the forests. In absence of literacy or communication, the local market serves as an important means for women to procure information about their natal village. The market thus supports the independent and individualistic behaviour of Garasia women by providing them with an environment with fewer social sanctions than their husband's village. Besides, 20% of tribal respondents had gone to their parents' home and 10% for regional outings to Ambaji.

While for majority (60%) of rural respondents, such outings were confined to local areas, such as Saipura (village fair), Ramgarh picnic spot, Andhi tehsil, 16% of them visited their parental village and another 20% other places such as Ajmer, Jhunjhunu, Udaipur, etc. In 4% cases, rural respondents had also visited distant cities of historical importance such as Bhopal and Agra.

Within the urban household sector, 10% respondents had gone for local outings while 20% visited regional locations. Such respondents were more affluent and had relatively much more free time, which reflected in 70% respondents visiting far-flung destinations within India.

In the urban formal class, none of the respondents preferred local outings and barely 10% had visited regional cities. Nearly half (45%) of respondents visited hill stations, 25% riverside/seashores and another 20% cities and places of historical importance. In sharp contrast, respondents from the urban informal segment lacked the financial capacity to visit distant locations. Half of such respondents satisfied themselves with local outings and 12.5% visited their parents' home for a break. However, 18.8% women had visited regional destinations and a similar proportion more distant locations.

Taking an overall perspective, the frequency and duration of such outings is much less in tribal, rural and urban (informal) segments as compared to household and formal counterparts in the urban society.

Cultural and Creative Activities

Amongst tribal respondents, singing emerged as the most popular activity being pursued by 81.3% of the respondents, followed by dancing (51.3%) and preparing *rangoli* (23.8%). Characteristics of culture of any community radiate through folk songs, music and dance. Folk songs reflect the person's relations with nature, society and family at different stages of life.

Leisure folk songs are composed by Garasias and sung by almost all members without any distinction of singer or listener. Regional words and dialects dominate these songs and they provide recreation and emotional outlet to Garasias.

Various types of Garasia folk songs are given below:

(a) Seasonal songs portray enthusiasm, joy and positive feelings that accompany seasons of spring and rains.
(b) Religious songs are sung as hymns in praise of local deities on religious occasions or while worshipping.
(c) Historical songs depict heroic stories and incidents of prominence within the community and are usually sung by elderly people to acquaint the younger generation with their predecessors.
(d) Moral songs personify human values and social norms within the Garasia community.
(e) Social songs are sung on specific occasions like marriage, birth, etc. Marriage songs are called 'Banna-Banni' and most are full of love practices between husband and wife and are full of humour and remarks on behaviour of newlyweds.

Folk dances of Garasias are a spontaneous rhythmic expression in which they willingly participate to express their love, affection and social involvement. Dances synchronize rhythmic movement of body parts to the beats of drums and other instruments. Males and females dance with equal enthusiasm and without inhibition in fairs, festivals and public gatherings and these opportunities increase their intimacy. Prominent dances of Garasias are described below:

(1) Valar Nach: It is the oldest form of Garasia dance and is associated with harvesting of crops and expresses solidarity of the tribe. The whole village participates and men and women form separate co-centric circles by joining hands. The innermost circle is of a few male dancers around a Nachiyo (leader), who is beautifully dressed and decorated. This is followed by an outer circle of women and the outermost circle again formed by men. All

participants move their right foot forward and backward in a rhythmic movement. As the momentum increases, the leader leads the group in singing and dancing. Songs connected with historical events are sung and this activity occurs without any musical instrument.

(2) Loor Nach: It is generally performed by women during Holi or on the occasion of marriage.

(3) Kood Nach: It is performed by young girls who go on jumping while singing Diwali songs.

(4) Mandal Nach: Mandal is a special drum which is narrow on one side and broader on the other. Drum player stands in the centre and produces a different sound for dances and is usually performed during a marriage ceremony.

(5) Rangal Khangal Nach: It is a group dance performed jointly by men and women accompanied by various musical instruments. This serves as a healthy competition between each village.

(6) Gaur Nach: In this, only young girls and women participate and men are not allowed to dance with them.

(7) Jhularu Nach: It is performed by young girls in pairs during the Diwali festival.

(8) Khema Nach: It is performed by boys and girls in pairs wherein the boy plays a small musical instrument called Ghosiyyun and the girl puts her left arm on the right arm of the boy and dances to the tune.

(9) Ghoomar Nach: It is performed in a group by men and women during Diwali and songs are sung to inspire them to face all calamities with courage.

(10) Berla Nach: It is performed by a girl who keeps a pitcher with numerous holes and a burning lamp inside. Balancing the pitcher while dancing and light coming out from the pitcher makes this dance very attractive.

(11) Moriyo Nach: This is the dance of marriage and symbolizes deep love and affection between the bride and the bridegroom.

(12) Dhol Nach: It is performed by men during Holi and they also act as drummers.

(13) Rayan Nach: It is performed by a single male dancer who appears dressed as a Goddess.

(14) Angura Nach: It is performed by young boys and men on day following Holi festival and they dance on half-extinguished fire of Holi.

(15) Bhopa Nach: It is performed only by Bhopas, especially during Navratras, Ratijaga and other festivals. They dance with full vigour before their deities.

Rangoli or paintings of tribals are also based on mythology of their Gods and Goddesses and are made to prevent from evil spirits and bring good luck.

Amongst rural respondents, singing is preferred by more than half the respondents (52.5%), followed by preparing *rangoli* (37.5%), playing musical instruments (12.5%), dancing (11.2%) and painting (5%). In the rural context, on the contrary, dancing is considered a demeaning activity and is never preferred by women in public. Women who value their reputation do not dance except under certain limited circumstances like family functions. A dancing girl is considered a prostitute in rural areas, hence they abstain from this activity. Instead, they prefer to decorate their homes through *rangoli* and paintings and play musical instruments such as harmonium, *dholak, majire,* etc. during family functions or religious gatherings.

In the urban context, amongst household respondents, preparing *rangoli* was preferred by 45% of women, followed by singing (40%), dancing and painting (27.5% each), playing musical instruments (25%) and drama (10%). It is interesting to note that these respondents are introvert in nature and try to satisfy their creative urges by indoor activities such as preparing *rangoli* or playing musical instruments.

Amongst informal respondents, singing was preferred by the majority (50%), followed by preparing *rangoli* (35%), playing musical instruments (12.5%), dancing (10%) and painting (5%). Since most of these respondents are uneducated, having low economic status and workload on both domestic and outside fronts, they express their joys and creativity through singing, playing instruments, etc.

In the formal sector, too, half of the respondents preferred singing, followed by painting (35%), dancing (25%), playing musical instruments (15%) and preparing *rangoli* (10%). These respondents are much more extrovert and creative, hence they prefer singing and dancing to more introvert activities such as preparing *rangoli*. Preference for painting exhibits their sensitive and creative as well as more intellectual bent of mind as compared to other counterparts.

Involvement in Miscellaneous Activities

In the tribal context, none of the respondents had any interest in activities such as games, morning walk or other exercises. Such activities have no relevance since their active lifestyle demands a great deal of physical labour and exertion in routine course. It is interesting to note that in tribal society, women do not worship at home or visit the temple regularly. They give vent to religious feelings only on special occasions when they worship and take part in religious ceremonies along with their husbands and family elders. A tribal woman worshipping all alone either at home or in a temple is viewed with suspicion and labelled a witch. An appreciable number (56%) of tribal women regularly sing devotional songs and a greater majority (75%) attend fairs and festivals. These fairs are regularly organized at the village level during occasions such as Holi, Diwali and Navratra. Gaur fair is observed on the festive occasion of Gangaur, which holds special relevance in the life of Garasia women as this relates to their special deity Lord Shiva and Parvati. Siyawa-ka-Gormela held during Baisakhi Krishna Panchmi in Siyawa village of Abu Road tehsil is the main fair of the Garasias.

Rural women shared a similar trend with their tribal counterparts as far as lack of interest in games, exercises or morning walk was concerned. However, majority (75%) of respondents worshipped at home regularly, followed by 50% of respondents who attended village fairs and 31% who sang devotional songs. Fairs for worshipping local deities such as Tejaji are organized on occasions such as *Asar, Sudi* Dashmi and other popular events are organized on Hanuman Jayanti and Janmashtami. They also come to cities like Jaipur on the occasion of Teej, Gangaur, Ganesh Chaturthi to take part in the *mela* and worship deities. A small number (2.5%) of respondents regularly went to the temples for worship.

An overwhelming majority (75%) of the household sector respondents also worshipped regularly at home, which is quite similar to rural respondents. However, their lifestyle is much more sedentary as compared to rural counterparts and hence these respondents make up for this lack of physical labour by regularly going for morning walks (55%) and exercises (15%). Only 5% of these respondents sang devotional songs and a similar proportion went to fairs and exhibitions. None of them have, however, exhibited any regular pattern in visiting the temples for worship.

In the informal sector, a big majority (85%) of respondents sang devotional songs, followed by half of the respondents who regularly worshipped at home. We also came across 37.5% respondents who regularly attended fairs and festivals such as Teej, Gangaur, Ganesh Chaturthi, etc. While 5% of such respondents regularly went to a temple, a similar number had formed a regular habit of going for morning walks.

Amongst formal sector respondents, while majority (70%) worshipped regularly at home and a similar proportion regularly went for morning walks, 10% regularly played games, followed by 5%, who exercised regularly and another 5% who sang devotional songs.

Satisfaction with Leisure Time

In the tribal context, majority (62.5%) of the respondents were satisfied with the leisure time available at their disposal. This is interesting as they have a more hectic and hard lifestyle. Another aspect can be limited options for recreation and leisure amongst tribal respondents. Due to this lack of exposure, they do not yearn for more leisure time. A good Garasia wife is one who works tirelessly at home and in the field without any complaint. This concept is grilled into young Garasia girls right from childhood and they try to portray this role to perfection. Satisfaction in view of leisure time diminishes from 43.7% in the rural context to 37.5% in the urban household and only 25% of urban informal sector respondents were satisfied with leisure time at their disposal.

This growing dissatisfaction can be correlated to increased exposure to means of recreation on one hand and moving to a more unorthodox set-up (i.e. more nuclear families instead of joint families) on the other hand. This leads to wants and desires boiling up and being curbed due to lack of time for these pursuits. This is more so in case of younger women who have more household as well as outside responsibilities. Older women are relatively more free and hence expressed satisfaction with the extent of leisure time available.

Proportion of urban formal sector respondents who expressed satisfaction with leisure time was 50% and much higher as compared to their household counterparts, which was only 37.5%. This is despite their stretched schedule and dual responsibilities of both household and workplace. However, half the urban formal respondents had the financial means and attitude to pursue leisure activities but they were unable to find enough time from their schedule to pursue these activities to their satisfaction.

Changes in Pattern of Leisure Activities after Marriage

After marriage, a girl leaves the familiar environment of her parents' house and moves to her in-laws' place, where she is expected to be tolerant, submissive and accommodative.

Did this changed scenario have any bearing on the leisure pattern of the respondents? Those who said that after marriage they found little time for leisure activities such as singing, dancing, games, sports, outdoor activities, wandering with friends, hobbies, etc. stood at 43.2% of the total sample. The proportion of such respondents was 42.5% in the urban sector, which witnessed a rise (50%) among rural respondents and dropped to 37.5% in case of tribal respondents. Even amongst urban respondents, this feeling was more prevalent in the informal sector (52.5%) as compared to household and formal sector counterparts (37.5% each). More than one-fourth, i.e. 27.5% of total respondents, said they faced restrictions on moving out after marriage and this affected their leisure pattern which existed before marriage. Although this feeling was limited to only 10% of urban respondents, it increased significantly to 31.3% of rural and half of tribal respondents.

More than one-fifth (20.4%) of the total respondents said their leisure pattern changed after marriage as they missed their circle of friends. This feeling emerged from 30.9% of urban respondents and only 12.5% each of rural and tribal counterparts. Even amongst the urban segment, this feeling was more predominant in formal and household segments (37.5% each) as compared to only 17.5% among informal sector respondents.

Women are by nature more conservative and take time in opening up with new people and environment, which restricts their leisure activities. Another 5.7% of respondents said they did not feel any perceptible difference in their leisure pattern after marriage. These feelings were limited to 25% of the formal sector and 15% of household sector respondents of urban society.

It is striking to note that one-fourth of urban formal sector respondents stand out as a glaring exception where leisure patterns remain unaffected even after marriage. This portrays their confident, independent and non-compromising outlook.

Optional Leisure Activity in Free Environment

By now, it is well realized that generally women are overloaded with household work or responsibilities of workplace and get very little free time to pursue their desires. The respondents were asked to specify the leisure activities they would preferably indulge in if they were given full freedom.

Respondents who said if given a chance they would prefer to move out for entertainment stood at 31%. These included more than 26.7% of urban respondents and this proportion increased to 31.3% amongst rural and 37.5% amongst tribal respondents. Even amongst the urban section, this feeling emerged from 37.5% of informal sector respondents, followed by 25% of household and only 17.5% of formal sector respondents. Rural and tribal societies are more conservative and orthodox and young women are not allowed to move freely and independently. So, majority of tribal and rural as well as urban informal sector respondents desired to be more outgoing for fun and entertainment along with friends, children or even alone.

More than one-tenth (10.4%) of the total respondents said they already had full freedom in their leisure time. All these respondents were confined to the urban set-up.

Nearly one-tenth (9.6%) were so overworked and exhausted that they preferred to rest/sleep if any free time was made available to them. This view was expressed by 15% of tribal, 16.2% of rural and only 1.7% of urban respondents. Amongst urban, such women mainly hailed from the informal sector. It is interesting to note that none of urban household and urban formal sector respondents expressed similar feelings. About 8.6% of the respondents said that if they got a chance they would prefer to watch a movie. These included 10% of tribal, 12.5% of rural and 5% of urban respondents. Similar proportion (8.6%) of respondents said that they had no wishes or preferred activities they yearned to pursue in their free time. In all, 11.3% from tribal, 12.5% from rural and another 12.5% from urban informal sector were included in this group of respondents. Only 5% of the total respondents said they would pursue religious activities in any free time, and included 12.5% tribal and 5% rural respondents.

Surprisingly, 4.6% of the total respondents also wanted to devote whatever free time was available to them for studying. This feeling emerged from 20% of urban informal sector respondents who were uneducated. A total of 12.5% of urban formal sector respondents also wanted to study in their free time. Nearly 2% of the total respondents had a burning desire to participate in games and sports. This feeling was confined to 12.5% of urban formal sector respondents.

So, while young tribal and rural women got little time for self-indulgence due to extended working hours, their middle-aged and older counterparts had selectively more time at their disposal. Rural and tribal respondents are less exposed and rely on traditional modes of leisure such as fairs, festivals, and group activities such as chatting and gossiping. This provided them with much needed emotional outlet to discuss family and societal issues. Family-oriented activities also occupied further available leisure time. Tribal respondents indulged in self-employing and economic activities.

In the rural segment, while the pattern of preferred leisure activities remained the same, the proportion of respondents preferring family-oriented activities declined significantly and the effect of modern audio-visual aids such as radio, TV and cinema halls was profoundly felt. Urban informal sector respondents faced dual pressure of household and outside responsibilities and scarce leisure time was utilized in family-oriented, self-employing and quietistic activities.

There is an emergence of a unique paradox wherein the time available and means of leisure are limited in tribal and rural segments, but the respondents are highly satisfied as regards utilization of leisure. Urban respondents have more disposable time and avenues for leisure and indulgence, yet they remain dissatisfied with it.

Notes

1. Warburton, I.W., 1989. 'The Work Leisure Paradox', *Australian Journal of Adult Education,* July, Vol. 8, No. 2, quoted in *Journal of Marriage and Family,* Vol. 51, No. 2.
2. Henderson and M.D. Bialeschki, 1991a. 'A Sense of Entitlement to Leisure as Constraints for Women,' *Society and Leisure*, 14(1), pp. 97–113.
3. Green, E., S. Hebron, and D. Woodward, 1987. 'Women's Leisure in Sheffield: Constraints and Opportunities,' in I Henry (eds). *Women's Leisure: Constraints and Opportunities*, Brighton: LSA, pp. 1–12.
4. Haworth, J.T., 1997. *Work, Leisure and Well-being,* London: Routledge;

   Csikszentmihaly, M., 1975. *Beyond Boredom and Anxiety,* San Francisco: Jossey-Bass;

   Driver, B.L., P.J. Brown, and G.L. Peterson, (eds), 1991. *Benefits of Leisure,* State College, P.A.: Venture Publishing;

   Iso-Ahola, S., 1980. The Social Psychology of Leisure and Recreation, Dubuque: W.C. Brown; and

   Wimbushch, E., 1987. 'Mothers with Young Children: Understanding their Leisure,' in I. Henry, (ed.), *Women's Leisure: Constraints and Opportunities,* Brighton: LSA, pp. 13–26.
5. Modi, I.P., 1985. *Leisure, Mass Media and Social Structure,* Jaipur: Rawat Publications, pp. 12–13.
6. Parker, Stanley, 1961. *The Future of Work and Leisure,* London: McGibben and Knee.
7. Modi, I.P., 1985. op. cit., p. 3.

8. Miller, Norman P. and M. Duane, Robinson, 1963. *The Leisure Age: Its Challenge to Recreation,* California: Wad-Worth Publishing Company, pp. 1–12.
9. Kaplan, Max, 1960. *Leisure in America: A Social Inquiry,* New York: John Wiley and Sons, pp. 1–22.
10. D'Amours, M., 1989. 'Free Time and Education: A Political Issue of the Coming Decade,' *Leisure and Recreation*, Vol. XXX, Nos. 3 and 4.
11. Kehinde, Eppo, 1991. 'Social-Cultural Views of Leisure in a Multi-Tribal Setting', *World, Leisure and Recreation,* Summer, pp. 13–16.
12. Mukerjii, D.P., 1951. 'The Status of Indian Women', *International Social Science Bulletin,* Vol. 3, No. 4, pp. 793–801.

8 Conclusion

The importance of evaluating the status of women in any society can hardly be overemphasized. It is the true index of its cultural, social, religious and spiritual levels. Obviously, it is the single-most important criterion for estimating with precision the degree of civilization attained by a particular society in various periods of its history.

In the present study, we have attempted to crystallize the 'status' of women belonging to the tribal, rural and urban society of Rajasthan based on their socio-cultural background, economic and educational levels, health, fertility and maternity, political participation, empowerment and development, concept of female body and sexuality, and concept of leisure.

Vedic period was a high point so far as the status of women in Indian society is concerned. During this period, women enjoyed freedom and equal opportunities in all aspects of life. They went to the *gurukul* and married after proper education. Educated girls had the freedom to marry as per their choice (love marriage or *swayambar)*. Women could be initiated into Vedic studies and could offer sacrifices to Gods. Widow remarriage was fairly common and had societal sanction.

Over a period of time, their position deteriorated and they were subjugated and marginalized to be considered as man's private property, had low legal status and were treated with ritual contempt. A span of 2,000 years (20 B.C. to 1800 A.D.) saw the revival of *sati,* prohibition of remarriage, spread of *purdah* system and greater prevalence of polygamy, which made women further insecure.

Social structure, cultural norms and value systems greatly determine women's position and status in societal sub-structure. It can both stimulate change and act as an impediment to change. It is indeed ironic that there is a great divide between theoretical possibilities of the status of women according to our law and Constitution and its actual realization. Religion goes a step further by providing the moral base for accorded and institutionalized roles that a woman plays in society, outlining her assumed virtues and vices.

Education has been widely recognized as a major instrument for elevating women's status, However, there is a serious imbalance in distribution of educational efforts among different sections of society. Education plays a major role in eliminating effects of socio-economic inequalities on one hand while increasing inequalities between haves and have-nots. Social attitude towards the education of girls varied from 'acceptance of need' to 'total indifference' at the other extreme. Prevalence of early marriage and motherhood in tribal, rural, and urban household and urban informal segments subjugates women and places them under severe physical and mental strain. In sharp contrast, majority of the urban formal sector women attach greater priority to their education and career and contemplate marriage much later in life. During the course of study, it emerged that the rate of literacy and level of education has progressively declined among rural and tribal women as compared to their urban counterparts. Even amongst urban women, there was a great dichotomy with widespread illiteracy in the informal segment at one end and majority of formal respondents being technically/professionally qualified on the other. It is thus evident that illiteracy is primarily responsible for the low status and insecurity amongst women.

Age at the time of marriage reflects the attitude of society in general and parents in particular towards the girl child. Besides, it is significant because it determines the level of fertility. In the urban formal segment, proper education and settled earning life are accorded higher priority before marriage, whereas the urban household segment was found to be more conservative and married off their daughters after routine school education or at best graduation. The outlook of the urban informal sector and rural respondents is further complicated due to acute poverty and they seemed keen to get free from their liability at the earliest. Majority of tribal marriages take place just after girls attain puberty.

Non-Sanctity of Virginity

The predominant mode of marriage in rural and urban set-ups is arranged marriage. However, exceptions exist in the urban formal setting where some women have gone in for love marriage. Though they have an appreciation for high-caste Hindus and are even keen to adopt their values, the Garasias still observe many of their age-old practices. For example, marriage by elopement is still popular and selection of a life-partner is a free choice for young boys and girls, who are allowed to mix with members of the opposite sex prior to marriage. A young Garasia girl is free from usual restrictions prevalent in the rural and urban societies. She can elope or even force herself on a person of her choice and this relation acquires social sanction once the brideprice is paid.

As observed in the upper and middle castes of both urban and rural communities, a girl child is kept under strict vigil and control. She is considered a scarce and genuine consumption good to be exchanged for her celibacy and leads a life of chastity till her marriage. When she is gifted away by her father to her groom, in a pure state, it is termed *Kanyadaan* (literally giving away of a virgin girl).

This sacrosanctity and hype around virginity diminishes amongst Garasias and lower castes of urban and rural segments and their uninhibited lifestyle can lead to varying degrees of physical interaction before marriage. This illustrates a new dimension and concept of *non-sanctity of virginity* amongst this segment.

Polygamous marriage is considered a matter of social prestige by successful, powerful and wealthy Garasia men. Joint family system has disintegrated in the urban society where couples seek more privacy and minimal interference even from blood relations. Transferable jobs in the urban society also force children to live away from parents. On the other hand, lack of exposure, easy lifestyle and interdependency among relatives, besides economy of scale in farming, are the major factors for cohesion amongst family members and wide prevalence of the joint family culture amongst rural respondents.

Unique Mix of Joint and Nuclear Family

A newly-wed Garasia bridegroom constructs his new hut in close vicinity of dwellings of other family members. So, his newly-wed wife does not live in a joint family and is devoid of usual restrictions from in-laws. He also aquires his share of land to cultivate and provide for his family. Though tribal households are nuclear as regards daily production, consumption of food, distribution of income and household labour, they converge as joint families for sharing well water, oxen for harvesting fields, collective labour in each other's fields or whenever any other collective effort is required. *Thus, the Garasia society personifies a unique synthesis of nuclear and joint family.*

It is evident that rigid restrictions and norms governing the institution of marriage that are sacrosanct in urban and rural sectors have little relevance in tribal society. Widow remarriage is quite common and even brideprice is less than usual in such cases. Even married Garasia women have the liberty to have a relationship *(nata)* with another man and such relationships are accorded societal sanction once the other man pays compensation (*dava)* to her husband after consent of the panchayat.

Dowry is a unique tradition in both rural and urban societies where the bride's parents give gifts and cash to the groom's family at the time of marriage. Over several decades, this has become coercive trauma and has led to various social, economic and ethical problems. The quantum of dowry is significantly higher in the formal and household sectors of urban society in comparison to the informal sector. It is indeed ironic that modernization and education have only added fuel to the fire. In sharp contrast, dowry has never existed in tribal society, which believes in the concept of *dapa* (brideprice) paid by the groom's family to the family of his would-be wife. While it was traditionally confined to gifts and animals, it now has added a dimension of cash also. Greed and materialistic attitude is on the rise since most of the older tribal respondents acknowledged giving minimal *dapa* compared to their young counterparts.

Brideprice (*dapa*) is higher for a girl who is thrifty, strong, hardworking and knows the art of home management. A girl who is clean, properly dressed and labourious at home and field is more desired. This is in total contrast to the norms of physical beauty and appearance prevailing in urban society.

Dynastic Ostracization

It is contradictory that even after marriage, a Garasia wife is considered an outsider in her husband's clan. She is not entitled to cook, distribute and eat in religious feasts, which remains a prerogative of their menfolk. In tribal society, children are considered to belong to the father's lineage and Garasias strongly believe that women mainly provide the space for child to be conceived and developed in the womb. Genetic content for the child is believed to be provided by *adami ka pani* (semen). At the time of marriage, she brings *vadku* (plate), *lota*, clothes and cheap jewellery. At her husband's house, she is given silver jewellery to wear but this remains the property of her husband and sons. It is mandatory to cover her face in presence of all seniors in the conjugal household, neighbourhood and even in the village. A Garaisa *vehu* (bride) cannot dare to sit on a cot in proximity of Garasia menfolk. Such unexpected behaviour would illustrate that she thinks of her own lineage (father) as superior to her husband. She is constantly forced to imbibe an inferiority complex that her husband's lineage is superior to her father's. She has to cook her own food and eat in utensils which she brings with her from her parents' house at the time of marriage. She is not allowed to eat food cooked by her mother-in-law, sister-in-law or their children. However, her husband and children face no such restrictions.

Tribal women are deeply God-fearing but restrain their religious feelings because a tribal woman praying all alone in a temple or making certain offerings is regarded with suspicion and considered a witch. They do not play any significant role during religious, family or community rituals, where only male members officiate. This is in total contrast to the norms of rural and urban set-ups where no religious activity can be performed without the presence of wife or *ardhangani*. A Garasia wife is expected to be reserved and does not go to houses of husband's relatives unless desired by womenfolk there.

In an overview, a women's status remains that of an outsider in her husband's home and this works to her advantage when she wants to separate from her husband. She has no right to her husband's property and has no right/obligation towards upbringing of her children and when her husband dies, she becomes free to plan her future life independently. Her children are looked after by parents and brothers of her deceased husband. Thus, the situation of women in the Garasia tribe is reflective of 'dynastic ostracization', wherein a woman, *on death of her husband, is denied any linkage with the family and dynasty of her husband.*

Another interesting revelation is that the proportion of urban formal sector respondents having religious faith is in consonance with rural counterparts and significantly higher than their urban household and informal sector fellows.

Existence of Parallel Faith

Beliefs regarding health and its related aspects prevailing in tribal and rural communities are interesting and typical. The health care practices are still primitive. They consider common ailments like cough, cold, fever, insect bites as unavoidable due to their living environment. They attribute sickness and disease amongst human beings and animals to the displeasure of deities and take recourse to appeasing Gods/spirits and visit Bhopa and Devla for charms and amulets (magico-religious treatment). Garasias strongly believe that ancestral or evil spirits (*vers*) cause similar affliction by casting their evil eye on people. They also believe that diseases are caused by witches and angry souls of the deceased persons and hence can be cured only by witch doctors and sorcerers. Respondents across all categories are convinced that jealousy of fellow human beings (evil eye) leads to several illnesses and women and children are particularly prone to this. Women wear black thread on the lower part of their legs and make a black spot on the forehead of their child with *kajal,* since they believe that an evil eye shall be distracted by this black spot and the impact of envy shall be reduced.

Garasias prefer indigenous herbal medication as per the advice of Bhopa for common ailments like cough, cold, fever, minor cuts, insect bites, etc. Prolonged and uncontrollable diseases are attributed to *vers* (evil spirts) for which they resort to magico-religious treatment. Allopathic doctors are consulted only as a last resort when the stage of disease is highly advanced and the condition of patient is critical. Although treatment given at PHC is free, medicines are usually not available and purchase of such costly medication is financially prohibitive for tribal respondents. In some cases, services of allopathic doctors are inaccessible, particularly in remote villages. It is, therefore, necessary to improve the services of such doctors.

Elderly women in villages give home remedy derived from items available in the kitchen in case of common illness. Private medical practitioners are more popular than government doctors since they provide value-added services like dispensing medicines and visiting houses of patients at odd hours. In urban areas, there are numerous PHCs, government and private hospitals and people have access to alternatives of ayurvedic, unani and homeopathic medication, besides widely popular allopathic treatment. Education and modernization in urban areas have not mitigated traditional beliefs of people who still take recourse to religious avenues to seek relief from chronic and critical diseases. This is a uniform ethos which runs through their culture and is evident amongst tribal, rural and urban segments in varying proportions. *They have simultaneous faith in modern and traditional forms of treatment and this illustrates the existence of 'parallel faith' and co-existence of modernity with tradition.*

Women's reproductive health status is greatly affected by the age at which she attains motherhood. Early marriage traps a woman in the vicious circle of conception-motherhood-nursing-more conceptions. This situation is further complicated since tribal and rural women refrain from discussing their gynaecological problems due to shame and embarrassment. Furthermore, it is the male members who still get preference regarding access to medical treatment.

Prevalence of unsafe motherhood is still a glaring reality in Rajasthan and its effect is more pronounced in the urban informal, rural and tribal segments. It is ironic that although statistically PHCs are increasingly present in rural and tribal areas, yet most of the deliveries in these segments are still conducted at home and administered by elderly household woman or *dai*. It is only in the urban community (with the exception of urban informal sector) where majority of respondents preferred to get deliveries conducted in hospitals.

In the Garasia community, there is no system of utilizing MCH services. *Dai* (*huhani*) is preferred to ANM for administering the delivery since she is one amongst them and well acquainted with their habits, family traditions and is always available within the village locality for emergency at odd hours. She also provides additional services such as cleaning effluvia and placenta, burying the placenta, cleaning the delivery room and mopping it with mud and cow dung, bathing the baby and giving post-natal massage to the child and mother. They approach the doctor only in case of any complication or abnormality.

The concept of pre-natal care is essentially confined to the well-educated and financially well-off respondents of urban formal and household sectors. This proportion drops significantly among the urban informal sector respondents, who were crushed between dual responsibilities of household and workplace.

In the rural set-up, non-availability of lady medical staff at PHC was the main hindrance in regular medical check-ups and vaccinations during pregnancy. Hesitation and communication gap between husband and wife in the joint family system was another reason for lack of care.

In the tribal community, a woman performs all normal household chores until she goes into labour. No special diet is given to a pregnant woman, though she is expected to increase her consumption since 'the one inside also needs food'.

Early marriage, low education, unawareness and inhibitions in usage of family planning measures lead to young women becoming mothers in rural and urban informal segments. In the urban community, however, the household sector to some extent and formal sector to much greater extent exhibits maternity patterns in a more matured age since the respondents are educated, working, economically self-sufficient and a major contributor to family income. Garasia men are insecure and believe that early and frequent offsprings will keep their wives fully occupied in domestic chores, ruling out any possibility of extra-marital affairs.

Idealism of Five

Another reason for Garasias to opt for more children could be their hard lifestyle, which is labour-oriented, and they want to strengthen their hold over their land and belongings with more helping hands. Disputes relating to landholding, adultery and brideprice payments are frequent amongst Garasia groups and persist for generations. Violence and arms are a way of life for Garasias and so they desire more sons to protect their family and resources from encroachment, besides maintaining the agnatic structure of the lineage.

Arising out of overall insecurity prevailing due to ongoing generational conflicts amongst Garasias is the concept of *idealism of five,* which prods Garasias to have more children. They yearn for a minimum of five siblings of which at least three should be sons to provide stability, security and carry forward the genetic lineage. After their birth, they look forward to at least two daughters for taking care of the household and bring *dapa* for their father at the time of marriage in order to increase their economic standing in the lineage. However, there is no taboo going beyond five siblings and this fits into their ideology of having larger families to combat various adverse situations.

Knowledge of family planning is almost universal in Rajasthan but the practice of contraception is low. Most of the urban respondents confirmed adopting family planning and this proportion dropped in the rural community but rose again significantly amongst tribal women. Even in the urban society, this trend was more prevalent amongst formal sector respondents as compared to their household and informal sector counterparts, respectively. Thus, it is evident that the use of birth control methods was proportionately higher amongst women with higher level of education, greater exposure and who were financially well-off. Usage of oral pills and condoms in tribal areas was even higher than in urban and rural areas. Undergoing of sterilization was popular in rural areas, while it is unthinkable for Garasia men and women as they can remarry at any stage of their life and fertility remains their main asset. People, particularly in rural and tribal areas, can be motivated if the extension work in these areas is strengthened. There is also a need to educate them so that misconceptions regarding adverse effects of various family planning methods can be allayed.

Female body and sexuality are tied to the reproductive process within the confines of marriage, in which the male normally dominates. Women are forced to accept societal practices and those not doing so are considered unnatural. A woman is considered a weaker sex being protected by father/brother in childhood, by husband in adulthood and by the son in old age. The cleavage between the mindset of the urban formal sector and other respondents is glaring as this segment is born and brought up in a less restrictive environment and hence radiates the confidence of being lesser than none. However, this confidence is totally lacking in tribal, rural, urban informal and household segments.

In the Garasia community, although unmarried girls are free from all restrictions, married women face many restrictions and are confined to their husband's home mainly because of the fear of extra-marital relations.

Production and Reproduction as Empowerment

Acceptance of a Garasia wife steadily increases if she is hardworking, both within the house and in the field. She can overcome her insecurity and strengthen her foothold by early and frequent childbirths to carry forward her husband's lineage. An ideal tribal wife is one who carries out domestic chores efficiently and is attentive towards the needs of the husband on his return home. Any lethargy regarding non-preparation of food or non-availability of water is deplorable and such irritants can lead to domestic violence and quarrels. Thus, women are considered a productive resource both in view of their fertility and capacity to work. This is indeed interesting that a woman gains security in married life through her hardwork and fertility. *Both production and reproduction strengthen her empowerment, leading ultimately to her secure position in the family.*

Active involvement of women in politics from the bylanes of the village panchayat to the corridors of national parliament remains a dream to be realized. With legislation in place, sporadically women have outshone as politicians. However, such stray instances cannot determine a trend and a total reorientation of the mindset is required to encourage women to embrace political activity, shunning their inhibition and predetermined roles.

For Garasia tribal women, perception of election is not more than a sponsored feast by political parties. They did not realize the gravity and implication of their involvement by voting or abstaining from the process. In spite of being a sarpanch, tribal women are still dependent on their husbands and other male members of family for decision-making. This was an eye-opener and made us realize that reservation in political structure alone cannot lead to empowerment. There has to be an emphasis on education and broadening the horizons of women across all sections. This would provide them enough confidence to start acting independently without inhibition.

Politics is considered an unsafe, corrupt field by even rural and urban respondents. This stark reality has been conveniently overlooked by the male-dominated society for several decades.

Women have outperformed men in fields as diverse as secondary board results to voyages in outer space. It is only a matter of time that the corridors of power see women politicians walking freely. This will be the pinnacle of women empowerment and liberation and would have a top-down effect on all other processes and systems in the country.

Emancipation of women and their equality with men is unimaginable as long as they are secluded from economically productive work and remain immersed and subjugated by household responsibilities.

As we probed into the daily schedule of Garasia women, we realized that their role stretched beyond the confines of home into the forests for collecting fuel, fodder, forest produce, etc. They actively participated in all cultivation activities except ploughing. They walked long distances to work as manual/unskilled labourers at mines, factories, etc. to substantiate family income.

In the rural segment, on the contrary, the outlook is more conservative and upper-caste women do not move out of the four walls of their house. However, lower-caste women work in fields and as manual labourers in factories and at construction sites. Options have evolved in the urban segment but majority of white-collared dignified jobs are restricted to urban formal sector respondents who are well-educated and professionally qualified. It is interesting to note that their husbands and other members supported them by sharing responsibilities of children and household. Urban informal sector and rural respondents were primarily engaged in unorganized jobs and were prone to exploitation.

In an overview, although women have moved out to work, they are unable to delegate or share their household responsibilities with their husbands. Thus, they are sandwiched between the pressing demands of workplace and home. Even at workplace, they are considered inferior to their male colleagues and at home their household work is never quantified or attached any economic significance.

Across all sections, women have limited control over their self-earnings and this usually becomes family contribution. Wants and desires of women are very limited and the concept of self-indulgence is hardly found. Similar is the case in the urban informal sector, where household economic needs remain unfulfilled even after contribution of the working respondents. Freedom to spend one's earning is more pronounced amongst tribal and urban formal sector women and across other segments, women are dependent on male members for even their basic requirements.

The aspirational level is also diverse in case of tribal, rural and urban women. In tribal and rural communities, women wish to accumulate jewellery, aspire to build a house and spend on needs of children and family. The urban informal sector had a rub-off effect of both the rural background and urban exposure; hence, their desires were a mix of conservative (accumulating jewellery, savings, building house, buying clothes) and modern (spending on leisure activities, needs of children and personal requirements). Across all segments, except for urban formal, mothers were more affectionate, accommodating and splurged money on children, whereas in the urban formal segment, majority opined that their husbands tended to spend more on the needs of their children.

Harassment as Fate Accompli

Respondents of tribal, rural and urban informal sector faced exploitation and harassment at the workplace. Even in the urban formal sector, where respondents were educated and qualified, they were dominated by male colleagues. Women workers also suffered humiliation of sexual harassment by workmates and employers. This varied from passing remarks, making suggestive gestures to outright physical molestation, which was confined to the urban informal sector and rural women, who suffer silently due to insecurity of losing their jobs. It is pertinent to note that none of the tribal women complained of such harassments since disrespect of any Garasia woman becomes a prestige issue for the entire community to take revenge. Thus, they *command fearful respect from their non-tribal colleagues at the workplace.*

The value of women's work in creating and maintaining the household's stock of human capital through cooking, cleaning, nursing, bearing and rearing children is never quantified as productive work and housewives are usually referred to as dependants or non-working members of society. Disintegration of the joint family system in tribal and urban societies has led to the shifting of household responsibilities to children, husbands, close relatives and even neighbours. Urban formal sector respondents were able to employ full/part-time servants to get relief from the pressure of household responsibilities.

Majority of working respondents regretted that they had little time for leisure activities due to their dual roles in the household and workplace. Perception and connotation of leisure differs as we move across cultures and habitats. While it symbolizes laziness to some, it is an opportunity for entertainment and self-cultivation for others. Apparently, it seems that leisure is a prerogative of males as they have the freedom to indulge without any inhibition. This does not imply that women do not have leisure; rather, what is more pertinent is the extent to which they are free to use this leisure time since freedom is an essential component of leisure. Importance of leisure can hardly be overemphasized since leisure is a source of relaxation from mental and nervous strain and fatigue caused by tensions. It keeps people free from psychosis and neurosis. It is the quality of human experiences with elements of choice and enjoyment associated with it. The phenomenon of leisure can be best understood and explained in the context of a social organization which not only determines the form and nature of leisure but also outlines the extent and limits of participants. The concept of leisure is an invaluable property of Garasias due to which they feel themselves free from the frustrations of their life. Garasias lead a simple and austere life and have limited opportunities and almost no exposure. The circle of concern for women respondents remains problems and topics related to family members, socio-cultural occasions and fairs and festivals. While the pattern of preferred leisure activities of rural respondents was quite similar to their tribal counterparts, the proportion of rural respondents preferring family-oriented activities reduced significantly. It is interesting to note the influence of modern audio-visual aids such as radio, TV and cinema, which also became a preferred source of entertainment for many rural respondents.

In the urban household segment, respondents are financially well-off and have pressure-free and an easy lifestyle. This was reflective in those respondents who idly pass away their leisure time literally doing nothing. Majority of respondents indulged in family-oriented, group-oriented and quietistic activities. Since this segment is educated and exposed, their sensitivity and creativity is illustrated by the pursuit of leisure activities such as reading, writing, gardening, painting, embroidery, etc. Urban informal sector respondents faced dual pressure of household and outside responsibilities and belonged to the lower economic class of society, which was struggling for basic necessities. They involved themselves in family-oriented, self-employing and economic activities in the scarcely available leisure time. A good number of informal sector respondents preferred to relax by quietistic activities so as to recoup their energy levels. Indulgence in audio-visual activities emerged sporadically as leisure activities amongst this group. Besides family-oriented, group-oriented or quietistic activities, urban formal sector women were inclined towards intellectual activities and this radiated their sensitive and creative quotient and intensity and urge to satisfy the same. Exposure and indulgence in modern means of recreation also found favour with these respondents.

It is really surprising that although the time available and means of leisure are limited in tribal and rural communities, the satisfaction of respondents is quite high with respect to utilization of leisure. Whereas urban respondents may have more time and avenues of leisure for indulgence, but they still remain dissatisfied with the content and quality of leisure.

The concept of leisure has direct relevance to the freedom of choice and we find that tribal and rural environments are more restrictive and married women do not have access to free movement. As a consequence, they have the constant burning of unfulfilled desires. Urban informal sector respondents are also sailing in the same boat but urban household and formal sector respondents are more liberated and free to indulge in multifarious leisure activities.

Thus, illiteracy, excessive involvement in domestic chores, household constraints, attitude of husband and society and dependency on males because of physical weakness and lack of social experiences are major impediments in the awareness of rights amongst women. We cannot absolve ourselves of our responsibilities by merely enacting laws. What is required is a total change in the mindset of society and its *perceived roles of women*. Women have to be encouraged to take initiatives and involve themselves in collective decision-making within and outside the family.

To conclude, although awareness and empowerment have risen amongst women due to increased literacy, exposure, economic emancipation and increased standard of living, yet the job is far from done. Empowerment has to be supplemented by a liberal dose of literacy, health awareness and socio-cultural changes which holistically would improve the status of women. This is a reality. It still remains a question whether we are willing to accept it or not.

It is obvious that the status of women is significantly determined by the structural and cultural realities of specific societies. Variations are also observed and illustrated within various sub-sections of this society. It is hoped that this study of the status of women in a wide spectrum of tribal, rural and urban society of Rajasthan would go a long way in understanding the process of social change.

Bibliography

Acharya, Meena and Lynn, Benett, 1983. 'Women and the Subsistence Sector: Economic Participation and Household Decision-making in Nepal', *Working Paper No. 526,* Washington, D.C.: The World Bank.

Acharya, Meena, 1982. 'Time Use Data and the Living Standards Measurement Study', *LSMS Working Paper No. 18,* Washington, D.C.: The World Bank.

Afshar, H. (ed.), 1985. *Women, Work and Ideology in the Third World,* London: Tavistock.

Agarwal, Sushila, 1988. *Status of Women,* Jaipur: Rawat Publications.

Ali, Mumtaz and Noor, Aysha, 1982. *Status of Rural Women in India,* New Delhi: Uppal Publishing House.

Almond and Colonan (eds), 1960. *The Politics of the Developing Nations,* Princeton University Press, pp. 27–28. Also see Richard Dawson and Kenneth Prewitt, 1960. *Political Socialization,* Boston: Little Brown & Co.

Anandhi, S. and A. Roychoudhary, 1994. 'Construction of Gender', *Social Action,* 44(2): 1.

Andal, N., 2002. *Women and Indian Society: Options and Constraints,* Jaipur: Rawat Publications.

Anderson, J.E., 1949. *The Psychology of Development and Fersonal Adjustment,* New York: Molt.

Apte, J.S., 1995. 'Education and Women's Empowerment', *Indian Journal of Adult Education,* Vol. 56, No. 3, July–September.

Baig, T.A. (ed.), 1955. *Women of India,* Delhi: Publication Division.

Baily, F.G., 1960. *Tribe, Caste and Nation,* Delhi: Oxford University Press.

Bang et al., 1989. 'High Prevalence of Gynaecological Diseases in Rural Indian Women', *Lancet,* 14 January.

Bang, R.A., and A.T. Bang, 1994. 'Women's Perceptions of White Vaginal Discharge: Ethnographic Data from Rural Maharashtra', in J. Gittellslobon et al. (eds), *Listening to Women Talk about Their Health: Issue and Evidence from India,* New Delhi: Har-Anand Publications.

Barge, Sandhya, 1997. 'Gynaecological Morbidity: The Ignored Tragedy', *Journal of Family Welfare*, 43(2), June.

Baroda Citizens' Council et al. *Prevalence of Clinically Detectable Gynaecological Morbidity in India: Results From Four Community Based Studies* (unpublished).

Basu, A.M. and K. Basu, 1991. 'Women's Economic Roles and Child Survival', *Health Transition Review*.

Basu, S.K., 1992. *Health and Culture among the Underprivileged Groups in India in State of India's Health*, Edited by Alok Mukhopadhyay, Voluntary Health Association of India.

Bathala, Sonia, 1998. *Women, Democracy and the Media*, New York: Sage Publications.

Batliwala, Srilata, 1995. 'The Meaning of Women's Empowerment', *Women's World*.

Bernstein, B., 1977. *Class, Codes and Control*, Vol. 3, London: Routledge and Kegan Paul.

Beteille, Andre, 1969. *Castes: Old and New,* Bombay: Asia Publishing House.

Bhasin, Kamla and Bina Agarwal (eds), 1984. 'Women and Media', *Kali for Women*, Delhi.

Bhasin, Kamla and Nighat, Said Khan, 1986. *Some Question on Feminism and Its Irrelevance in South Asia*, New Delhi: Raj Press.

Bhasin, Kamla, 1992. 'Education for Women's Empowerment: Some Reflections', *Adult Educational Development*, March, Number 38.

Bhatia, J.C., 1988. 'A Study of Maternal Mortality in Anantpur District, Andhra Pradesh, India, Bangalore', *Indian Institute of Management*.

Bhave, Anjali, 1995. *Of Women Caste: The Experience in Rural India*, Calcutta: Stree Publications.

Bose, A., 1988. *From Population to People*, Vol. 1, Delhi: B.R. Publishing.

Boserup, Ester, 1970. *Women's Role in Economic Development,* New York: St. Martin Press.

Chakrapani, C. and S. Vijay Kumar, 1994. *Changing Status and Role of Women in Indian Society*, New Delhi: M.D. Publications.

Chambers, R., N.C., Saxena and T. Shah, 1989. *To the Hands of the Poor: Water and Trees*, London: Intermediate Technology Publications.

Chandrakala, P. Hate, 1969. *Changing Status of Women in Post Independent India*, Bombay: Allied Publishers Pvt. Ltd.

Chant, S., 1992. 'Woman and Poverty in Urban Latin America, Mexican and Costa Rican Experiences', *London School of Economics and Political Science*, United Kingdom.

Charcot in Chaudhary, Buddhadeb, 1974. *Tribal Health: Socio-Cultural Dimensions*, New Delhi: Inter-India Publications.

Charlton, S.E.M., J. Everett, K. Staudt, (eds), 1989. *Women, the State, and Development*, Albany: State University of New York Press.

Chomsky, Noam (et al.), 1986. *Liberating Theory*, Boson: South End Press.

Conclusions of All India Conference on Women, 1976. *Social Scientist*, Vol. 4, No. 6, February.

Cormack, M., 1961. *She Who Rides a Peacock*, Bombay: Asia Publishing House.

Cormack, M., 1981. *The Hindu Women*, Bombay: Asia Publishing House.

Csikszentmihaly, M., 1975. *Beyond Boredom and Anxiety*, San Francisco: Jossey-Bass.

D'Amours, M., 1989. 'Free Time and Education: A Political Issue of the Coming Decade,' *Leisure and Recreation*, Vol. XXX, Nos. 3 and 4.

Dak, T.M. (ed.), 1988. *Women and Work in Indian Society*, Delhi: Manohar Publications.

Das, Veena, 1988. 'Feminity and Orientation to the Body', in Kaurna Chanana (ed.), *Socialization, Education and Women*, New Delhi: Orient Longman.

Das. R.M., 1993. *Women in Manu's Philosophy*, Jalandhar: ABS Publication.

Davis, Kingsley, 1964. *Human Society*, New York: Macmillan.

De Lauretis, Teresa, 1989. *Technologies of Gender*, Bloomington: University of Indian Press.

Dean, Jaros, 1973. *Socialization to Politics*, Nelson.

Delamont, S., 1980. *The Sociology of Women*, George Allen and Unwin.

Desai, Neera, 1957. *Women in Modern India*, Bombay: Vora & Co. Publishing Pvt. ltd.

Dharuvajan, Vanaja, 1989. *Hindu Women and the Power of Ideology*, New Delhi: Vistar Publications.

Driver, B.L., P.J. Brown, and G.L. Peterson, (eds), 1991. *Benefits of Leisure*, State College, P.A.: Venture Publishing.

Dube, L., 1983. 'Misadventures in Aminocentesis', *Economic and Political Weekly*, 18.

Dube, Leela and Rajni, Palriwala (eds), 1990. Structure and Strategies: Women, Work and Family, New Delhi: Sage.

Dube, Leela, 1997. *Women and Kinship: Comparative Perspectives on Gender in South and South-East Asia*, New Delhi: Vistar Publications.

Dube, S.C., 1967. *India's Changing Villages*, Bombay: Allied Publishers.

Dube, S.C., 1967. *Indian Village*, Bombay: Allied Publishers.

Dumont, L., 1970. *Homo Hierarchicus*, London: Weidenfeld and Nicolson.

Durnazedier, J. Ohre, 1967. *Towards a Society of Leisure*, London: Collier Macmillan.

Durnazedier, J. Ohre, 1974. *Sociology of Leisure*, Amsterdam: Elsevier.

Elenora, B.M., 1987. 'Women as Builders of the Future', *Future*, August 19.

Elise, B., 1977. *Women of 21st Century*, New Delhi: Sage.

Engle, Patricia L., 1983. 'The Effect of Maternal Employment on Children's Welfare in Rural Guatemala', *Child Development and International Development: Research Policy Interfaces, New Directions for Child Development*, Vol. 20, San Francisco: CA.

Engles, 1978. 'Origin of Family', in *Women and Communism*, Calcutta: New Book Centre.

Evans, Mary, 1997. *Introducing Contemporary Thought*, Cambridge: Polity Press.

Everet, Jane Mason, 1979. *Women and Social Change in India*, New Delhi: Heritage Publishers.

Field, D., 1984. 'The Social Definition of Illness', in David Tuckett (ed.), *Introduction to Medical Sociology*, London: Tavistock Publications.

Fisher, Sue, 1987. 'Good Women After All: Cultural Definitions and Social Control,' in J.F. McDonough and R.C. Saari (eds), *The Trapped Women: Catch 22 in Deviance and Control*, Newbury: Sage.

Fortes, M., 1953. 'The Structure of Unilineal Descent Groups', *American Anthropologist*, Vol. IV, No. 1.

Ganatra, B.K., and S.S. Hirve, 1995. 'Unsafe Motherhood: The Determinants of Maternal Mortality', *Journal of the Indian Medical Association*, 93, 2.

Gandhi, M.K., 1925. *Young India*, February 9.

Gandhi, M.K., 1942. *Women and Social Injustice*, Ahmedabad: Navjivan.

Gathaskar, Sujata, 1992. *Struggles of Women at Work*, Delhi: Vikas Publishing House.

Ghadially, Rehana, 1988. *Women in Indian Society: A Reader*, New Delhi: Sage.

Ghurye, G.S., 1959. *The Scheduled Tribes*, Bombay: Popular Prakashan.

Giddens, A., 1993. *Sociology*, Cambridge: Polity Press.

Goldschmidt-Clermont, Luisella, 1987. *Economics Evaluations of Unpaid House Work: Africa, Asia, Latin America and Oceania*, Geneva: International Labour Office

Green, E., S. Hebron, and D. Woodward, 1987. 'Women's Leisure in Sheffield: Constraints and Opportunities,' in I Henry (eds). *Women's Leisure: Constraints and Opportunities*, Brighton: LSA.

Greentien, Fred, I., 1968. 'Political Socialization', *International Encyclopedia of the Social Sciences*, 14, New York.

Greer, G., 1984. *Sex and Desting*, London: Secker and Warburg.

Gupta, A.R., 1976. *Women in Hindu Society*, Delhi: Jyotsana Prakashan.

Gupta, Amit Kumar, 1986. *Women and Society: The Developmental Perspective*, New Delhi: Criterion Publication.

Gupta, Mala, 1993. 'Let Mass Media Help Build Positive Public Opinion about Women's Concerns', *Kurukshetra,* December.

Gupta, Nirmal, K., 1990. *Women at Work in Developing Economy*, New Delhi: Anmol Publications.

Hall, C. Margaret, 1990. 'Patriarchal Values', in Margaret, C. Hall (ed.), *Women and Identity,* Washington: Hemisphere Publishing Co.

Harvey, L., 1990. *Critical Social Research*, London: Unwin, Hyman.

Hasan, K.A., 1967. *The Cultural Frontier of Health in Village India,* Bombay: Manaktalas.

Haworth, J.T., 1997. *Work, Leisure and Well-being,* London: Routledge.

Henderson and M.D. Bialeschki, 1991a. 'A Sense of Entitlement to Leisure as Constraints for Women,' *Society and Leisure*, 14(1).

Heptulla, Najma (ed.), 1992. *Reforms for Women: Future Options*, Calcutta: Oxford and IBH Publishing Co. Pvt. Ltd.

Hiremath, S.L. and Shahida, 1999. 'Choice of Indian Women: A Study of Reproductive Behaviour' in R. Indira and Deepak Kumar Behera (eds), *Gender and Society in India*. Vol. I, New Delhi: Manak Publications Pvt. Ltd.

Hodding, Carter. Jr., 1984. Cited in Jeanve H. Block in *Sex Role Identity and Ego Development*, Jossey Bass Publishers.

ICMR. 1989. *Illegal Abortion in Rural Areas: A Task Force Study,* New Delhi: ICMR.

Ide, Arthur Frederick, 1985. *Women Before History was Written*, Dallas: Monument Press.

India, 1975. Ministry of Education and Social Welfare, *Towards Equality: Report of the Committee on the Status of Women in India.* Delhi.

Indira, R. and V. Shanti, 1997. 'Gender Dynamics in the Context of a Tribal Society: The Case of Jenukuruba', in *Georgepfeffer* and Deepak Kumar Behra (eds), *Contemporary Society and Tribal Studies,* Vol. I, New Delhi: Concept Publishing Company.

International Institute of Population Sciences (IIPS), 1995. National Family Health Survey (MCH and Family Planning), India 1992–93. Mumbai, *IIPS*.

Iso-Ahola, S., 1980. *The Social Psychology of Leisure and Recreation,* Dubuque: W.C. Brown.

Jaggar, A.J., 1983. *Feminist Politics and Human Nature*, Sussex: Harvester.

James, Col. Tod, 1920. *Annals and Antiquities of Rajasthan or the Central and Western Rajput States of India*, edited by William Crooke, Oxford: Oxford University Press.

Jayawardena, Kumai, 1986. *Feminism and Nationalism in the Third World*, Zed Printers.

Jeffery, R., P. Jeffery and A. Lyon, 1984. 'Female Infanticide and Aminocentesis', *Social Science Medicine*, 19, 11.

Jejeebhoy, S.J., 1997. 'Addressing Women's Reproductive Health Needs, Priorities for the Family Welfare Programme', *Economic and Political Weekly*, XXXII (9 & 10).

Johnson, H.M., 1963. *Sociology*, New Delhi.

Johnson, M. Harry, 1962. *Sociology: A Systematic Introduction,* London: Routledge and Kegan Paul Ltd.

Kakar, S., 1981. *The Inner-World: A Psychoanalytic Study of Childhood and Society in India,* New Delhi: Oxford University Press.

Kanitkar, Tara and B.N. Murthy, 1983. 'Factors Associated with Contraception in Bihar and Rajasthan: Findings from Recent Sample Surveys', in K. Srinivasan and S. Mukerji (eds), *Dynamics of Population and Family Welfare*, Mumbai: Himalaya Publishing House.

Kaplan, Max., 1960. *Leisure in America: A Social Inquiry*, New York: John Wiley and Sons.

Kapur, Promilla, 1974. *Marriage and the Working Women in India,* New Delhi: Vikas Publishing House.

Kasturi, Leela (et al.) (eds), 1990. *Women, Workers in India: Studies in Employment and Status*, Delhi: Chanakya Publications.

Kaur, Inderjeet, 1983. *Status of Hindu Women in India,* Allahabad: Chugh Publications.

Kaur, P.C., 1993. 'Curb this Obscenity Galore in Mass Media!', *Kurukshetra,* December.

Kehinde, Eppo., 1991. 'Social-Cultural Views of Leisure in a Multi-Tribal Setting', *World, Leisure and Recreation,* Summer.

Kemp, Sandra and Judith, Squires, 1997. 'Introduction', in Sandra Kemp and Judith Squires (eds), *Feminisms*, New York: Oxford University Press.

Khan, M.E. et. al., 1983, 'Women and Health. A Case Study of Sex Discrimination', *Paper presented at Joint ICMR-Ford Foundation Workshop on Child Health*, Nutrition and Family Planning, Bangalore.

Khan, M.E., Irfan, Khan and Nupur, Mukerjee, 1997. 'Involving Men in Safe Motherhood', *Journal of Family Welfare*, 43, 2, June.

Khare, R.S., 1972. 'Hierarchy and Hypergamy: Some Interrelated Aspects among the Kanya-Kubja Brahmans', *American Anthropology*, 74.

Klein, P., 1979. 'An Institutional View of Development Economics', *Journal of Economic Issues*, XI (4).

Kosambi, D.D., 1991. 'Historical Perspective of Women', in H.C. Upadhyay (ed.), *Status of Women in India*, Vol. I, New Delhi: Anmol Publications.

Krishan Raj, Maithreyi, 1986. *Women Studies in India: Some Perspective*, Bombay: Popular Prakashan Pvt. Ltd.

Krishan Raj, Maithreyi, 1989. 'Women's Issues in India: Is the Feminist Perspective of the West Totally Irrelevant to India', *Seminar Abstract, Research Unit on Women's Studies.* UGC Project No. 38.

Krishan Raj, Maithreyi, 1988. *Role of Rural Women in Development*, Bombay: S.N.D.T. University.

Kulkarni, S., 1986. 'Sex Determination Tests in India: A Survey Report', *Radical Journal of Health*, 1, 3.

Kumar, Ashok (ed.), 1993. *Women in Contemporary Indian Society*, Vol. I, New Delhi: Anmol Publications.

Kumar, D., 1983. 'Amniocentesis again', *Economic and Political Weekly*, 18.

Kumar, Kirti, 1993. 'Mass Media is Promoting Gender Inequality', *Kurukshetra,* December.

Kumar, N. (ed.), 1994. *Women as Subject*, Calcutta: Stree.

Kumar, Shubh K., 1978 'Role of Household Economy in Child Nutrition at Low Incomes: A Case Study of Kerala', *Occasional Paper No. 95*, Cornell University and US/AID Tad-c-1327.

Kuppuswamy, 1972. *Social Change in India*, Delhi: Vikas.

Law, B.C., *Ancient Indian Tribes*, Vol. II.

Lengermann, P.M. and J.M.N. Brantley, 1988. 'Contemporary Feminist Theory,' in George Ritzer, *Contemporary Sociological Theory,* New York: Alfred A. Knopf.

Lewis, Gilbert, 1976. 'A View of Sickness in New Guinea', in J.B. Loudan (ed.), ASA, *Social Anthropology and Medicine*.

Lieban, R.W., 1973. 'Medical Anthropology', in J.J. Honigman (ed.), *Handbook of Social and Cultural Anthropology*, Chicago: Rand McNally College Publishing Company.

Lingam, L., 1991. 'Sex Determination Tests and Female Foeticide Discrimination before Birth', *Indian Journal of Social Work*, 3, 1.

Linton, R., 1936. *The Study of Man,* Appleton Century-Crafts.

Lt. Col. Erskine, 1910. *Gazetteer of Sirohi*, Ajmer: Scottish Mission ind.

Lucy, T.V., 1995. 'Empowerment of Women for Sustainable Development', *Social Action*, Vol. 45, April–June.

Macdonell and Keith, *Vedic Index*, Vol. I.

Mair, Lucy, 1972. *An Introduction to Social Anthropology*, Oxford: Clarendon Press.

Majumdar, D.M., 1960. *Applied Anthropology*, Lucknow: Rajkamal Publications.

Majumdar, V., 1978. *Role of Rural Women in Development*, Bombay: Allied Publishers Pvt. Ltd.

Majumdar, Veena, 1985. *Emergence of Women's Questions in India and the Role of Women*, New Delhi: Centre for Women's Development Studies.

Mann, R.S., 1984. *Anthropological and Sociological Theory Approaches and Applications*, Jaipur: Rawat Publications.

Martin, Emily, 1987. *The Woman in the Body: A Cultural Analysis of Reproduction,* Boston: Press Boston.

Marwar Raj ki Mardumshumari, Vol. I.

Mechanic, D., 1967. *Medical Sociology*, New York: The Free Press.

Meharda, B.L., 1985. *History and Culture of the Girasias*, Jaipur: Adi Prakashan.

Mehrotra, Nilika, 2000. 'Perceiving Feminism: Some Local Responses', *Sociological Bulletin*, Vol. 5., No. 1, March.

Mehta, A. and K. Jayant, 1981. 'Perinatal Mortality Survey in India (1977–79): Part I – Identification of Health Intervention Needs', *Journal of Obstetrics and Gynaecology*, 32(2), April.

Mehta, B.C., 1994. *Fertility Behaviour of Tribals in Rajasthan*, New Delhi: M.D. Publication Pvt. Ltd.

Mencher, John P., 1988. 'Women's Work and Poverty: Women's Contributions to Household Maintenance in South India', in Daisy Dwyer and Judith Bruce (ed.), *A Home Divided: Women and Income in the Third World,* Stanford CA: Stanford University Press.

Merton, R.K., 1976. *Sociological Ambivalence and Other Essays*, New York: Free Press.

Meyer, Fortes, 1970. *Time and Social Structure and Other Essays,* University of London: The Athlone Press.

Miller, Norman P. and M. Duane, Robinson, 1963. *The Leisure Age: Its Challenge to Recreation,* California: Wad-Worth Publishing Company.

Mitra, Jyoti, 1997. *Women and Society: Equality and Empowerment*, New Delhi: Kanishka Publishers.

Modi, I.P., 1985. *Leisure, Mass Media and Social Structure,* Jaipur: Rawat Publications.

Modi, Ishwar (ed.), 1986. *Emerging Trends in Indian Sociology,* Jaipur: Rawat Publications.

Modi, Ishwar and Shalini, Modi, 1996. 'Women Leisure and Family in Indian Society', in Nicole Samue (ed.), *Women, Leisure and the Family in Contemporary Society: A Multinational Perspective,* Oxon (UK): CAB International.

Modi, Ishwar, 1996. 'Contemporary Patterns of Leisure in India', *Paper Presented at the Leisure Asia 96 and Trends in Leisure and Entertainment International Conference,* Singapore, March 21–23, 1996.

Modi, Ishwar, 1996. 'Cultural Implication of Tourism in 21st Century', in Frank H. and Partick. E. Cohn (eds), *Recreation, Sport, Culture and Tourism for the 21st Century,* Department of Physical Education, Hong Kong: Hong Kong Baptist University.

Modi, Ishwar, 1996. *Indian Parks Next to Boom,* Inter Park (UK), June.

Moghadam, Valenline M., 1990. *WIDER Research for Action – Gender, Development and Policy: Towards Equity and Empowerment,* World Institute for Development Research of the United Nations University.

Mohanty, S. and N. Mohanty, 1999. 'Empowering Elected Woman Representatives of Village Panchayats: An Urgent Need', in R. Indira and Deepak Kumar Behera (eds), *Gender and Society in India,* New Delhi: Manak Publications Pvt. Ltd.

Moi, Toril, 1989. 'Feminist, Female, Feminine', in Catherine Belsey and June Moore (eds), *The Feminist Reader: Essays in Gender and the Politics of Literary Criticism,* London: Macmillan.

Mukerjii, D.P., 1951. 'The Status of Indian Women', *International Social Science Bulletin,* Vol. 3, No. 4.

Mukherjee, Subrata and Sushila Ramaswamy, 1995. *The Subject of Women,* New Delhi: Deep and Deep Publications.

Murli Manohar, K., V. Shoba, 1981. *The Status of Women in India – Some Trends and Issues,* Department of Public Administration, Kakatiya University.

Murray, Last, 1976. 'The Presentation of Sickness in a Community of Non-Muslim Hausa', in J.B. Loudan (ed.), ASA 13, *Social Anthropology and Medicine.*

Myres, Robert and Cynthia, Indriso, 1987. 'Women's Work and Child Care: Supporting the Integration of Women's Productive and Reproductive Roles in Resource-Poor Households in Developing Countries', *Paper prepared for the Rockefeller Foundation/IDRC Workshop on Gender, Technology and Development,* February, 26–27.

Nair, K.S., 1970. 'Women's Two Roles', *Social Welfare,* December.

Nash, J., 1960. *Philosophy of Recreation and Leisure*, IOWA: Brown, Duboque.

National Perspective Plan For Women, 1988. '1988–2000 A.D. Report of the Core Group Set Up by the Department of Women and Child Development', Ministry of Human Resource Development, Government of India.

NE 113 Regional Research Committee, 1981. 'Family Time Use: An Eleven-State Urban/Rural Comparison', *Bulletin VPI-2,* Blackburg, VA: Virginia Agricultural Experiment Station.

Nichal, Kamlesh, 1978. *The Invisible Women*, New Delhi: Amaltar.

Nickols, Sharon Y. and Kamala, Srinivasan, 1994. 'Women and Household Production', in Romy Borooah (et al.), *Capturing Complexity*, New Delhi: Sage Publications India Pvt. Ltd.

NSS, 1992. 'Morbidity and Utilization of Medical Services', *NSS* 42nd Round (1986–87), *Sarvekshna*, Vol. XV, No. 4, Government of India, April–June.

Offen, K., 1992. 'Defining Feminism: A Comparative Historical Approach', in G. Book and S. Jove (eds), *Beyond Equality and Difference*, London and New York: Routledge.

Omvedt, Gail, 197. 'Women and Rural Revolt in India', *Social Scientist*, Vol. 6, Nos. 1 and 2, August and September.

Oommen, N., 1996. *Poverty and Pathology: Comparing Rural Rajasthan Women's Ethnomedical Models with Biomedical Modes of Reproductive Morbidity: Implications for Women's Health in India.* Dissertation submitted to the School of Hygiene and Public Health, Baltimore: Johns Hopkins University.

Ortner, S.B., 1974. 'Is Female to Male as Nature is to Culture?', in M.A. Rosaldo and L. Lamphere (eds), *Women, Culture and Society,* Stanford: Stanford University Press.

Palriwala, R., 1990. 'Introduction' in Leela Dube and Raja Palriwala (eds), *Structures and Strategies: Women, Work and Family,* New Delhi: Sage Publications.

Pande, Mrinal, 1991. *The Subject is Women*, New Delhi: Sanchar Publishing House.

Pandey, Rekha, 1989. *Women from Subjection to Liberation*, Delhi: Mittal Publications.

Papanek, H., 1973. 'Men, Women and Work: Reflections on the Two Persons Career', in J. Huber (ed.), *Changing Women in a Changing Society*, Chicago: University of Chicago Press.

Papanek, Hanna., 1989. Socialization for Inequality: Entitlements, the Value of Women and Domestic Hierarchies, *Mimeo, Centre for Asian Development Studies,* Boston University.

Parenti, M., 1978. *Power and the Powerless*, New York: St. Martin's Press.

Parker, Stanley., 1961. *The Future of Work and Leisure,* London: McGibben and Knee.

Patel, Tulsi, 1994. *Fertility Behaviour, Population and Society in a Rajasthan Village*, Bombay: Oxford University Press.

Patel-Ahooja, Krishna, 1995. *Women and Sustainable Development: An International Dimension*, New Delhi: Ashish Publishing House.

Popkin, Barry M., 1983 'Rural Women, Work and Child Welfare in Philippines', in M. Buvinic, M.A. Lycette and W.P. McGreevey, (ed.), *Women and Poverty in the Third World*, Baltimore, M.O.: The Johns Hopkins University Press.

Prabhu, Pradid, 1993. 'Working with Tribals', *Seminar*, 412, December.

Pye, L.W., 1968. *International Encyclopedia of Social Science*, 12, The Free Press.

Quoted from Duncan Mitchell (ed.), 1968. *A Dictionary of Sociology,* London: Routledge & Kegan Paul.

Radcliffe-Brown, A.R., reprinted 1971. *Structure and Function in Primitive Society,* Cohen and West Ltd., Roadway House.

Raghavendra Rao, J.V., 1999. 'Panchayati Raj, Women and the Problematic of Empowerment', in R. Indira and Deepak Kumar Behera (eds), *Gender and Society in India*, New Delhi: Manak Publications.

Ramanana, A. and U. Bambawale, 1980. 'The Mania for Sons: An Analysis of Social Values in South Asia', *Social Science Medicine*, 14B, 2.

Ramu, G.N., 1990. *Women Work and Marriage in Urban India*, New Delhi: Sage.

Rao, Nina, 1985. 'The Woman Question: Perspective for Today', *Social Scientist*, Vol. 149–50, October–November.

Rao, Sudha and M.D. Gayatri Devi Dutt, 1999. 'Gender Bias and Socialization through the Primary School Curriculum in Karnataka', in R. Indira and Deepak Kumar Behera (eds), *Gender and Society in India,* New Delhi: Manak Publications Pvt. Ltd.

Raz, S.M., 1976. *The Process of Socialization*, New Delhi: Chetna Publications.

Reid, Margaret G., 1934; *Economics of Household Production*, New York: Wiley and Sons.

Rheingfold, H.L. and K.V. Cook., 1975. 'The Contents of Boys and Girls Rooms as an Index of Parents' Behaviour', *Child Development,* 46.

Rowbotham, Shiela, 1981. *The Trouble with 'Patriarchy' in No Turning Back: Writing from the Women's Liberation Movement 1975–80.* London: The Woman's Press.

Roy, Aruna, 1990. 'A Women's View', *Seminar,* December.

Royston, E. and A. Armstrong, 1989. *Preventing Maternal Death,* Geneva: WHO.

Sai, F.T., 1986. 'Family Planning and Maternal Care', *World Health Forum,* 7(4).

Santhya, K.G., and G.L. Das Varma, 1988. 'Spousal Communication on Reproductive Illness: A Case Study of Rural Women in Southern India', *Paper presented at the IUSSP Seminar on Gender Inequalities and Reproductive Health: Changing Priorities in an Era of Social Transformation and Globalization,* Brazil, November.

Sapru, R.K., 1989. *Women and Development,* New Delhi: Ashish.

Schlesinger, P. (et al.), 1992. *Women Viewing Violence,* London BFI.

Schur, E., 1971. *Labelling Deviant Behaviour,* New York: Harper and Roue.

Scott, James C., 1986. *'Weapons of the Weak: Everyday Forms of Peasant Resistance',* New Heaven Conn.: Yale University Press.

Scott, W.P., 1988. *Dictionary of Sociology,* Delhi: Goyal Saab Publishers and Distributors.

Scott, William, P., 1997. *Dictionary of Sociology,* New Delhi: Goyalsaab.

Seal, K.C., 1974. 'The Family Planning Programme in India', in A. Bose (et. al.), *Population in India's Development 1947–2000,* Delhi: Vikas Publishing House.

Sen, Amartya K., 1990. 'Gender and Cooperative Conflict', in Irene Tinker (ed.), *Persistent Inequalities,* New York and London: Oxford University Press.

Sethi, Rajmohini, 1999. *Globalisation, Culture and Women's Development,* Jaipur: Rawat Publications.

Sharma, B.M., 1996. 'Lok Tantra ke Unnayan Mein Panchayati Raj Ki Bhoomika', *Yojana,* Vol. 40, No. 3, June.

Sharma, Ursula, 1980. *Women, Work and Property in North West India,* London: Tavistock.

Shiva, Vandana, 1995. 'Women, Ecology and Economic Globalisation – Searching for an Alternative Vision', *IAWA,* Jaipur.

Singh, J.P., N.N. Vyas and R.S. Mann, 1988. *Tribal Women and Tribal Development,* Jaipur: Rawat Publications.

Sinha, B., 1982. *Society in Tribal India,* Delhi: B.R. Publishing Corporation.

Srinivas, M.N., 1991. *Indian Social Structure,* Delhi: Hindustan Publishing Corporation.

Srinivas, M.N., 1998. *Village, Caste, Gender and Method: Essays in Indian Social Anthropology*, New Delhi: Oxford University Press.

Stalin, 1978, 'Anarchism or Socialism', in *Women and Communism*, Calcutta: New Book Centre.

Stromquist, Nelly P. (ed.), 1998. *Women in the Third World: An Encyclopedia of Contemporary Issues*, New York: Harland Publishing Inc.

Sykes, J.B. (ed.), 1993. *The Concise Oxford Dictionary of Current English*.

Thaddeus, Sereen and Deborah, Maine, 1994. 'Too Far to Walk: Maternal Mortality in Context', *Social Science in Medicine*, 38.

Thapar, Romila, 1975. 'Looking Back in History', in Devaki Jain (ed.), *Indian Women*, New Delhi: Ministry of Information and Broadcasting, Government of India.

They lived in groups and still follow the principles of 'Giroh' (group cohesion and unity). Bajrang Lal Lohia in his book *Rajasthan-ki-Jatiya*.

Thomas, P., 1964. *Indian Women Through the Ages,* Bombay: Asia Publishing House.

Thorbek, Susane, 1994. *Gender and Slum Culture in Urban Asia*, New Delhi: Sage Publications.

Turner, Bryan S., 1984. *The Body and Society: Explorations in Social Theory,* New York: Basil Blackwell.

U.N., 1996. *Platform for Action and Beijing Declaration Fourth World Conference on Women*, New York, U.N. Dept. for Public Information.

U.N., 1998. *Too Young to Die: Genes or Gender,* New York: UN.

United Nations, 1994. Declaration on the Elimination of Violence Against Women, U.N., Resolution No. A/Res/48/104.

Unnithan Kumar, Maya, 1997. *Identity, Gender and Poverty,* Oxford: Berghahn Books.

Upadhyay, H.C., 1991. *Status of Women in India*, (Vol. I), New Delhi: Anmol Publications.

Van Gennep, A., 1960. *The Rites of Passage*, Chicago: University of Chicago Press.

Verba, Sydney, 1972. 'Comparative Political Culture', in L.W. Pye, and S. Verba (eds), *Political Culture and Political Development*, Princeton.

Vidyarthi, L.P., 1997. *The Tribal Culture of India*, Delhi: Concept Publishing Co.

Visaria, L., 1988. *Levels, Trends and Determinants of Infant Mortality in India*, in Jain and Visaria.

Vishwanathan, Maithili, 1994. *Women in Agricultural and Rural Development*, Jaipur: Printwell.

Walters, S., 1991. *Her Words on His Lips: Gender and Popular Education in South Africa*, ASPBAC Counter 52.

Warburton, I.W., 1989. 'The Work Leisure Paradox' *Australian Journal of Adult Education,* July, Vol. 8, No. 2, quoted in *Journal of Marriage and Family,* Vol. 51, No. 2.

Waylen, Georgina, 1996. *Gender in Third World Politics*, Buckingham: Open University Press.

Wignaraja, Pooja, 1990. *Women, Poverty and Resources,* New Delhi: Sage.

William, K., 1976. *Key Words,* London: Fontana Croom Helm.

Wimbushch, E., 1987. 'Mothers with Young Children: Understanding their Leisure,' in I. Henry, (ed.), *Women's Leisure: Constraints and Opportunities,* Brighton: LSA.

World Bank, 1981–1991, 'Living Standards Measurement Projects', Various titles, Washington, D.C.: World Bank.

World Bank, 1996. *Improving Women's Health in India,* Washington, D.C.: The World Bank.

World Health Organization Report, 1984.

Young, F.L. Fort and M. Danner, 1994. Moving from the Status of Women to Gender Inequality, *International Sociology*, 9(1): 55–77.

Zaniecki, F., 1940. *The Social Role of the Man of Knowledge*, Columbia: Columbia University Press.

Zaveri, Saroj, 1993. 'Stop Negative Portrayal of Women in Mass Media!', *Kurukshetra,* December.

Index